AUSTRIA

NATIONS OF THE MODERN WORLD: EUROPE
edited by Rand Smith and Robin Remington

This series examines the nations of Europe as they adjust to a changing world order and move into the twenty-first century. Each volume is a detailed, analytical country case study of the political, economic, and social dynamics of a European state facing the challenges of the post–Cold War era. These challenges include changing values and rising expectations, the search for new political identities and avenues of participation, and growing opportunities for economic and political cooperation in the new Europe. Emerging policy issues such as the environment, immigration, refugees, and reordered national security priorities are evolving in contexts still strongly influenced by history, geography, and culture.

The former Eastern Bloc nations must cope with the legacies of communism as they attempt to make the transition to multiparty democracy and market economies amid intensifying national, ethnic, religious, and class divisions. West European nations confront the challenge of pursuing economic and political integration within the European Union while contending with problems of economic insecurity, budgetary stress, and voter alienation.

How European nations respond to these challenges individually and collectively will shape domestic and international politics in Europe for generations to come. By considering such common themes as political institutions, public policy, political movements, political economy, and domestic-foreign policy linkages, we believe the books in this series contribute to our understanding of the threads that bind this vital and rapidly evolving region.

BOOKS IN THIS SERIES

Austria: Out of the Shadow of the Past, Anton Pelinka

Albania in Transition: The Rocky Road to Democracy, Elez Biberaj

The Czech and Slovak Republics: Nations Versus State, Carol Skalnik Leff

The Politics of Belgium, John Fitzmaurice

Great Britain: Decline or Renewal? Donley T. Studlar

Spain: Democracy Regained, Second Edition, E. Ramón Arango

Denmark: A Troubled Welfare State, Kenneth E. Miller

Portugal: From Monarchy to Pluralist Democracy, Walter C. Opello Jr.

AUSTRIA

Out of the Shadow of the Past

ANTON PELINKA

UNIVERSITY OF INNSBRUCK

Westview Press

A Member of the Perseus Books Group

Nations of the Modern World: Europe

Copyright © 1998 by Westview Press, A Member of the Perseus Books Group

Published in 1998 in the United States of America by Westview Press, 5500 Central Avenue, Boulder, Colorado 80301-2877, and in the United Kingdom by Westview Press, 12 Hid's Copse Road, Cumnor Hill, Oxford OX2 9JJ

Library of Congress Cataloging-in-Publication Data
Pelinka, Anton, 1941–
    Austria : out of the shadow of the past / Anton Pelinka.
      p.   cm. — (Nations of the modern world: Europe)
    Includes bibliographical references and index.
    ISBN 0-8133-2918-3
    1. Political culture—Austria.   2. National characteristics,
Austrian.   3. Historiography—Austria.   4. Austria—Politics and
government—20th century.   5. National socialism—Austria—
Psychological aspects.   I. Title.   II. Series.
JN2026.P44   1998
306.2'09436—dc21   98-22740
                                                                          CIP

The paper used in this publication meets the requirements of the American National Standard for Permanence of Paper for Printed Library Materials Z39.48-1984.

10   9   8   7   6   5   4   3

Contents

Tables and Illustrations

Tables

Figures

Maps

Acronyms

B-VG	Federal Constitutional Law (Bundes-Verfassungsgesetz)
CA-BV	Credit-Anstalt Bankverein
CFSP	Common Foreign and Security Policy (EU)
CSCE	Conference for Security and Cooperation in Europe
EC	European Community
ECU	European Currency Unit (will change to Euro in 1999)
EEA	European Economic Area
EEC	European Economic Community
EFTA	European Free Trade Association
EU	European Union
FCG	Organization of Christian Unionists (Fraktion Christlicher Gewerkschafter)
FPÖ	Freedom Party of Austria (Freiheitliche Partei Österreichs)
FSG	Organization of Social-Democratic Unionists (Fraktion Sozialdemokratischer Gewerkschafter)
IGC	Intergovernmental Conference (EU)
KPÖ	Communist Party of Austria (Kommunistische Partei Österreichs)
LIF	Liberal Forum (Liberales Forum)
NAPOLAs	National Political Educational Institutions
NATO	North Atlantic Treaty Organization
NDP	National Democratic Party (Nationaldemokratische Partei)
NSDAP	National Socialist German Workers' Party (Nationalsozialistische Deutsche Arbeiterpartei)
ÖAAB	Austrian League of Workers and Employees (Österreichischer Arbeiter- und Angestelltenbund)
ÖBB	Austrian Farmers' League (Österreichischer Bauernbund)
OECD	Organization of Economic Cooperation and Development
OEEC	Organization for European Economic Cooperation
ÖGB	Federation of Austrian Trade Unions (Österreichischer Gewerkschaftsbund)
ORF	Austrian Broadcasting Corporation (Österreichischer Rundfunk-Fernsehen)

ÖVP	Austrian People's Party (Österreichische Volkspartei)
ÖWB	Austrian Business League (Österreichischer Wirtschaftsbund)
SDAP	Social Democratic Workers' Party (Sozialdemokratische Arbeiterpartei)
SPÖ	Social Democratic Party of Austria (Sozialdemokratische Partei Österreichs), until 1991 Socialist Party of Austria (Sozialistische Partei Österreichs)
VDU	League of Independents (Verband der Unabhängigen)
VF	Fatherland Front (Vaterländische Front)
VÖEST	United Austrian Iron and Steel Industries (Vereinigte Österreichische Eisen- und Stahl AG)
VÖI	Association of Austrian Industrialists (Vereinigung Österreichischer Industrieller)
WEU	West European Union

Preface

Austria usually considers itself "between": between East and West, between North and South, at the crossroads of Europe. Because it is located at the very center of Central Europe, Austria is necessarily involved in all the significant developments taking place in Europe. Since 1989, Austria's neighbors to the east have been undergoing dramatic transitions. During the same period, Austria applied for membership in the European Union, the main organization of Western European integration, and joined the EU in 1995.

This is just one of many important aspects of the transformation of Austrian society and the Austrian political system. Austria is not the same Austria it used to be: It is neither the Austria of the Habsburgs nor the Austria that was part of Nazi Germany. Nor is it the same Austria that came into existence when the Second Republic was founded in 1945. The realities of present-day Austria are different from those of the past.

This book takes the same approach used in the comparative analysis of political systems. It is a twofold comparison: It compares contemporary Austria with other political systems, especially those that are at about the same stage of development; and it compares contemporary Austria with the Austrias that existed in the past. The dynamism of the changes currently taking place in Austria can be described and analyzed with this double focus of comparison.

I am grateful to Professor W. Rand Smith of Lake Forest College for inviting me to publish this book in his series "Nations of the Modern World: Europe." I thank Lee Anne Oberhofer for editing the English version and getting it ready for publication. Ellen Palli has been as helpful and efficient as ever in dealing with the manuscript. Sylvia Greiderer provided the index.

Anton Pelinka
Innsbruck

1

AUSTRIA'S COMPLEX IMAGE

Austria's identity has many contradictory aspects: It is sometimes seen from the viewpoint of its imperial past—as a great European power, full of stories of the Habsburgs and their rule over most of Central Europe for so many centuries. It is sometimes perceived as the hotbed of Nazism, from which came many of the racist and genocidal trends and ideas that led to Auschwitz. It is sometimes defined by its complex relationship to Germany, which-—especially from 1848 to 1938—was not just a neighbor, but an idea, the "Reich," which many Austrians wanted to belong to or even felt part of. And sometimes Austria is seen as a small country, a kind of second Switzerland, that has been able to develop a formula for combining internal welfare and external security.

Only the last of these images concentrates on contemporary Austria—Austria as it has existed since 1945. And it is this republican Austria, claiming to be a liberal democracy, that is now participating in the transformation of Europe at the end of the twentieth century as a member of the European Union and as a nation confronted—due to its geopolitical position—by the changes in the former Communist countries.

For historians and social scientists, especially for political scientists, this Austria of the Second Republic is of particular interest. But this interest has followed certain patterns reflecting political developments:

1. First, there was the interest in Austria's peculiar status during the Cold War period. From 1945 to 1955, Austria was not *between* the Cold War fronts; these fronts went directly *through* Austria. Liberated by the allies in 1945, Austria was still occupied ten years later. The occupation and the liberation from the liberators stimulated research and analysis. How did

1

the Austrians do it? How was it that such a briefly opened "window of opportunity"—between Stalin's death in 1953 and the events in Hungary in
1956—had been used in such an efficient manner? Especially from a
Western point of view, the outcome of the year 1955—the State Treaty
and the Declaration of Neutrality—was seen as the somewhat miraculous
retreat of the Red Army from occupied territory, a phenomenon almost
unheard of before (Bader 1966; Schlesinger 1972; Rauchensteiner 1979;
Cronin 1986; Bischof and Leidenfrost 1988).

2. Then came the interest in the reasons for Austria's stability. How did Austria manage its own "economic miracle"? How did democracy work in such
   a stable manner in a country with a clear deficit in democratic experience?
   Corporatism, Austro-corporatism, became the password for this second
   wave of interest. Austria was considered to be the model case of (neo-)cor-
   poratism, the network of cooperation between business and labor under
   the auspices of a benign government. Especially in the 1970s, during the
   years of social democratic dominance, Austria competed with Sweden to be
   the model case, to find a way to combine the best of all worlds: democracy
   and welfare, capitalism and union power, economic growth and full employment—but without significant inflation. Was there an Austrian model,
   an Austrian "way of (political) life"? Was Austria really an "island of the
   blessed"? (Schmitter and Lehmbruch 1979; Lehmbruch and Schmitter
   1982; Katzenstein 1984; Bischof and Pelinka 1996).

3. Later, in the 1980s, the picture darkened. Austria was seen not so much as
   the former empire that turned out to be an interesting, successful small
   nation in Europe, neutral but nevertheless a Western democracy; rather
   the world and academia started to remember the time between the great
   days of the Habsburgs and the success story of the Second Republic. Austria became the country that, together with Germany, was responsible for
   Nazism but, unlike Germany, was able to escape this responsibility after
   1945. The Germans, it was thought, had learned from their past; the Austrians had not. The "Waldheim affair" became the antithetical story—
   antithetical to all the positive interpretations of Austria, which had dominated the earlier perception (Parkinson 1989; Mitten 1992; Uhl 1992).

In the 1990s, Austria started to change its international outlook by joining the
European Union and by rethinking neutrality. Austria began to lose much of its
(positive or negative) charm and to stop insisting on its special status. Its profile
became "normal," that is, normal in the sense of average West European. But this
normalization, this Westernization must not be seen as the work of a public relations agency; it is the product of several domestic and international factors
(Schneider 1990; Pelinka, Schaller and Luif 1994; Luif 1995).

Contemporary Austria can be analyzed from different viewpoints, using different perspectives. There is the perspective of a country that did not seem to fit into

a Europe based on ethno-national sovereign states. Austria, defining itself in 1918 as a part of Germany, did not accept its independence and its specific role among nation states before losing its independence. This comparative delay in developing a national identity is one aspect that must be considered.

There is also the aspect of democratic delay. Austria did not become a constitutional state until 1867, when all West European states had already been in that league for quite some time. The Austrian Empire, even after 1867, was in the same league of constitutional latecomers as Russia and Turkey and Germany: monarchies with an underdeveloped form of parliamentarism—that is, with an underdeveloped form of democracy. The Austrian political parties, however, did not come late: They already had strong, well-developed organizations with multiple functions, and they functioned as substitutes for a strong parliament and a developed democracy before the semiparliamentarism of the monarchy made room for the parliamentary rule established by the republic. But this republic, with its parliamentary constitution, was not able to create a basic consensus, upon which any democracy must be built. It needed the experience of authoritarian and totalitarian rule to establish the conditions for such a consensus.

The instruments of consociational democracy (Lehmbruch 1967; Lijphart 1977), which were used after 1945 to establish the national and the democratic consensus, can be described and analyzed with respect to their Austrian peculiarities: grand coalition on different levels, balanced clientelism throughout most of society, and corporatist arrangements in the field of economic interests. Consociational democracy, as a set of political techniques, has come under scrutiny since the techniques have reached their goal. The stabilization of the Second Republic can be interpreted as indicating that the historical shortcomings have been overcome. Does that mean that there is no longer any need for these techniques?

This question is related to the main instruments of consociational democracy: the party state and corporatism. The strong, even decisive, position that political parties had (and still have) in Austria is related to the development of consociational democracy in Austria. Due to the delays, which still characterized Austria at the time, political parties had to fulfill functions that in other democracies do not belong to the sphere of parties. During the first decades of the Second Republic, the Austrian parties functioned as "gatekeepers" not only for politics but for society as well (Pelinka and Plasser 1989). Almost all important and even unimportant positions in Austria were under the control of the parties, that is, the two major parties, the SPÖ and the ÖVP. If consociational democracy is in decline, is the party state in decline, too? (Plasser 1987). And if it is, what about corporatism and social partnership? Are they also in decline? (Tálos 1993; Karlhofer and Tálos 1996).

As Austria stands poised on the brink of a new century, it is losing its peculiar characteristics, losing its special features. This is, perhaps, the other side of winning its identity as a state and a nation and one that must be considered "normal."

Basic Features

Austria is a rather small country with a rather small population at the crossroads of Europe, where the East-West axis intersects the North-South axis. In the decades since World War II, Austria has been one of the easternmost countries of Western Europe. It has been a Western democracy since the Second Republic, established in 1945, was able to stabilize competitive democracy and a market economy. It has been on the border of Eastern Europe; among its neighbors were two founding members of the Warsaw Treaty Organization (Czechoslovakia and Hungary) and the nonaligned Communist Yugoslavia. Together with Switzerland, Austria constituted a kind of special geopolitical case: As neutral countries, Austria and Switzerland abstained from military alliances and thus physically separated NATO's northern (Germany) and southern (Italy) sectors; but as liberal democracies, they were nevertheless part of Western Europe.

The collapse of the Communist regimes changed Austria's geopolitical position dramatically. It was no longer possible to describe Austria's position with some of the old terms: Austria was no longer a "bridge" between East and West; nor could it be considered a "bridgehead." Most of Austria's neighbors underwent significant transformation. All the Communist countries became liberal democracies during a very short period around 1990. This transformation not only resulted in a radical change in the political system; it also included the violent breakup of Yugoslavia and the peaceful breakup of Czechoslovakia. Austria's neighbor to the northwest, Germany, became united: The regions that until 1990 belonged to the Communist German Democratic Republic joined the Federal Republic of Germany.

Parallel to this European drama, Austria had been assessing the impact of its changing geopolitical conditions. After a waiting period of five years, Austria became a member of the European Union on January 1, 1995. This has to be seen as part of a process of Westernization. Austria did not perceive its neutrality as an obstacle to integration into a community that is part of the Western bloc and that also includes security (that is, military) aspects. At the end of the century, Austria is, more than ever before, a part of Western Europe.

Among the 8,055,000 inhabitants of Austria (see Table 1.1), almost 10 percent—713,500—are estimated to be non-Austrians, among them legal migrant workers and refugees from the post-Yugoslav wars (Fischer Almanach 1995: 475). The number of non-Austrians living in Austria has significantly increased during the late 1980s and early 1990s. In 1981, the number of "foreigners" in Austria was 291,448; in 1991, it was 517,690 (Reiterer 1995: 265); and three years later, the number was over 700,000. The reason for this development can be seen in the dramatic changes in Europe. The collapse of Communist regimes in Austria's neighborhood—in combination with the incentives offered by Austria's socioeconomic situation to Central and East Europeans—resulted in a mass migration. Austria, bordering four former Communist states, was a logical destination for such an economically motivated migration.

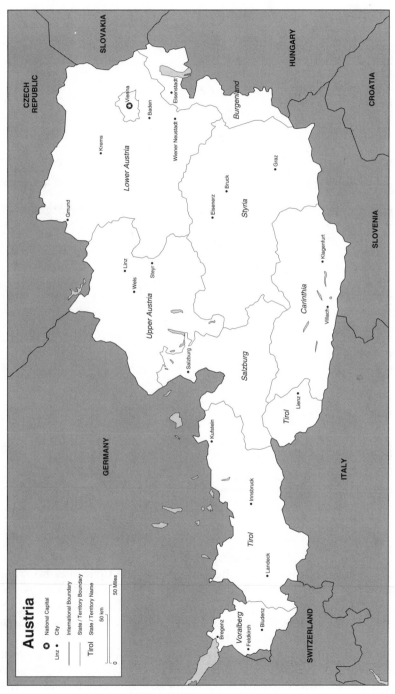

Map of Austria

TABLE 1.1   Austria: Size and Population

Bundesland (state)* Capital	Size (in square km)	Population (in thousands)
Burgenland Eisenstadt	3,966	274.8
Kärnten (Carinthia) Klagenfurt	9,533	562.2
Niederösterreich (Lower Austria) St. Pölten	19,173	1,521.5
Oberösterreich (Upper Austria) Linz	11,980	1,383.8
Salzburg Salzburg	7,154	508.4
Steiermark (Styria) Graz	16,388	1,207.8
Tirol (Tyrol) Innsbruck	12,648	659.9
Vorarlberg Bregenz	2,601	343.8
Wien (Vienna) Vienna	415	1,592.6
AUSTRIA Vienna	83,857	8,054.8

SOURCE: Population, official estimation for 1995 (latest census 1991) from *Österreich-isches Statistisches Zentralamt.*

* Names in parentheses are the English translation of the state or bundesland.

German is the official language of Austria. More than 90 percent of the Austrian population (including non-Austrian citizens) speak German as their mother tongue; that means almost all Austrian citizens born in Austria are German speaking. The largest traditional linguistic minorities (that is, not including non-Austrians) are the Croats in Burgenland and the Slovenes in Carinthia, each consisting of about 20,000 Austrians (Reiterer 1995: 263 f.).

The census also gives a clear picture of the traditional Catholic hegemony that has characterized Austria for so many centuries. In the population of about eight million people registered by the 1991 census, 78 percent were Catholics, 5 percent

Protestants, and 2 percent Muslims. Only 0.1 percent were Jewish. Most of the rest were nondenominational (Fischer Almanach 1995: 475). But there is a clear long-term trend against Catholic dominance. In 1951, the percentage of Catholics in Austria was 89.0 percent (Reiterer 1995: 265). The decline to 78 percent is the result of non-Catholic migration to Austria and of a trend among Austrian Catholics toward leaving the church.

Austria is a rather homogenous country as far as language and religion are concerned. This is, of course, the result of history. The Republic of Austria has been shaped out of the German-speaking parts of Habsburg Austria as it existed under different political arrangements up to 1918. And Habsburg Austria was the heart of the Counter Reformation, which fought Protestant Reformation in the seventeenth century and even later. The Counter Reformation, organized by the alliance of the Catholic Church and the Habsburgs, marginalized the Austrian Protestant element. Protestantism, the dominant denomination in the late sixteenth and early seventeenth centuries in many parts of Habsburg Austria, became a minority phenomenon. It was repressed until the Tolerance Act of 1782 and even after that it was discriminated against, like all non-Catholic denominations, including and especially the Jewish community. Only the constitution of 1867, which included a basic guarantee of religious freedoms ("Staatsgrundgesetz"), ended the legal prerogatives of the Catholic Church in Austria in comparison with other creeds.

Austria is a country with a balance between urban and rural areas. For a long period, especially during the First Republic (1918–1934), Vienna was considered too big for Austria. The capital, which developed as the center of a vast empire, seemed demographically too dominant for the small republic. At the beginning of this republic, Vienna—with about two million inhabitants at the time—accounted for almost one-third of Austria's population. Politically, Vienna was considered to be "red" (due to its social democratic dominance); the other states were "black" (Catholic-conservative). This led to tension and conflict and fed political prejudices.

This balance has changed in favor of the non-Viennese parts of Austria, especially the western states of Upper Austria, Salzburg, Tyrol, and Vorarlberg. These regions had the highest population growth during the decades of the Second Republic, after 1945. One reason for this shift from eastern to western Austria was the geopolitical situation of the Cold War: In many respects, eastern Austria was seen as a dead end, and the economic dynamism of these years was directed toward western Austria. Therefore, in the 1990s, not one-third but only one-fifth of the Austrian population lives in Vienna (see Table 1.2). The old reference to Vienna as Austria's "hydrocephalus" has lost its meaning.

Urbanization is still ongoing in Austria, but after decades of westward drift, European mobility seems to be changing this pattern to a more balanced trend. Since the downfall of Communist regimes, millions of Central and Eastern Europeans have been trying to migrate to Western Europe. Austria, politically and economically part of Western Europe, is especially challenged by this migration

TABLE 1.2   Demographic Trends in Austria, 1991

Population	Rural Communities up to 5,000 Inhabitants	Small and Medium-Sized Cities	Vienna and State Capitals
Proportion	44.8%	23.3%	31.9%
Tendencies	decline	growth	growth (but not Vienna)

SOURCE: Fassmann 1993: 260.

due to its geographical position. During the first years of the 1990s, the number of registered foreigners (noncitizens) living in Austria increased from 515,000 (census 1991) to 713,500 (official estimates, 1995) (Fischer Almanach 1995: 475). This has not only produced (or brought into the open) waves of xenophobia, it also balanced the east-west demographic situation in Austria. It is especially responsible for reversing the trend that had been observed since 1918: the decline of Vienna's population. Because the dynamism that accompanies the migration is to a great extent directed toward the Viennese metropolitan area, this area is profiting demographically.

The transformation that Europe is going through has had and is still having a significant impact on Austria:

- With the end of the East-West conflict, Austria is trying much harder than before to integrate itself—politically, economically, and perhaps even militarily—into the Western world. This is the international, especially European, precondition of Austria's general trend toward Westernization.
- With the end of the Cold War, Austria's borders were opened to the former Warsaw Treaty countries. This new openness has influenced Austria in economic but also demographic and political terms, which is reflected in the xenophobic issues of Austrian politics.

Austria is participating in the general European trend toward new concepts of internal as well as external security, especially through its membership in the European Union. But as a country and a nation with special problems that have nothing to do with this general trend, Austria has to deal with some specific issues, especially the problem of competing identities. There are identities based on political consensus and/or ethno-linguistic communities; identities based on subsocieties of class, religion, or nation ("Volk"); and identities based on general "Austrian" references.

The Second Republic can be characterized as a program of social, political, and economic stabilization. Having achieved this goal during the first five decades of its existence, the Second Republic of Austria is now faced with overall European mobility, which creates a general uncertainty. Having come to terms with its existence as a small, rather ordinary country on the eastern fringes of Western Europe and its own transformation, Austria now has to deal with a European transformation, which it cannot escape—especially after saying farewell to the old illusion of being an "island of the blessed."

Changing Identities

There is no other European country at the end of the twentieth century whose identity has changed so many times, whose objective, as well as subjective, substance has been altered so often and so significantly since 1800. What Austria is— or should be—has been defined in so many different and completely contradictory ways that being "Austrian" means very little, if nothing is added to indicate which of the many Austrias is meant. In less than two centuries, many different versions of Austria have made their impact on the mind and the souls of the people living in Central Europe. Austria is not Austria is not Austria. Present-day Austria and its political system are the result of many breaks in history.

When speaking about Austria, it is necessary to define which Austria is being discussed. The Austria of the late twentieth century is, in geographic, linguistic and political terms, so different from the Austria of the early nineteenth century that they seem to have little in common except for the name. And even Habsburg Austria up to the end of World War I was characterized during its last century by significant breaks in political continuity, as was the Republic of Austria, founded in 1918. Modern Austria is a chain of periods that differ not only—like France— on the political and/or constitutional level but also in regard to size, population, languages, and identity. The most important periods of this chain of discontinuity consist of the following:

1. The Austrian Empire ("Kaisertum Österreich"), created in 1804 out of the different provinces ruled at that time by the Habsburgs and consisting of a great variety of linguistic or ethnic identities: German, Polish, Czech, Hungarian, Italian, Slovakian, Slovenian, (Serbo-)Croatian, Ukrainian, Romanian, Yiddish, and Romani, just to name the most important ones. Austria was, after Russia, the second largest state in Europe. Austria was administered by one of Europe's most conservative political systems. It was a regime without a constitution under the absolute rule of the Habsburg emperors, who claimed the tradition of the Holy Roman Empire, which officially was dismantled in 1806 after centuries of pure symbolic status without any significant political importance. This Austria was one of the pillars of the Holy Alliance, the order the Congress of Vienna established in 1815 to roll back history and to undo the consequences of the French Revolution. The Austrian Chancellor Prince Metternich was primarily responsible for the program and the strategy this alliance was bound to follow (Kissinger 1957).

This Austria was an empire defined not only by the dynasty but also by its antirevolutionary standing. It opposed on principle any democratic or national innovation in the not totally unfounded belief that democratic changes would destroy the absolute rule of the Habsburgs and that national changes would destroy the complex balance among the different nationalities living under the Habsburg umbrella. This Austria was the perfect antithesis to the concept of both a constitutional ("Verfassungsstaat") and an ethnically homogenous state ("Nationalstaat"). This twofold antithetical character created a long-lasting situation: Any modern democratic or modern nationalistic movement or concept had to be "anti-Austrian." Austria became a synonym of antidemocratic and antinationalistic reaction. The failure of the 1848 revolution and its democratic and national ambitions (which were of special importance in Hungary) emphasized this reactionary picture of Austria even more.

2. The Austrian part of the dual monarchy of Austria-Hungary, as established in 1867. The change from the Austrian Empire ("Kaisertum Österreich") to the Austro-Hungarian Empire ("Österreich-Ungarn") was the result of defeats the Habsburgs endured in the wars of 1859 (against Piemonte and France) and 1866 (against Prussia and Italy). They were forced not only to surrender provinces such as Lombardy and the Veneto to the newly founded Italian kingdom but also to find a compromise at home with the Hungarian gentry. This compromise significantly changed the nature of Austria. Austria was now the sum of the Habsburg provinces minus the countries of the Hungarian Stephan's crown, claimed by Hungary on the basis of historic experience. The dual monarchy consisted of two highly autonomous parts, "Cisleithanien" (Austria) and "Transleithanien" (Hungary), which had only foreign, defense, and financial policies in common. Austria was now, much more than before, dominated by its strongest national (linguistic) minority, the Germans. Austria also ceased to be ruled without a constitution: The constitution of 1867 permitted the development of a parliament in which different parties competed, but without jeopardizing the still-hegemonial rule of the emperor, who alone was responsible for appointing the government. The party system soon became completely fragmented following ethno-linguistic cleavages. Even the Social Democrats, by their very nature bound to represent an international understanding, were not able to maintain their multinational organization. Before World War I, there was no Austrian Social Democracy, but rather there existed a Social Democratic Party dominated by Austro-Germans and an Austro-Czech Social Democratic Party, a separate party since 1911 as the result of Austro-German domination and non-German reaction within Social Democracy (Kann 1950; Mommsen 1963). In 1918, the military breakdown was followed by the collapse of the multinational framework: The idea of the ethno-na-

tion state had triumphed over the idea of the multinational state. Because the empire could not become reconciled with democratic ideas in time, it could not overcome the tensions between the different nations (May 1966).

3. The (First) Republic of Austria started in 1918 by declaring itself the "German-Austrian Republic" and a part of the German Republic. The dominant orientation of the "rest," which did not belong to the other successor states of the old empire (Czechoslovakia and Hungary, as well as the regions that became parts of Poland, Romania, Yugoslavia, and Italy), was German. After the elimination of the multinational umbrella, there seemed to be no other choice but to do what the Czechs, Poles, Italians, and Slovenes, as well as the Croats, Slovaks, and Romanians in the Hungarian part of the empire had done: claim self-determination according to national principles. And in view of the majority of the (now) Austrian population, the small republic did not want to remain independent—but to become part of democratic, republican Germany. It was not the will of the people that was responsible for the independence of the Republic of Austria but rather the strategic interests of the Entente. The victorious powers did not want to add something to Germany that had never belonged to a German national state but nevertheless claimed to be German.

   The Anschluss question was born. Before 1918, the idea of unifying Austria with Germany had been the sectarian program of smaller groups within the pan-German camp; now it became the national consensus of the First Republic. The Entente's veto, as expressed in the conditions of the Treaty of St. Germain of 1919, had to be accepted, but Social Democrats and Christian Socials agreed with pan-Germans that the veto must be overridden at the first opportunity. This opportunity did not come before 1938—and then under circumstances quite different from those in 1918. The First Republic was a state that nobody in Austria really accepted: For the conservatives, it was the product of (old) Austria's defeat; for the left, it was just a temporary arrangement until unity with Weimar could be implemented; for the extreme right, it was a nightmare phase between reality and the great myth of a Greater German Empire.

4. The authoritarian state, modeled by the Christian Socials in 1934 after the Italian fascist example and after the doctrine formulated in the papal encyclicals of 1891 ("Rerum novarum") and 1931 ("Quadragesimo anno"), was the dictatorship of one camp (the Christian conservatives) over two others, the socialists and the pan-German camp, the latter already more or less identical with the Nazi Party (Pauley 1981). As the Anschluss could not be viewed independently from the fact that Germany had been under Nazi rule since January 30, 1933, the Anschluss was no longer the intention that united all camps. Only the pan-Germans fa-

vored annexation to Germany by any means, even if this included a Nazi takeover of Austria. The Social Democrats had officially eliminated the Anschluss from its party manifesto in 1933; the Christian Socials (the authoritarian regime) legitimized their rule as the only realistic alternative to occupation by Nazi Germany.

The government, led by Engelbert Dollfuss and (after Dollfuss's assassination by Nazis on July 25, 1934) by Kurt Schuschnigg, defined the nature of their regime as Christian and German and Austrian—Austrian not as a contradiction to German but as the resumption of pre-republican traditions with a distinct Catholic flavor. This kind of Austrian identity was a minority program: The Nazis fought for the real German thing, the Anschluss; the left opposition, the Social Democrats, and the (small number of) Communists could not forget the violation of the constitution, the brutal destruction of the leftist organizations in the civil war of February 1934, and the experience of an authoritarian dictatorship, directed against the left as well as against the Austrian Nazis (Gulick 1948).

Habsburg Austria, the First Republic, and the semifascist regime of Dollfuss and Schuschnigg lived with an understanding of Austria that did not correspond to the reality of a small country the size of Portugal inhabited by about seven million people. For generations—in the nineteenth century and up to the year 1938—Austria had been too grand an empire; later, the legacy of that past prevented Austrians from identifying with the small, unloved republic the Allies had forced them to live in. Deeply influenced by a tradition that defined nation as a "cultural" entity, German-speaking Austrians considered themselves German. In the tradition of Herder, national identity was not seen as the result of political consensus but as more or less independent from political institutions and political developments. And as "culture" was defined not so much by sociological terms (as the result of milieu or caste or class) as by linguistic categories (Reiterer 1988), the fact that from 1918 onward all Austrians spoke German was enough for them to define themselves as Germans.

As Germans in Austria, they fell into the ethno-nationalistic trap. Nazi rule did not prevent many Austrians—many more than the Austrian NSDAP (National Socialist German Workers' Party) was able to recruit—from accepting the Anschluss, even under Nazi terms. Because "nation" was not seen as the product of political development and consensus building but rather as a kind of ironclad law, an eternal and mystic bond, the Austrians were unable to defend Austria against the Nazis—the Nazis who came as Germans, as Germany.

Of course, many other factors have to be taken into account in order to understand the lack of self-esteem that characterized Austria on the eve of Anschluss (Dokumentationsarchiv 1988). The Austrian version of rabid racism, expressed in the hatred against Jews, was not a sentiment that divided the Nazis from the non-Nazis. Anti-Semitism was deeply rooted in Austria (Pulzer 1988). Before 1938, especially within the Christian-conservative camp, there was a tendency to claim anti-Semitism as a Catholic tradition and to challenge the Nazis to a competition to prove who was the better anti-Semite. But even the Social Democrats, their doctrine officially free of all anti-Semitic rhetoric and therefore political home to most of Austria's Jews, did not fight anti-Semitism offensively because so many among the party's rank and file were not immune to anti-Jewish sentiment (Pauley 1992: esp. 131–172).

There was a striking parallel between the lack of an Austrian identity and the lack of democratic stability. After 1918, Austrians did not seem to be able to direct their political loyalty to the small republic on an emotional level, in the sense of national identity. They could not bring themselves to accept the smallness of their country. As it was impossible either to reestablish the old empire or to reconcile the old empire with the needs of the different nations in a democratic way, the Austrians longed for another empire: Germany. Not so much the real Germany of Weimar or of the Nazis but the Germany of romantic fairy tales: a Germanic empire able to dominate the non-Germanic parts of Europe as the pan-Germans hoped; or the Christian "Reich," successor to Charlemagne's empire and defender of Christendom and "Abendland" against the old and the new heathen forces; or a progressive republic in the tradition of German enlightenment—the very tradition the name Weimar stood for and the cornerstone of a future socialist Europe.

None of these was real. The real Germany was not only the antithesis to an independent Austria; it was also the antithesis to all the democratic and religious values the two major camps represented. Consequently, the response—made possible by the defeat of Nazi Germany—had to come from those major camps.

Greatness does not pay. This was the lesson Austria and the Austrians had to learn first. The Nazi years were the most catastrophic in Austria's history. Austrians defined as Jews were exiled or persecuted. Austrians defined as gypsies followed the Jews into the gas chambers. Austrians seen as political opponents of the regime were oppressed. Austrians, as citizens of the Greater German Empire, had to follow the call to arms—voluntarily or not—and fight and be killed, from Stalingrad to the Atlantic. Austrian civilians had to endure the horrors of war as the populations of other countries had. Austria was destroyed by the war that the empire so many Austrians wanted to belong to had started (Luza 1975).

The outcome of World War II provided the entity that—much against the will of its population—had been called Austria between 1918 and 1938 with its second chance to build a democratic republic. It was not so much the result of decisionmaking in Austria itself. Austrian resistance to Nazi dictatorship was not at all united by a common political purpose beyond overthrowing the Nazis. The two strongest resistance groups, the Communists and the Habsburg loyalists or "legitimists" (Luza 1984), existed more on the fringes of the Austrian political mainstream. It was the political intention of the Allies to reestablish Austria within its borders of 1937 (the year before the Anschluss) as an independent and sovereign state.

This decision of the victors was accepted by the political traditions, which started to reorganize at the end of the war and which to a greater degree than the Communists or the legitimists represented what politically motivated most Austrians: the Social Democrats and the Christian Socials, the socialists and the Christian-conservative camp. The two major camps, which were also the main forces behind the foundation of the First Republic of 1918 and of the constitution of 1920, had changed their attitude during the four years of the "authoritarian state" and during the seven years of totalitarian dictatorship. The period between 1934 and 1938 was considered a lesson: The forceful exclusion of one of the two camps destroyed the possibility to stabilize Austria. Therefore the victims of February 1934, the left, had to be accepted as partners on a permanent basis by the victors of this civil war, the Catholics of the Christian-conservative camp. And the socialists also had to accept their former oppressors as partners. The period between 1938 and 1945 was regarded as a lesson in practical, real Anschluss: The annexation by Germany, which so many Austrians had rejoiced at, did not fulfill their expectations. Austrians, who had survived political oppression and the war and the Holocaust, had to realize that to be German was to be on the losing side and that being a loser in 1945 had a very different flavor than it had in 1918. The fate that awaited conquered Germany now was to be ostracized by the international community.

The years of the real Anschluss had also strengthened the feeling of being different from the Germans who came from the "Reich," from pre-1938 Germany. The Anschluss worked as a catalyst for the development of a distinct Austrian identity—distinct from the ethno-national identity that made German-speaking Austrians consider themselves German, distinct from the imperial identity that made Austrians members of a supranational entity with no special Austrian national identity (Kreissler 1984: 316–374; Hanisch 1994: 395–398).

The combination of international factors—the intentions of the Allies—and domestic factors created the atmosphere of 1945, one very different from that of 1918. Austria did not have to be forced to accept its independence from Germany; Austria did not have to be forced to accept its existence as a small, distinctly nonimperial state. Austria did not change its size or geographic shape from the interwar period, but Austria did change its attitude toward its own independence and its own smallness.

The formula that the new Austria of the Second Republic started to follow in 1945 was the formula of "consociational democracy." This formula was not developed from textbooks, nor was it developed from theory. It was a pragmatic combination of different compromises, which only later came to be known as "Proporzdemokratie" or "Konkordanzdemokratie," and it evolved out of the tradition established by the Netherlands and Switzerland (Lijphart 1977).

2

POLITICAL CULTURE

Austria's political culture was considered the model of change. The First Republic was the prototype of centrifugal democracy: The political elites were not able and/or willing to bridge the deep fragmentation that characterized Austrian society. The Second Republic became—together with Switzerland and the Netherlands—the main European model for consociational democracy: The elites, highly interested in establishing a network of cooperation, agreed to share power within a principal arrangement (Steiner 1972: 155–189).

The most recent developments indicate a new quality of Austria's political culture. Consociationalism is weakening, while the competitive character of Austrian democracy is becoming more prevalent. The Austrian society seems to be less fragmented, at least as far as the traditional cleavages are concerned. Consequently, the elites' behavior is becoming less consensus oriented. The distinctly Austrian way of dealing with challenges—a pattern characterized by the search for compromise—is in retreat.

Nation Building Through Consociationalism

Consociational democracy should be seen as a technique that has always to do with the integration not only of different interests but also of different identities. Consociational democracy is a technique for healing the wounds history has inflicted (Lehmbruch 1967). Fragmentation is the result of such deeply inflicted damage, and healing a fragmented society means bridging the past. Consensus building through power-sharing arrangements is more than power obtained by distributing positions and supporting all who are part of such an arrangement.

Consensus building must also deal with the symbols, the mystique, and the perception of historic truth, all of which divide a fragmented society.

How to deal with Austria's past, how to come to terms with the contradicting aspects of the Nazi past? The Second Republic first tried an approach that must be called apologetic in its substance and elitist in its methods. The Second Republic's official description of Austria's fate between 1938 and 1945 was influenced by the interests of the political elites of 1945 and after, especially by foreign policy interests in fulfilling the expectations of the Allies and by domestic interests in integrating the most important segments of Austrian society into the political system.

The technique the elites used was that of divided truth. Like the power the Catholic-conservatives and the socialists had agreed to divide among themselves, the truth was divided horizontally as well as vertically. On the top, especially for international purposes, the elites ("black" and "red" alike)—the Renner government ("Provisorische Staatsregierung") and its successor, the coalition cabinet led by Leopold Figl and by Adolf Schärf—did their best to depict Austria as a victim. Austria had been invaded in March 1938, and the Allies had recognized Austria as a victim—as the first victim—of Hitler's aggressive expansionist policy. The Austrian government never tired of quoting the Moscow Declaration of November 1, 1943, defining Austria as a victim whose independence must be reinstated by the victorious powers. Simultaneously, the Austrian government had to play down the fact that there was more to the Moscow Declaration than the paragraph defining Austria as a victim (". . . Austria, the first country to fall victim to Hitlerite aggression"); it also contained the following: "Austria is reminded, however, that she has a responsibility which she cannot evade for participation in the war on the side of Hitlerite Germany, and that in the final settlement account will inevitably be taken of her own contribution to her liberation" (Keyserlingk 1988: 207 f.).

In Austria's Declaration of Independence, dated April 27, 1945, and signed by the representatives of the "antifascist parties" that made up the Renner government, the first part of the Moscow Declaration was mentioned very prominently, but the second part was almost hidden at the end and, with a significant use of terminology, was called a "postscript" ("Nachsatz"), a term nowhere to be found in the Allies' document.

This official position was aimed especially at the Allied Powers. It was designed to influence public opinion in foreign countries, thereby having an impact on the negotiations for the reestablishment of full Austrian sovereignty, the negotiations that led to the State Treaty of May 15, 1955. Consequently, between 1945 and 1955 official Austria attempted to extinguish the historical interpretation formulated in the final paragraph of the Moscow Declaration. Austria should be depicted as a victim, not as a perpetrator or as an accomplice of the Nazi criminals. On the eve of the signing of the Austrian State Treaty, at the foreign minister's conference on May 14, 1955, the Austrian government finally succeeded in eliminating the offending paragraph from the preamble of the treaty. The draft of the preamble had included the very precise wording that gave Austria a "certain responsibility" for the Nazi war—the very same interpretation that was included in the Moscow Declaration (Stourzh 1975: 121). This aspect seemed to be extinguished—at least on a formal, diplomatic level.

For ten years, official Austria fought to establish Austria's innocence and for its role as a victim. It took a full ten years before Austria was able to acquit itself of responsibility for the crimes of Nazism. On the surface, it was a great success. The Austrian elites were able to define truth—on the surface.

But at the very same time, the elites contradicted their own position significantly—for domestic reasons. Beginning in 1948, those Austrians who, in 1938 and the seven years thereafter, had been on the other side, who had jubilantly welcomed the occupation of Austria by German troops and had interpreted the outcome of the war as a defeat, began once again to be of some interest as voters in domestic politics. The shadows of the 1949 general elections were predictable. More than 500,000 "Ehemalige" (former Nazis) got back their voting rights (Riedlsperger 1978). And now the other side of the truth became part of the official, collective memory: Austria was a country that had not defended itself militarily; many Austrians—not only the true believers in Nazism but even the Catholic bishops and prominent Social Democrats such as Karl Renner—had welcomed the Anschluss. Austria's Nazi Party had been extremely successful in organizing and integrating a large number of Austrians even before 1938 and, in the seven years up to 1945, had about the same number of members as the Social Democrats had before 1934 and after 1945.

In the official documentation the Austrian government published to back its claim as a victim of Nazi aggression, neither the behavior of the bishops nor Renner's pro-Anschluss declaration was mentioned. Despite one reference to a certain opportunism that some Austrians demonstrated in 1938, the official response sidestepped culpability: "But the Austrian people didn't go over to Nazism, even during that period. Anybody who knows anything about Austrians understands and accepts that Prussianism, militarism, and Nazism are basically as alien to Austrians as to any other people in Europe. Prussia's military cult, the idea of totalitarianism and the perfect control of the individual by the government have always been and still are in total contradiction to Austrian nature" (Rot-Weiss-Rot-Buch 1946: 71 f.).

The official Austrian attitude was leaning toward ethno-national clichés: "Prussianism" ("Preussentum"), identical with Nazism, contradicted "the Austrian nature"—as if Hitler, Kaltenbrunner, Seyss-Inquart, Globocnik, Eichmann, and so many others had not been Austrian. However, it is this balance of unspoken aspects, of taboos, that has been especially important for the implementation of consociational democracy. The official documentation of 1946 (Rot-Weiss-Rot-Buch 1946) and other documents did not speak about the appeasement that representatives of both major camps had offered the Nazi rulers or about the NSDAP propaganda before the "plebiscite" of April 10, 1938, which used the "yes" of the bishops as well as that of Karl Renner. Not speaking about the major failures both camps had to hide was instrumental in establishing mutual trust: Both sides—the Catholic-conservative and the socialist elite—were necessarily grateful for this official silence. Each side had taken the other hostage: If you dare to speak about Renner or other aspects of social-democratic weaknesses, we will expose the truth about the bishops and other leaders of the Catholic camp.

Not that the truth about the days of March and April 1938 could have been kept secret—anybody who wanted to could clearly remember the open letter the bishops wrote and the interview Renner gave (Hanisch 1994: 337–347). It was the mutuality of being ashamed of past propaganda and the mutuality of being grateful for the present silence that worked as a kind of confidence-building measure. There was not so much to hide, but there was something both sides had in common: an interest in ignoring some aspects of history.

History—and especially the history of Austria's involvement in Nazism—was divided horizontally: At the top, the government insisted on the role of victim, stressing the first part of the Moscow Declaration. At the bottom, the elites soon started to pay tribute to the hundreds of thousands of Austrians who did not feel liberated but rather defeated and conquered by the outcome of the war. But history was also divided vertically. The politics of silence corresponded with the interests of both camps, namely, to forget what could have compromised either side. There was a "left" version of history and there was a "right" version; and there were "left" taboos and "right" taboos. At the beginning of the Second Republic, there were different Austrian histories—but there was no Austrian history.

Both major parties agreed that the Second Republic should be a democracy according to liberal Western standards. Therefore, the reality of the political market could not be fully and permanently ignored. And the reality of the political market was characterized by the fact that many more independents were to the right of the elite cartel the ÖVP and the SPÖ had built than were to its left. The Communists were not able to mobilize more than 5 percent of the electorate—not even in November 1945, when the future of Austria seemed to be dependent on the USSR. But the former Nazis, the "Ehemalige," represented about 15 percent of the electorate. And as they were refranchised, the logic of the market took over despite consociational democracy. Both major parties, the ÖVP as well as the SPÖ, tried to win as many former Nazis as possible. The SPÖ, thinking that the ÖVP, as a "bourgeois" party right of the center, would be in the better position, helped to establish the "Verband der Unabhängigen" (VDU), the League of Independents, designated to represent the former Nazis and to revive the tradition of the pan-German camp (Riedlsperger 1978: 47–49; Rathkolb in Meissl et al. 1986: 73 –99).

The background of this behavior was the specific Austrian method of denazification. Austrian denazification differed significantly from German denazification. Immediately after liberation, the three "antifascist parties" took over the task of ridding political and other institutions of former Nazis and to free the Austrian society from the ideological remnants left by the old regime. From the very beginning, the specific Austrian roots of Nazism were largely ignored: Nazism was to be considered only as an organizational phenomenon—membership in the National Socialist German Workers' Party (NSDAP). In 1945, it was up to the three parties of the Provisional Government to decide who was to be registered as a Nazi and to what degree he (or she) should be denied certain rights, for instance exclusion from certain professions. This denazification, based on the "Verbotsgesetz" ("Prohibition Act") passed by the Provisional Government in 1945, was mainly directed toward NSDAP members in the public service sector. It was up to "special commissions" to decide who was a "big" Nazi, who was just a "hanger-on" ("Mitläufer"), and who was perhaps not a Nazi at all despite "formal" party membership. The members of the "special commissions" were directly recruited by the political parties (Stiefel 1981: 48–77).

It was this first period of denazification that established a certain pattern: Members of the NSDAP felt invited to seek the protection of one of the three parties. And from the start, the ÖVP and the SPÖ (and to a lesser degree the Communist Party of Austria—the KPÖ) developed a tendency to claim certain "smaller" Nazis as the clientele they wanted to protect. And when the KPÖ had lost most of its power, following the elections of November 1945, this pattern became part of the consociationalism upon which the "grand coalition" of the ÖVP and the SPÖ was built. It became customary to argue that most of the Austrian members of the NSDAP were only misguided patriots who had already suffered enough. Both coalition partners tried to win as many of them as they could for their own party.

The Allies had a stronger interest in rigid denazification than the Austrian government. It was the pressure from the Allied Council, the supreme institution of the four powers in Austria, that was responsible for the "Entnazifizierungsgesetz" ("Denazification Act") of 1947 (Stiefel 1981: 101–124). But soon, the Cold War with its new philosophy took over: East and West, Communist or anti-Communist became more important, perhaps even more than being a (former) Nazi or an antifascist (Knight in Meissl et al. 1986: 37–50). The common interest linking the Western powers and the USSR and all the parties that constituted the Austrian government ceased to exist. In 1947, the KPÖ left the coalition and became an opposition party in parliament—a phenomenon then taking place all over Western Europe. The Cold War overshadowed denazification. Consequently, there was not much opposition when the majority of the former Nazis, the "less incriminated" ("Minderbelastete"), were invited to participate in politics again, as was the case in 1948, with particular impact on the elections of 1949.

But even during the first years of the Cold War, the ÖVP-SPÖ coalition and the Western Allies followed policies with different interests concerning denazification. The question of reparation ("Wiedergutmachung") was a source of conflict, especially between the United States and the Austrian government. The United States put pressure on the more than hesitant Austrian government to satisfy the claims of Austrian Jews, especially those pertaining to property in Austria. The minutes of the cabinet meetings clearly show that as early as the summer of 1945 the Austrian government was inclined to do everything it could to slow down the reparation process (Sternfeld 1990: esp. 85–122; Bailer 1993). It is obvious that among the cabinet members, some—such as Foreign Minister Karl Gruber (ÖVP) and Interior Minister Oskar Helmer (SPÖ)—were influenced by anti-Semitic prejudices (Knight 1988: esp. 59, 140, 211).

The coalition cabinet behaved democratically insofar as many more of their voters stood to lose than to gain if reparations were made by restoring Jewish property and responding positively to Jewish claims, for instance as concerned housing. Too many Austrians had profited from "aryanization"—and too many of them were voters again (Etzersdorfer 1995). It was not at all a consistent "antifascist" or anti-Nazi sentiment that was responsible for the consensus upon which the coalition was built. It was a pragmatic consensus to be rhetorically anti-Nazi for international purposes and to be survival oriented for domestic purposes. One factor that suited all these interests was Austrian patriotism.

Austrian patriotism in 1945 and the years after was—like all identity formulas—full of contradictions because it was fed by very different traditions:

- by the nostalgic pro-Habsburg sentiment the authoritarian system had tried to revive between 1934 and 1938;
- by the programs for an Austrian (that is, non-German) nation formulated in the 1930s by such different intellectuals as the Catholic-conservative Ernst Karl Winter and the Communist Alfred Klahr and designated to give anti-Anschluss policies an emotional background;
- by the experience of the real Anschluss, which many or perhaps most Austrians had seen—at least in 1945—as a negative one;
- by the incentives the international political arena had ready for an Austria that did not consider itself German.

Sentiments, intellectual programs, popular experience, and the international arena—the common link between all those factors was an Austrian patriotism centered around the Austria that existed then, the republic. This was the significant difference between the beginning of the First and the Second Republics. In 1918, there was almost nothing to reconcile Austrians with the artificially created, small, new Austria. The Habsburg nostalgics could not overcome their longing for the empire. To them, in 1918, it seemed grotesque to call a remnant nobody wanted Austria. There was no program or strategic plan to call this small Austria a national entity different from that of Germany. Pan-Germanism was the national feeling that united Austrians in 1918. Consequently, from 1918 on, they were looking for a way to follow their national feelings to a logical conclusion: the Anschluss. But that experience was to come later. The international incentives that existed in 1918 did not work—primarily due to the fact that at the beginning of the First Republic there was a democratic Germany, Weimar, which attracted most progressive, republican, democratic, and even socialist interests.

In 1945, there was no Germany, let alone a respected one. In 1945, it was obvious that any positive future for Austria could not be linked to any future of Germany, whatever that might be. In 1945, it was also obvious that any restoration of a greater Austria was not in the cards of global politics. Resentments over the reality of the seven years of Nazi power could easily be channeled into an anti-German feeling: Being Austrian became different from being German (Kreissler 1984: esp. 375–391; Bruckmüller 1994: esp. 73–78; Bruckmüller 1996: esp. 384–396).

The result was a change in Austrian identity. For the second time in the twentieth century, what it meant to be Austrian changed significantly. After the identity typical of Habsburg Austria (which saw Austria as a non-national umbrella identity, above the ethno-national identities all belonging to and fitting into Austria) and the identity typical of the years between 1918 and 1938 (which regarded Austria as a German state, perhaps even the "better" German state), Austrians became reconciled with the existing small republican state.

The results can be seen in public opinion data: From 1945 on, an increasing majority of Austrians declared themselves members of an Austrian nation (see Table 2.1). And because the term "Austrian nation" had always been a key word in conflict with pan-Germanism, this meant a dissociation from a pan-German identity as well as from a supranational identity. To deny the existence of a special Austrian nation meant especially to deny this connotation. It can be assumed that the denial of an Austrian nation reflects the strength of hard core pan-Germanism in Austria: Those who did not believe in the existence of a specific Austrian nation demonstrated their pan-German creed (Bruckmüller 1994: 15–25).

This must also be interpreted as the result of consociational democracy. Despite the identities on which the Habsburg Empire and the First Republic were built—the former supranational, the latter pan-German—there was a strong subidentity with the existing ideological camps. The majority of Austrians at the beginning of the twentieth century and during the First Republic were politically motivated and mobilized not only and perhaps not even primarily by their government or by their state, which in any case did not correspond with the dominant national (pan-German) feeling. Most Austrians were emotionally linked to their respective camps. A Social Democrat in the 1920s was first and foremost a Social Democrat. A politically active Catholic around 1930 considered himself (or herself) first of all to be bound to the alliance between church and party, the Christian-conservative camp. And a pan-German Austrian, socialized by pan-German "Turnerbünde" (gymnastics clubs with highly developed ideologies) and dueling fraternities, did not feel loyal primarily to Austria–neither to Habsburg Austria, nor to the republic–but to the myth of Germany represented by the organizations of the pan-German camp (Pelinka 1990: 81–126).

"Building an Austrian nation" (Bluhm 1973) was therefore the task of the traditions and organizations that were the sources of this secondary, subnational identification–the ideological camps. And because in 1945 the pan-German camp was immobilized due to its almost total participation in the Nazi regime, the task

TABLE 2.1   National Identity of Austrians As It Developed in the Second Republic

Out of the representative samples, the percentage of Austrians who identified with the following statements:

Year	1964	1970	1980	1990	1993
The Austrians are a nation	47	66	67	74	80
The Austrians are beginning to feel like a nation slowly	23	16	19	20	12
The Austrians are not a nation	15	8	11	5	6
No response	14	10	3	1	2

SOURCE: Bruckmüller 1994: 15.

fell to the two other major camps, now represented by the ÖVP and the SPÖ. They had to cooperate on all levels: not only making pragmatic daily decisions and sharing power by dividing positions within all the social subsystems but also arriving at a common understanding of what Austria was about, what the Austrian identity should include and exclude. Consociational democracy not only had to answer bread-and-butter questions; it also had to deal with highly emotional factors of national identity.

It was not the intention of the two major parties to implement a certain semantic understanding of Austrian identity. It was general patriotism, linked with Austria, the coalition cabinets from 1945 on had in mind. But this Austrian patriotism competed with pan-German nationalism. And this competition turned out to be quite successful for Austrian patriotism. The consequence was the erosion of pan-German nationalism.

Arend Lijphart describes four essential characteristics of consociational democracy (Lijphart 1997: 25):

- grand coalition,
- mutual veto or "concurrent majority" rule,
- proportionality as the principal standard of political representation, and
- a high degree of autonomy for each segment of the political system.

The basic philosophy behind this type of democracy in plural societies is to reduce the rule of competition in favor of a balance between competitive and coalescent elements, between conflict and consensus orientation. The rules of the game are not "the winner takes all" but rather that the loser gets something too.

The history behind this philosophy lies in the deep fragmentation caused by violent domestic conflict. The Swiss Civil War between Catholic and Protestant cantons in 1847 is probably the best example of a civil war that greatly exacerbated an already existing fragmentation. Consociational democracy did not come as a specific constitutional answer. On the contrary. The Swiss constitution of 1848 is neither the product of nor the reason for Swiss consociationalism. Consociational democracy is a specific political culture that exists independently of the written rules of the constitution (Lehmbruch 1967).

It is not the Swiss constitution that is responsible for Swiss-style consociational democracy. The political element that was considered the winner of the civil war, the liberal Protestant, started to develop the political culture later described as consociational democracy only after 1848. This culture was based on a mutual understanding between the winners and the losers, the latter being the predominantly conservative Catholics. This pattern, later seen as "typically Swiss," came out of the realization of both winners and losers that their country needed a new balance of power if the wounds of the war were to heal. The result was and still is the perpetual grand coalition, which binds Catholics and Protestants as well as German-, French-, and Italian-speaking Swiss by uniting the four major parties in a coalition cabinet (Linder 1994).

It is not the Austrian constitution that explains the Second Republic's inclination toward consociational democracy. After 1945, the constitution was still the same as it had been during the years of the First Republic, years that certainly cannot be called "consociational." Consociational democracy is the specific political culture as it developed after the catalyst years of authoritarian and totalitarian rule.

The First Republic's political culture fits the pattern of centrifugal democracy in that it was already fragmented along the lines of the camps. Three subcultures divided the Austrian society and its political system: the two major ones, the socialist and the Christian-conservative, and the smaller pan-German one. The leaders of those three camps responded to this situation by competing according to the rules of liberal democracy. Because nothing could be gained by adopting a moderate attitude toward the political center, this competition set in motion a trend away from the center: centrifugal democracy.

The most striking aspect of this development was that the camps treated each other according to the logic not of domestic but of foreign policy. This included an arms race that led directly to the civil wars of 1934. Centrifugal democracy had brought about the destruction of democracy.

After 1945, the fragmentation still did not disappear. In his study of Hallein, a town near Salzburg, G. Bingham Powell, Jr., described and analyzed the deep hostility that still characterized the relationship between "black" and "red" Austrians in the 1960s (Powell 1970). There was still an identity between party functions and functions in all the secondary groups that dominated social life. There was no independent life beyond the ideological camps. And the camps were still characterized by strong hostile stereotypes. Powell summarized the finding of his study:

- partisan distrust and hostility are indeed associated at the individual level with pure or cumulative (rather than mixed or cross-cutting) cleavage position and with membership in partisan secondary groups; and
- hostility and distrust between major political groups complicate and reduce the effectiveness of political decision-making (Powell 1970: 138).

After twenty years of consociational democracy, the fragmentation and the "Lager-Mentalität" (camp mentality) were still there. Politics was still considered to be a battle between the forces of good and evil. The two major camps, in a coalition cabinet jointly responsible for Austria's development, still took a dichotomous view of society. To put it more precisely, because the old stereotypes still worked in society, in the "masses," the elites were free to behave according to the model of consociational democracy.

The most basic necessity of consociational democracy is deep mutual enmity among the masses. Fragmentation is the first and most vital precondition of consociational democracy in Austria and elsewhere. The Second Republic developed very differently from the First not because "the people" had a different perception of politics but because high-ranking politicians behaved differently.

The political leaders who counted in 1945 and the years immediately thereafter were the elites of the SPÖ and ÖVP, of the socialist and of the Christian-conservative camps. The Communists did not really count: As soon as it was obvious that the USSR did not plan to integrate Austria into its Marxist-Leninist realm by force, the influence the KPÖ had enjoyed in 1945 dwindled. The KPÖ was not strong enough to build a camp for itself. The SPÖ kept its de facto monopoly on the political left because the Social Democrats were able to reestablish their camp with all the familiar structures and organizations of the last decades of imperial Austria and the First Republic: socialist organizations for everyone, fulfilling every social function, from child care to provisions for a true socialist burial. And the pan-German camp was paralyzed. Identified for good reasons with the Nazi regime and without a voice until the birth of the VDU in 1949, the camp that had been the Christian Socials' coalition partner between 1920 and 1933 simply did not exist in political terms.

Austrian-style consociational democracy was the result of elitist learning. Christian Socials, now organized as the ÖVP, and Social Democrats, now the SPÖ, reversed their mutual attitude—at the top level. Instead of competition with no restrictions, their policy was cooperation with some competitive elements. This cooperation had two outside enemies that provided the new alliance with the necessary coherence:

- Nazism, especially for foreign policy purposes.
- Communism, at first especially for domestic purposes, and later, under the influence of the Cold War, also for foreign policy purposes.

The ÖVP-SPÖ alliance had to prove that this new kind of cooperation was the patriotic Austrian answer to the Nazi experience. And the alliance also had to prove that it was the only alternative to Communism. Without this alliance, there would be chaos and dictatorship and foreign rule. This was the message both parties tried to deliver, especially to their own. The coalition became popular by explaining how dreadful any alternative would be.

The Austrian consociational democracy consisted from the very beginning of two levels or two focal areas: the cooperation between the ÖVP and SPÖ on the government level, including a parliamentary alliance; and cooperation between employers and employees, or between their respective interest organizations. These two elements were characterized by different logics and capacities:

- Government and parliament followed the rule of liberal democracy, which the grand coalition simply by its existence restricted until 1966. This rule followed the logic of a zero-sum game. If you don't want to lose, make sure that someone else will. Majority rule existed, electoral victories had an impact on parliament, and elections were a competitive procedure in a political market, the same as in other liberal democracies. Government and parliament dominated all noneconomic matters, and both government and parliament were under the control of political parties, namely the ÖVP and SPÖ.
- Business and labor established their own rules of corporatism. Majority rule was abolished, and a mutual veto made compromises unavoidable. The zero-sum game did not exist, and elections had no or at least no immediate influence. Corporatism dominated all economic matters, including most aspects of social policy. The corporatist level was controlled by economic interest groups organized to represent employers, employees, or agriculture.

Both levels were integrated by virtue of their amalgam of political parties and economic interest groups. Political decisionmaking was synchronized by the identity of political personnel: The two major camps controlled not only the parties but also the organized economic interests. There was no significant voice on the corporatist level that was not controlled by the parties, and no significant voice was heard on the government level unless it was under the control of the major economic interest groups (see Table 2.2).

This synchronization had structural and personal aspects. The structural aspect was and is the participation of all major interest groups in the preparliamentary legislative process by means of a formalized invitation to evaluate any draft coming from any ministry ("Begutachtungsverfahren"). Major parties and major interest groups are linked together by factions ("Fraktionen") and cannot be distinguished clearly.

These structural linkages were responsible for the personal ones. The presidents of the major employees' associations, the Austrian Trade Union Federation (ÖGB) and the Federal Chamber of Labor, were always SPÖ leaders, usually representing their party directly (and their interest group indirectly) in parliament. The leadership of the Chamber of Economics and of the different Chambers of Agriculture were always prominent members of the ÖVP who also had a seat in parliament. Following the same pattern, some key govern-

TABLE 2.2   The Two Logics of Government and Corporatism

	Government	*Corporatism*
Differences:		
Players	Political parties	Economic associations
Arenas	Parliament	Social partnership
Philosophies	Competitive	Coalescent
Rules	Majoritarian	Unanimity
Tendency	Public disclosure	Little disclosure
Powers	Noneconomic	Economic
Similarities:		
Stuctures:	Both institutions have party factions within interest groups	
Personnel:	Both are controlled in an elitist, cartel-like way	

ment ministries were virtually reserved for certain functionaries: The minister of Labor and Social Affairs was always a member of the ÖGB leadership, and as long as the Ministry of Agriculture was (and is) led by someone from the ÖVP, the minister was (and is) always linked with the Chambers of Agriculture.

The combination of structural and personal links necessitated the pattern of multiple functions. Because government and corporatism had to be synchronized and because this synchronization included a number of persons fulfilling roles on both levels, there had to be more roles than persons. The often criticized "multiple functionaries" were the consequence.

The structural and personal links prevented the two areas from moving apart. The differences concerning majoritarian versus unanimity rule also implied different tendencies in self-promotion and self-perception: Parties in parliament competing for votes are always inclined to go public as much as possible. On the other side, interest groups that have to preserve their ability to compromise are always interested in avoiding publicity if possible.

Without the strong bonds that guaranteed their political synchronization, the balance between the competitive and the coalescent elements would not have been maintained for such a long time. The atmosphere of constant campaigning typical of majoritarian rule always jeopardizes the much more intimate atmosphere of the compromise-seeking arena corporatism needs. Party politicians always fighting for positions would jeopardize the intimate understanding corporatist decisionmaking requires. By nature, the relationship between government and corporatism is not a harmonious one. Government and corporatism would not be compatible in the long run—if there were not strong bonds to hold together forces that naturally move apart.

The grand coalition established corporatism from 1945 on, step by step:

- In 1945, Social Democratic, Christian, and Communist trade union representatives founded the ÖGB. This gave labor a strong, centralized institution capable of overcoming the competition between labor unions, which depended on the different camps and could not develop a political suprastructure such as the ÖGB was designed to become.
- In 1946, the law establishing the Federal Chamber of Commerce (now the Austrian Chamber of Economics) gave the traditional chambers of commerce, which had existed on the regional level since 1848, an umbrella organization. Business got the suprastructure similar to what labor had with the ÖGB.
- Between 1947 and 1951, the major interest groups (ÖGB, Federal Chamber of Commerce, Chambers of Labor, Chambers of Agriculture) and the government produced a total of five agreements on wages and prices. For the first time, government and corporatism had formally cooperated in political decisionmaking.
- In 1957, the Joint Commission on Wages and Prices was established (Tálos 1993; Bischof and Pelinka 1996). This Commission, founded by Chancellor Julius Raab and ÖGB president Johann Böhm, was the epitome of corporatism in Austria: The four major interest groups, which run the Joint Commission and were responsible for the five agreements between 1947 and 1951, emancipated themselves from government control.

After the end of the first grand coalition, mutual veto, as one of the main characteristics of consociational democracy, had to be reinterpreted. Until 1966, either of the two coalition partners could veto a cabinet decision. Despite the competitiveness that defines parliament, the Austrian federal cabinet is not modeled on majoritarian rule but on the rule of unanimity. On the government level, the veto between the two camps was based on their participation in the cabinet. When the first one-party cabinet was installed in 1966, there was no veto power left in government for the opposition party—from 1966 to 1970 for the SPÖ, and from 1970 to 1986 for the ÖVP. The emphasis on consociationalism had to swing toward corporatism.

But there was still much left in government to provide an interparty balance. State and local politics continued to follow the model of grand coalition. In seven of the nine states, the state constitution differs from the federal with respect to cabinet appointments. In these seven states, the cabinet ("Landesregierung") is constituted according to proportional representation, that is, all major parties have to be represented not only in parliament but also in the cabinet. On the local level, municipalities use approximately the same model (Nick and Pelinka 1996: 61–64).

On the federal level, corporatism did become more important after the end of the first grand coalition. Josef Klaus, chancellor and ÖVP party chairman during the four years of the Second Republic's first one-party cabinet, remembers the informal contacts he had established with Anton Benya, president of the ÖGB and a leading SPÖ figure. Klaus and Benya used these contacts not only to exchange views but also to reach agreements concerning policy matters (Klaus 1971: 88 f., 388). At the very same time when, on the official government level, Westminster-style confrontation had replaced the grand coalition and the SPÖ was behaving like a traditional opposition party, consociational links between the head of the ÖVP government and the head of the SPÖ-dominated labor federation were working.

The importance of corporatism, especially from 1966 to 1987, the interim years between the two grand coalitions, is illustrated by the history of the Labor Act ("Arbeitsverfassungsgesetz") from 1974. The bill did not include constitutional amendments and therefore did not require a two-thirds majority in parliament. At the time, the SPÖ commanded an overall majority in the National Council so it theoretically should have been no problem to pass the act without having to compromise with anyone outside the SPÖ. The SPÖ and the ÖGB were programmatically committed to the idea of "parity co-determination," which meant giving labor representatives 50 percent control of the boards ("Aufsichtsräte") of all joint stock corporations ("Kapitalgesellschaften"). But the SPÖ did not want to push parity co-determination through parliament. Instead, it first tried to work out a compromise with the employers' associations (Federal Chamber of Commerce, Association of Austrian Industrialists). And only after reaching a compromise, which gave labor representatives one-third of the positions on the boards and included further restrictions, did the act pass in parliament with the votes of the opposition party, the ÖVP (Atzmüller 1985: 75–101).

Consociational democracy Austrian-style had (and to a lesser extent, still has) the possibility to change arenas. If elections resulted in a parliament that followed the Westminster model of a one-party cabinet facing a strong opposition, the power share shifted to the corporatist arena of social partnership. The government was always anxious not to alienate the "other side" too much, especially in all matters concerning general arrangements of great interest to the "other side." The Westminster model was significantly softened by the pattern both parties accepted, as expressed by Klaus in his contacts with ÖGB president Benya and by Kreisky in his preparliamentary dealings to reach a compromise on the Labor Act. The grand coalition had ceased to exist in 1966—but it lived on in different forms in different arenas. And this was possible because the very same elite groups were able to control both levels, government and corporatism. The dominant camps, still in control of politics and society, had different ways and means of balancing their power by sharing it. The "winner takes all" philosophy so important in the First Republic never made a comeback in the Second.

Consociational democracy Austrian-style was characterized by its great elasticity and flexibility. Top-ranking politicians were able to move from one arena to the other and had full control over the game of politics. They could shift decisionmaking from the government level to corporatism and back to government. They were able to combine parliamentary and preparliamentary elements. They lived in the best of both worlds: liberal democracy to fulfill the expectations of enlightenment, human rights, and Western traditions; and corporatism to plan and control with little or no disturbance from democratic upheaval or intense class warfare.

Little wonder that it was a pope who called Austria an "island of the blessed" (Luther and Müller 1992: 8). Pope Paul VI realized that Austria was able to combine some of the doctrines the church preached with the traditions of Western democracy. The Austria of the 1970s was a fully developed Western democracy that at the very same time could escape some of the less attractive effects of being such a democracy. "Social peace" expressed itself in an absence of significant strikes and a broad consensus including all main aspects of foreign and domestic politics. Other countries might have their conflicts, but Austria was happy being different.

Consociational democracy Austrian-style was not only a set of institutions and procedures designed to reduce the competitiveness of liberal democracy. It was also an opportunity to reduce the illusions of greatness and dreams of power that the ideological camps had nurtured for such a long time. For Social Democrats, power sharing was unavoidably linked to accepting limits on socialist expectations. Tied to a Christian-conservative partner with veto power, the SPÖ had to accept the impossibility of implementing the theory of true democratic socialism. Austromarxism had to be watered down. For the ÖVP, accepting the Social Democrats as permanent partners meant lowering the expectations the Christian-conservative camp had for a Christian Austria.

By lowering expectations and destroying illusions, the political leaders had taken the first step in the direction of reconciling Austria and Austrians with reality. But their clients, the voters, had difficulty following. In the years following 1945, the voters still held to the old creeds and dichotomous pictures of "good" and "evil." But after decades of power sharing, nobody really believed that a true socialist or a true Christian society was just around the corner. Consociational democracy had harmonized the overstretched ideologies with a reality that was significantly more modest than anyone had been led to believe.

That was the moment when consociational democracy in Austria had to start crumbling. The preconditions for consociational democracy were undermined by the successes of the concept. By reducing social fragmentation, it had also reduced political hostility. The auto- and heterostereotypes had lost their dichotomous significance; the "reds" had a less negative impression of the "blacks" (and vice versa); the enemy stopped being so dreadful anymore.

It was the attitude of the younger generation and the significant changes it underwent in the 1980s that made the walls of consociational democracy start to crumble. When the younger generation realized that the old perception of two hostile camps no longer fit the political reality, they started to leave the camps. For them, the old fragmentation along traditional cleavages was history.

Consociational democracy Austrian-style is the history of self-elimination by success. The old elite groups were able to bridge the deep gaps from the past so successfully that the gaps disappeared. But in closing those gaps, the elites destroyed their power base. The cleavages responsible for the old camps disappeared—and so did the old camps.

The Forces of Change and Transformation

The elections of the Nationalrat on December 17, 1995, gave clear evidence of the social factors that were decisive for the election outcome. The most visible (and most decisive) factor was the generation gap; additional factors important in the outcome were education (and correspondingly, occupation) and gender.

Age has divided Austria into two almost completely different societies. Generational replacement played an important role in the dramatic increase in volatility. The parties representing the two traditional, major camps—the SPÖ and the ÖVP—still have an overwhelming hold on the older generation. The third traditional party, the Freedom Party of Austria (FPÖ), and to an even greater degree the two nontraditional parties, the Liberal Forum (LIF), and the Greens, attract a significantly younger electorate. In the subsociety of the older generation, the old party system, the two-and-a-half-party system, is still alive—two major parties and one medium-sized third party. In the subsociety of the younger generation, a much more competitive situation has transformed the party system toward a five-party system, with the SPÖ and the FPÖ competing for the leading roles and the ÖVP in danger of becoming number five (see Table 2.3).

During this period of political transformation, in the mid-1990s, political attitudes were sharply divided by the generation gap, by a deep cleavage created by traditional loyalties to the parties of the traditional camps and by loyalties of a new, distinctly more volatile type.

This deep cleavage signifies the end of the "camps." For about one hundred years, beginning with the 1880s, the Austrian camps and their respective parties were able to pass on political loyalties within the borders of the camps. An Austrian was born usually into a particular camp and stayed within it, in turn handing down this loyalty to the next generation. Being born into a camp meant undergoing a political socialization: Through youth groups, cultural organizations, educational programs, and leisure activities, a person was more or less completely bound to this camp. A person was either "black" (politically Catholic, that is, Christian-conservative), or "red" (Social Democrat), or "blue" (pan-German—in the 1930s and later often described as "brown" due to the almost complete takeover of this camp by the NSDAP).

In the 1930s, however, there was a break in this chain, in this continuity: The Austrian Nazi Party attracted voters (up to 1933, the year of the last free local elections), members, and sympathizers in numbers far beyond the strength of the traditional pan-German camp. Even before 1938, the Austrian Nazi Party became a successful catchall party, winning acceptance among the traditional Christian

TABLE 2.3   The Correlation of Party Vote and Age Group, 1995

	SPÖ	ÖVP	FPÖ	LIF	Greens
Percentage of voters:					
Aged 18–29	18	15	31	39	52
Aged 60 and older	31	32	19	13	3
Aged 30–59	50	52	51	49	45

SOURCE: Plasser, Ulram, and Seeber 1996: 178.

Social and the traditional Social Democrat electorate by invading political Catholicism and labor. In the 1930s, the traditionally closed camps were no longer so closed.

Between November 1945 and April 1946, the Allies had registered 428,249 Austrians, or about 10 percent of the adult population, as (former) members of the NSDAP (Stiefel 1981: 34). If the many Austrians who were still outside of the country during the first year after World War II (for example in prisoner of war camps) are taken into account, this figure must be adjusted even higher. About 600,000 Austrians had joined the Nazi Party (Luza 1975), a number that corresponds almost exactly to the membership of the best-organized party of the First Republic, the Social Democrats. Considering that the pan-German camp in the First Republic attracted only one-third as many votes as the Social Democrats (and the Christian Socials) were able to get between 1919 and 1932, these membership figures emphasize the success the Austrian NSDAP had even with Austrians who did not come from the traditional pan-German camp. And it is also clear that it was especially the younger generation born into either the "black" or the "red" camp who went over to the Nazi Party (Pauley 1981: 91–96).

But in 1945 and especially in 1949, when most of the former NSDAP members got back their voting rights, the old pattern was fully reestablished: The two major parties, strengthened by the rejuvenated socializing powers of their respective camps, were able to win about the same share of votes as in the First Republic: Together they received 82.7 percent of the vote in 1949. The pan-German VDU (League of Independents, predecessor of the FPÖ) got 11.7 percent, or 489,273 votes (Plasser, Ulram, and Ogris 1996: 344 f.)—approximately the same number the two smaller parties of the pan-German camp had received in the First Republic. Compared with the 600,000 members—not voters—the NSDAP had in Austria, the reestablishment of the traditional camp system and of the two-and-a-half-party system had an interesting impact: A significant number of former Nazis had joined the two major parties—at least as voters, but in many cases as members, too. The camp system was back. But nobody, least of all the ÖVP and the SPÖ, wanted to be reminded of the power of attraction the Austrian Nazi Party had enjoyed with the young generation of politically active Catholics and blue-collar workers in the 1930s.

Once reestablished, the traditional party system and its tradition of socialization within the camps worked rather smoothly to control Austrian politics by means of its hereditary system. Everybody had his (or her) place in the party system, and in most cases, this place was defined by birth and was therefore for life. It worked for about four decades, and only then did things start to change. In the 1980s, the combined voting share of the two major parties started to decline. The FPÖ, the Greens, and later also the LIF were attracting more and more voters. But it was not so much the general electorate that started to leave the SPÖ and ÖVP; it was mainly the young voters who, no longer content to remain within the borders of the camps they were born into, went over to the FPÖ, to the Greens, and to the LIF.

Because this is happening under the conditions of liberal democracy, it must have a different meaning from the generation gap that was responsible for the rise of the Austrian Nazi Party. In both cases—in the 1930s as well as in the 1980s and 1990s—the socialist and the Christian-conservative camps were (and are) losing control over political socialization. But in the 1980s and 1990s, this cannot be the by-product of political instability as was the case in the 1930s. It must be seen in correspondence with the stability of the Second Republic. The younger generation's inclination to leave the two major parties is based on a feeling of (political) stability, not instability. They do not go over to a totalitarian party with militant structures like the Nazi Party. They are attracted either to the Greens or the Liberals, parties with no permanent organization or structure reminiscent of the strict organizations the camps were famous for, or to the FPÖ, which is a traditional party with vestiges of the pan-German camp that are still important for political recruitment within this party. But the FPÖ does not attract its new electorate by binding it through membership or organization. During the eight years when the FPÖ's share of the vote exploded from 5 to more than 20 percent, its membership did not increase significantly. In 1985, the official data for FPÖ membership was 37,057, and in 1994, it was 42,200 (Nick and Pelinka 1996: 75). Since 1986, the FPÖ has been a much less traditional party than it was prior to that time.

The explanation is that the younger generation is not leaving the major parties to join parties of the same type, nor is it leaving traditional parties. An increasing number of the younger generation has not been effectively socialized by the traditional structures of political parties and ideological camps. They never "belonged" to such traditional parties and camps and are now demonstrating their preference for a much looser alliance—for example, by not voting at all; voter turnout is on the decline in Austria, falling from 92.9 percent in 1975 to 81.9 in 1994, but going up again to 86.0 in the 1995 general parliamentary elections (Plasser, Ulram, and Ogris 1996: 344 f.). Younger voters are quite flexible, changing party affiliations much more easily than the older generation, and do not view casting a vote as a lifetime decision.

The political behavior of the younger generation must be seen as a process of political polarization. The parties that significant numbers of younger voters prefer (with the exception of the Liberals) are seen by the electorate as less centrist than the SPÖ or ÖVP. The Austrian electorate perceives the Greens as the most left-wing party and the FPÖ as the most right-wing (see Table 2.4).

The young vote is a polarized and polarizing vote. This can be seen in correspondence with the education gap. Education as an electoral factor, according to

TABLE 2.4 Perception of Political Parties on the Right-Left Scale, 1996

1.00=very left *5.00=very right*	*Greens*	*SPÖ*	*LIF*	*ÖVP*	*FPÖ*	*Self-perception of the electorate*
	2.26	2.37	2.86	3.37	4.02	2.93

SOURCE: Plasser, Ulram, and Seeber 1996: 166.

traditional assumptions about the correlation between class and education, followed for decades a well-established pattern: Voters with a higher level of education, thanks to their bourgeois background, showed a significant preference for the ÖVP, the party of the moderate right, whereas an overproportional number of voters with less education, as a consequence of their nonbourgeois background (that is, the labor vote, with the exception of the agricultural vote), voted for the SPÖ, the party of the moderate left. This is still the case with older voters but no longer true of the younger generation.

Among younger voters, the left-right dimension is completely reversed: Higher levels of education mean an overproportional tendency in favor of the Liberals and the Greens—both of which, according to the dominant perception, are to the left of the ÖVP, and the Greens even left of the SPÖ. The lack of higher education means an overproportional tendency in favor of the FPÖ, which is seen as the most right-wing of all the Austrian parties (see Table 2.5).

If the education gap is correlated with the generation gap, the differences become even more significant. Among the youngest blue-collar voters, the FPÖ is already the party of choice, ahead of the SPÖ; among the youngest voters with a high school education, the Liberals and the Greens are at least as strong as the ÖVP. But that means that a high school or a university degree is no longer correlated with voting right of the center, and lack of higher education, especially in the case of the blue-collar vote, is no longer correlated with voting left of center.

This reversal of the traditional correspondence between education and the left-right scale calls for an explanation, which can be found by analyzing the blue-collar vote. Between 1986 and 1995, the blue-collar vote shifted dramatically from the SPÖ to the FPÖ. With respect to the generation gap, this means that as a group, the younger blue-collar voters have changed their preference from a moderate left-wing party to a not-so-moderate right-wing party (see Table 2.6).

The education gap must be interpreted as an indicator of a general trend toward modernization. As early as 1960, Seymour Martin Lipset analyzed the authoritarian tendencies among blue-collar workers in the United States (Lipset 1960). In other Western democracies, the impact of significant numbers of working-class voters casting their ballots not for traditional left-wing parties but for those from the right, especially for authoritarian rather than moderate right-wing parties, was felt much earlier than in Austria. The traditional perception of the labor vote as being inclined toward leftist parties had already been corrected, first in the United States and then in Western Europe, before the Austrian party system ever felt the effects of this reversal.

TABLE 2.5 The Correlation of Party Vote and Education, 1995

Parties preferred by the following groups	SPÖ	ÖVP	FPÖ	LIF	Greens
Compulsory education only	45	27	18	1	2
Additional (not higher) education	38	25	27	4	3
Higher education	30	32	16	11	9

NOTE: The share of voting that is not included among the given percentages consists of voters who did not answer the exit poll questions. The group with additional education includes skilled blue-collar workers.
SOURCE: Plasser, Ulram, and Seeber 1996: 172–175.

The percentage of party votes from the following groups	SPÖ	ÖVP	FPÖ	LIF	Greens
Compulsory and additional education	76	65	78	38	42
Higher education	24	35	22	62	58

SOURCE: Plasser, Ulram, and Seeber 1996: 178.

TABLE 2.6 The Blue-Collar Vote for the SPÖ and FPÖ, from 1986 to 1995

	General Parliamentary Elections in			
	1986	1990	1994	1995
SPÖ	57	52	47	42
FPÖ	10	21	29	34

SOURCE: Plasser, Ulram, and Seeber 1996: 172, 175.

The background of the labor vote's rightist tendency has to be seen in light of the effects that modernization—in the sense of general social progress—has on different social groups. For decades now, modernization has not worked for labor—at least not for blue-collar workers. The general trends with which Western societies are confronted favor the well-educated middle class. Education has become the key to upward mobility. The Marxist assumption that progress more or less automatically favors the labor movement has not been verified by the social developments of the late twentieth century. The weaker members of the working class, the less well educated blue-collar workers, are increasingly confronted with the threat of unemployment and cutbacks in social services. They are tempted to blame certain groups for this decline, and xenophobic and racist explanations provide them with scapegoats.

But it is not only imaginary enemies that make blue-collar workers the losers in the modernization process. It is real wage competition, brought on by the globalized economy and by the international division of labor. Migrant workers are able and willing to work for less. Production in former Communist countries or in Asia is cheap. And blue-collar labor is responding in the same way as the small middle class responded to the economic crisis in the 1930s: by moving not to the left, as Marxists predicted, but to the right. Austrian politics has no instruments to prevent the logical consequences of this global trend from coming to Austria.

It is not at all remarkable that this trend can be observed in Austria. What is remarkable is that this trend is so delayed in Austria. The delay can be explained by the preservative effects that the traditional ideological camps–in the case of labor, the socialist camp—had for such a long time. The strength of social democracy in Austria provided the blue-collar element with a political and ideological home that workers claimed as their own. Now that home is no longer providing shelter—at least not for the majority of the young blue-collar workers. They consider themselves homeless. Now that the camp has lost its function as a subsidiary home for young blue-collar workers, they are responding as workers have done already in other comparable societies: They are moving toward the right and evolving authoritarian tendencies.

Because the socializing powers of the camps and their ability to stabilize political beliefs and behavior within their borders are in decline, the effects of modernization are setting in. But this decline is the impact of modernization. The demographic trend toward the cities (urbanization) and the economic trend toward the tertiary sector (service-oriented industries) are feeding the need for education. Education and social as well as geographical mobility are destroying the ability of traditional camps to control political loyalties. Social modernization provokes political transformation—even in Austria.

This can also be seen with respect to the political attitudes that distinguish male and female behavior. The gender gap, long an insignificant factor in Austrian politics, has reached Austria.

The gender gap expressed by the difference between the male and female vote is especially significant for the FPÖ. The FPÖ is a male party: The probability of an Austrian man voting for this party is significantly higher than it is for an Austrian woman. The upswing enjoyed by the FPÖ since 1986 must be attributed mainly to the male vote (see Table 2.7).

The gender gap can be explained by means of international comparison. In most Western European countries, the "postmaterialist" type of political party the Greens are representing is especially attractive to women. On the other hand, "rightist-populist" parties—a category that clearly includes the FPÖ—attract significantly more men than women (Plasser, Ulram, and Seeber 1996: 188; Hofinger and Ogris 1996). The European division between the "harder," more materialistic orientation of male voters and the "softer," postmaterialist orientation of female voters has finally come to Austria.

The surfacing of the gender gap is also an indicator of modernization. Austrian politics is more and more explainable by patterns already established in other so-

TABLE 2.7   The Correlation of Party Vote and Gender, 1995

	SPÖ	ÖVP	FPÖ	LIF	Greens
Percentage of male voters	35	26	27	5	4
Percentage of female voters	40	29	16	6	5
Difference	+ 5	+ 3	−11	+ 1	+ 1

SOURCE: Plasser, Ulram, and Seeber 1996: 188.

cially and economically advanced societies. The idea of specific Austrian behavior and Austrian uniqueness is vanishing.

The increasing importance of generation, education, and gender means a decrease in the impact of factors such as religion, "Volk" (ethnocentrism), and class—at least in the traditional sense. The SPÖ, the party of the traditional labor movement, has already lost the majority of the young (blue-collar) labor vote. The upswing of the FPÖ, the party of the pan-German tradition, cannot be attributed to pan-Germanism and traditional ethnocentrism. The FPÖ's recent popularity can be explained by the amalgamation of the remnants of pan-German ideology with general Austrian patriotism and the populist protest agenda that the FPÖ has represented since 1986 (Plasser and Ulram 1995). The SPÖ has retained the old blue-collar vote and much of the new middle-class vote, but this cannot be analyzed as the effect of traditional class orientation. And the decline of the ÖVP can be explained by the decline of political Catholicism and the resulting diminished impact religion as such has on political behavior.

The general picture of the transformation process still going on in Austria is that of a delayed political secularization. The subsocieties and the substitute fatherlands that the ideological camps provided are no longer necessary. Society has taken over these roles and functions, and the fragmentations so typical for Austria during the first half of the century are no longer so deep.

There are, of course, visible new fragmentations. The transformation is not changing Austria into a realm of perfect harmony; in fact, quite the opposite is true. There is a deep-seated conflict between the winners and the losers of modernization, expressed in the xenophobic attitudes of the latter. There is a significant increase in the importance of gender and education in political behavior. And hidden behind the generation gap, there is an explosive potential.

But this has almost nothing to do with the old cleavages that constituted and defined the traditional camps. It has everything to do with Austria's integration into Europe—not with Austria's membership in the European Union but with Austria's full participation in the dynamism that Western societies have developed, transgressing borders. Austria is not an island—neither of the blessed nor of the damned.

3

THE CONSTITUTIONAL STRUCTURE

In terms of constitutional law, the Austrian political system is based on the laws of the First Republic, a term that merely signifies a historical period (1918 to 1933–1934). Thus, the Second Republic differs from the First Republic not because of different constitutional documents but because its specific political culture is different. Consociational democracy, characterized by a pronounced predominance of parties and associations, is the key element of this political culture. Changes in this culture in the 1990s have opened a discussion of the possibility of a Third Republic (Dachs et al. 1997; Luther and Müller 1992; Mantl 1992; Nick and Pelinka 1996).

Two things are necessary to describe and explain Austrian politics: the constitution, and the understanding of the way politicians use it, following certain trends and informal rules that are the essence of Austrian political culture. One aspect of these unwritten rules is that the Austrian constitution is constantly being amended. The constitution of 1920 is merely a formalistic frame, which the political players, that is, the parties, are willing and able to change very easily. The constitution itself allows for this flexibility in dealing with constitutional matters, which may explain why the Second Republic has not seen the need to frame its own constitution. Constitutional flexibility is an important feature of the Austrian political system (Adamovich and Funk 1985: esp. 16–18).

The Constitution

The Austrian constitution is based on the Federal Constitutional Law (Bundes-Verfassungsgesetz: B-VG) of 1920, which has been modified numerous times. It was particularly the constitutional amendment of 1929 that significantly changed the character of the constitution. In combination with the constitutional amendment of 1929, the Federal Constitutional Law of 1920 lends the Austrian political system a parliamentary character, which is supplemented by presidential components. This parliamentary character is expressed by the fact that the federal government is politically responsible to the first chamber, the directly elected chamber of parliament, the National Council.

By a simple majority vote, the National Council can express its no-confidence against the federal government or any of its individual members and thus "overthrow" the government. Thus the institutional separation of powers between the government and parliament is eliminated by virtue of the de facto identity between the government and the parliamentary majority. There can be no basic conflict between a majority of the National Council and the federal government. The election of the National Council, in combination with the subsequent formation of a government, determines the makeup of the government. Thus, as in all parliamentary systems, parliamentary elections assume the character of governmental elections.

Yet the "normality" of parliamentary government is relativized by the powers of the directly elected president, as legislated in 1929. The federal president, who is not responsible to the parliament, appoints both the federal chancellor and—according to the chancellor's recommendations—the members of the federal government, and he can dismiss them as well. The Austrian constitution is very similar to both the Weimar constitution and the constitution of the French Fifth Republic in that the head of state is elected directly and has the power of government appointment. In contrast to these other two political systems, which integrate (or integrated) "mixed," that is, parliamentary and presidential, elements in their constitutions, Austria's constitutional reality reflects a development that has given significantly more importance to the parliamentary than the presidential element. Public perception has always seen the federal chancellor rather than the federal president as the key person, one reason being that top party functionaries have traditionally tried to become chancellor, not president.

A clear and stable majority in the National Council is the prerequisite for the de facto preponderance of the parliamentary over the equally constitutionally based presidential character of the political system. The concentration of the party system—until the 1980s a significant element of Austria's political system—favors clear parliamentary majorities, against which a president trying to strengthen his position stood little chance of success. However, the significant decrease in the concentration of the party system now taking place may slowly alter these conditions. If that happens, there is more likely to be a competitive relationship between the parliament (National Council) and the head of state (federal president), both of whom draw on the same legitimacy, that is, direct election by the people.

The federative element laid down in the constitution can be termed "mixed," as well. On the one hand, the constitution ensures the general powers of the nine states, which means that all powers and responsibilities not expressly given to the federal administration are automatically those of the states. However, there are so many federal responsibilities that Austrian federalism can be regarded as underdeveloped: Austria is a "centralistic federation" (Adamovich and Funk 1985: 122–129).

The Austrian constitution is the product of certain historical constellations, the result of a compromise between the socialist camp (the Social Democratic Workers' Party) and the Christian-conservative camp (the Christian Social Party). There was little consensus, however, on basic human rights. The Social Democrats favored more social entitlements than the Christian Socials were prepared to concede, and there was also disagreement about the principal aspects of the church-state relationship. Since no consensus could be reached, the lawmakers simply took over the basic rights as laid down during the monarchy in the form of the basic law of state of 1867 ("Staatsgrundgesetz").

From 1945 onward, in the Second Republic, various attempts to reformulate the basic rights were unsuccessful. As a consequence, the basic rights are still an expression of the era in which they were formulated: They are meant to be liberal (in the sense of noninterventionist) but do not have a social (interventionist) orientation. Thus, in Austria the principles of the social and welfare state are not included in the catalogue of basic rights; rather they are the products of political developments from 1945 onward, without being formalized as basic rules. There is every indication that Austria will enter the twenty-first century with a charter of basic rights from the nineteenth century (Adamovich and Funk 1985: 358–433).

This explains a great deal about the culture of the Second Republic. Political leaders are not very interested in such topics as the codification of basic rights. The reality of social and political development is rather independent from whatever is written down and agreed on in a formal charter. The welfare state in Austria, for example, developed without any constitutional guarantees of social security, a minimum wage, or the right to work. The pragmatism that the elites of the two major camps have come to prefer over ideological attitudes has had little impact on the constitution.

In 1929, the presidential component was added to the originally exclusively parliamentary focus of the federal constitution. This was the consequence of a shift in party power relations. The Social Democrats, who had not been represented in the federal government since 1920, were on the political defensive. In an era of antidemocratic tendencies in many European nations, the Christian Democrats, who together with smaller parties formed the ruling "bourgeois block," increasingly turned against the parliamentary character of the constitution, which Social Democrats predominantly supported. Since a constitutional amendment required the votes of the Social Democrats, who held more than one-third of the seats in parliament and thus had a minority veto power, a compromise was negotiated. On the one hand, the parliamentary character was maintained in the form of the political responsibility of the federal government to the National Council; on the other hand, parliamentary power was weakened by expanding the powers of the federal president (Adamovich, Funk, and Holzinger 1997: 79–82).

The compromise of 1929 was retained after 1945 because directly following the declaration of independence on April 27, 1945, the two dominant parties—the Austrian People's Party (ÖVP), the successor of the Christian Socials, and the Socialist Party of Austria (SPÖ) as successor of the Social Democratic Workers' Party—were not interested in a debate on constitutional principles. In addition, the two parties formed a common front against the Communist Party of Austria (KPÖ), which wanted to repeal the 1929 amendment and return to the original, thoroughly parliamentary structure of the constitution (Rauchensteiner 1979: 112 f.).

The decision of 1945 is a good example of the elitist understanding the two major parties had developed, especially regarding important matters such as the constitution. The ÖVP and SPÖ avoided any broad discussion of the formal principles of Austrian democracy for fear of two possible consequences:

- They feared that debate might revive old controversies between the two major camps, thus making it much more difficult to represent the elitist consensus to their respective electorates. The socialist rank and file would have expected the restitution of the pre-1929 constitutional status minus the presidential component, which the left had only accepted out of necessity, not out of conviction. The People's Party would have had problems explaining to its followers why it had caved in to pressure from a "united" socialist-Communist left. So both sides agreed not to debate.
- They did not want to give the KPÖ a voice of any importance. The KPÖ was isolated within the Provisional Government of 1945. The KPÖ's strength was also its weakness: For good reasons, the party was identified with the USSR. The Soviet Union was perhaps the most important power factor in Austria at this time, but the Red Army was rather unpopular with most Austrians. The ÖVP and SPÖ strategy was to give the Communists exactly the share of power the USSR seemed to expect, but nothing more. Even in the summer of 1945, it was obvious what the ÖVP and SPÖ hoped to do and that their plans did not include any significant role for the KPÖ.

The Austrian constitution is characterized by the existence of "basic principles" (Baugesetze). This term appears nowhere in the constitutional document itself or in any constitutional amendment. It was coined by legal scholars as a way of providing a certain systematic structure for analyzing the constitution (Adamovich and Funk 1985: 98–140). It was necessary to define a "complete" constitutional change ("Gesamtänderung der Bundesverfassung"). Changing the constitution "completely" requires both a two-thirds majority in parliament and a simple majority in a referendum. Such a referendum is obligatory—as was the case in the 1994 referendum on Austria's entry into the European Union.

Leading experts on constitutional law agree that the following principles are considered "basic": the democratic principle, the republican principle, the federal principle, the principle of the rule of law, and the principle of the separation of powers. The last one creates some problems because of the relationship between the government and parliament. The cabinet (federal government) is politically responsible to the National Council. The result is a rather strong connection between the parliamentary majority and the government, formed by the identity of the party or parties that democratic elections have entitled to command the majority in parliament and which therefore is/are the party or parties in government.

According to a traditional typology of constitutions, the Austrian constitution can be characterized as follows (Loewenstein 1965: 136–163):

- The Austrian constitution is an extremely flexible one, and it is legally and politically very easy to amend (Adamovich, Funk, and Holzinger 1997: 11–13). It has always been part of the political culture of consociationalism to change the constitution as often as the two major parties deem it useful. This degree of flexibility will decrease if the SPÖ and ÖVP no longer command a two-thirds majority in parliament. That, in turn, limits the scope of those two parties, which represent not only the "party state" but also the "corporate state" of social partnership, to apply the constitution according to their interests. This was the situation following the general elections of 1994. In 1995, SPÖ and ÖVP narrowly regained the two-thirds majority.
- The Austrian constitution is "original" as far as the B-VG 1920 is concerned, but it is "derivative" with regard to the amendment of 1929. The 1920 constitution was the result of political compromises between the main Austrian parties, edited according to the "legal positivism" of Hans Kelsen. This positivistic side of the constitution implied that the constitution should not express specific value orientations. In general, the constitution can be called "original" because it does not follow a given pattern. But the amendment of 1929 was obviously based on the Weimar constitution. This was the result of Austria's general orientation toward Germany at that time, but also of the strong tendency to move away from the consistent parliamentary system toward a presidential one, a tendency all parties to the right of the Social Democrats had. The Weimar-style "dual executive" was a necessary compromise (Loewenstein 1965: 95 f.).
- The constitution of 1920 has, for the same reasons, a "utilitarian" character, whereas the amendment of 1929 is "ideologically programmatic." The B-VG was not shaped according to a certain political platform. Neither the Christian Social Party nor the SDAP used the constitution to write their respective ideologies in stone. One indication of this nonprogrammatic, pragmatic attitude was the omission of the catalogue of basic rights because coming to a decision on it would have triggered too much ideological debate. But the amendment of 1929 was purely the product of ideology—of the antiparliamentary, proto-authoritarian agenda of the

political right. The necessity of compromising with the Social Democrats moderated the "ideologically programmatic" quality, but it is still there.
- Within the triad of "normative," "nominal," and "semantic" constitutions, the Austrian constitution must be qualified as "nominal." "The factual state of affairs does not . . . permit the complete integration of the constitutional norms into the dynamics of political life" (Loewenstein 1965: 149). The overpowering weight of the Second Republic's political culture of consociationalism and especially the corporatist elements that were intentionally omitted from the constitution reduce the amount of control the constitution has over the political process. But the decline of consociationalism would also mean the decline of the "nominal" element. The constitution and the political process are, in the long run, bound to converge.

The political culture of the Second Republic could be called an example of the "erosion of the constitutional conscience" (Loewenstein 1965: 158)—if there had been such a thing as a strong constitutional conscience in the past. A better description may be a "delay in the development of the constitutional conscience."

The Austrian political system represents a combination of direct and indirect democratic elements. In the first decades of the Second Republic, direct democracy was seldom applied. The first popular initiative was not started until 1964, and the first referendum on the federal level did not take place until 1978. The constitution was not responsible for this delay; in fact, it is the constitution that provides instruments of direct democracy.

The constitution foresees direct democratic decisionmaking on the federal level in cases involving two kinds of political questions:

- In the case of "basic changes" in the constitution, that is, changes in the principles of the constitution, an "obligatory referendum" is held. To date, this has been necessary only once: in the course of the debate over whether Austria should become a member of the European Union. In June 1994, more than 66 percent of all eligible voters cast their ballots in favor of Austrian membership.
- In the case of a majority decision of the National Council to hand over its legislative power to the people, a "facultative referendum" is held. Again, such a popular referendum has taken place only once: in November 1978, a slim majority of all eligible voters voted against putting the first Austrian atomic power plant into operation, which effectively meant a rejection of atomic energy.

This stringent plebiscitary variation of the political decisionmaking process on the federal level is significantly limited by a clause stipulating that any referendum not absolutely necessary in terms of global constitutional changes must be initiated by a majority of the National Council. (In the case of a constitutional amendment, which does not imply "basic changes," one-third of parliament is entitled to initiate a referendum.) This means that the popular referendum is a governmental instrument (with the exception of the obligatory referendum) and not an effective opposition instrument (which theoretically could also be the case). Although there have been many popular initiatives, popular referenda are hardly ever used. The explanation is simple: In calling for a (nonobligatory) popular referendum, the government—conforming to the principle of parliamentary systems closely connected with the parliamentary majority—has to renounce its decisionmaking power.

Popular referenda and other instruments of direct democracy (popular initiatives and consultative referendums, which are nonbinding polls to determine public opinion) are used not only on the federal level but also on the state and municipal levels. In the past twenty years, the state constitutions have increasingly integrated such elements of direct democracy—an expression of the general tendency to strengthen the plebiscitary components of the political system.

In this respect, the state constitutions follow the model of the federal constitution: The state diets vote on popular initiatives started by qualified minorities of the voting population. Popular referenda are decisionmaking instruments that focus directly on certain issues (Esterbauer 1995: 86).

The constitutional provisions for direct democracy have been underused because the party state has traditionally taken care of democracy. For several decades, Austria was an example of an extremely unbalanced mixture of plebiscitarian and representative elements. Political activity was channeled through the party and the corporate state. Almost all Austrians identified with one of the traditional parties; almost all Austrians were members of at least one economic association. There was not much interest left over for activity outside the camps.

The first indication that the camps were about to crumble came during the 1970s, when informal citizens' initiatives became more and more frequent. Citizens' initiatives—in combination with new social movements—started to influence the legislative as well as the general political process, especially issues concerning the environment (Natter 1987) and the position of women in Austrian society (Rosenberger 1992, 1997). As a consequence, the informal aspects of direct participation in politics have become increasingly recognizable.

This tendency explains the emergence of the Greens, whose foundation was rooted in three social movements:

• The environmental movement, which voiced its opposition to prevailing economic policies by pushing for more ecologically responsible thinking. Two political triumphs were important in shaping environmental policies: the "no" majority in 1978, when the Austrians decided by a very small margin not to produce nuclear energy; and the government's 1985 decision not to build a dam on the Danube east of Vienna—the result of massive protests against the dam.

- The peace movement, which gained momentum when the arms race escalated to new levels of destructive capability in the first half of the 1980s. As a consequence of Austria's neutrality and its comparatively low level of armament, pacifists in Austria had less impact on domestic politics than pacifists elsewhere. The peace movement was nevertheless instrumental in shaping the Greens' attitude from their very beginnings as a party.
- The feminist movement, which became evident in the 1970s, especially during the conflict between "pro-life" and "pro-choice" forces in Austria. Independent feminists challenged the SPÖ, whose claim of being the women's liberation party was based on its party history and platform. The Greens also adopted this feminist tradition.

All these movements and citizens' initiatives were based on an expanded understanding of democracy. The technique they used, putting pressure on the political machine from the outside, was rather new for Austria. Austria had had its share of extraparliamentary politics in the past, but it had always been controlled by political parties and their camps. Now the pressure on the political system was coming not from any of the traditional camps but from a new force, which no traditional understanding of politics could explain.

But the challenge the constitutional agencies had to face also changed the party system and the corporate system. Both had always had the power to be in full control of the demands and supports that affected the political system. Now they began to lose control.

The Legislature, Executive, and Judiciary

The Legislature: National Council and Federal Council

Austria has a "pseudo" two-chamber system: There are two chambers of parliament, but there is no balance of power between them. The first chamber is, according to the constitution, the decisive one (Adamovich and Funk 1985: 214–216). The two chambers (the National Council and the Federal Council) have very different powers:

- The National Council (Nationalrat) is directly elected by the people. Federal Council (Bundesrat) representatives are delegated by the state parliaments (state diets) in proportion to the number of seats each of the parties holds there. This difference gives the National Council a higher or at least a more visible form of democratic legitimation.
- The federal government is politically responsible only to the National Council, not to the Federal Council. Thus, the federal government depends on majority conditions in the first chamber only. The federal government cannot exist if confronted with a hostile majority in the National Council, but it can rather easily survive a hostile Federal Council.

- If there is dissent in legislative procedures, the National Council can, in principle, always overrule the Federal Council, since the latter has only a suspensory veto right. The Federal Council is dispensable in legislative matters.

The preponderant authority of the National Council is reflected in public perception and career orientation. What happens in the National Council receives significantly more attention than what happens in the Federal Council. A seat in the Federal Council is normally regarded as a merely intermediary step on the way to the National Council.

The National Council (since 1971, made up of 183 representatives) is a working parliament and thus fulfills the normal functions of any parliament in a liberal democracy: legislation and control. In addition to these two main functions, the Austrian parliament also serves as a means of cooperation with the government and as a public tribune (Fischer 1997: 107).

The National Council is structured in various ways:

- It consists of the plenary meeting and of the committees.
- It consists of factions that are in control of nominating members of parliament for certain functions.
- It consists of the Presidential Conference (Präsidialkonferenz), which functions as a kind of steering committee.
- It consists of government and opposition, that is, of members who are loyal to the government and members who oppose the government.

Permanent legislative committees have been established largely following the structure of the government: Each ministry has a corresponding National Council committee. In order to fulfill its control function, the National Council also has ad hoc investigation committees. Both the permanent committees and the investigative committees are open to the media. The work of both types of committees is sent to the plenary body, which in principle always has the final decision-making power.

Factions (in Austria termed "clubs") basically correspond to the political parties and are an important structural component of the National Council. The factions determine the individual division of labor in parliament, such as membership in committees or speaking times in plenary sessions. The factions are headed by chairpersons who hold a high position in their own party hierarchy. In the opposition parties, the "club" chair is often reserved for the party chairperson. This gives the leading figure of an opposition party the best possible position to compete with the leading figures of government.

Factions have a hierarchical structure. Despite the formal equality of the members of each faction, their structure is determined by the necessary division of labor. Different tasks have to be fulfilled, different roles have to be played. Being in a more prestigious committee or having better and more opportunities to speak at the plenary session reflects a better position in this hierarchy. Seniority is just one factor determining the position of a specific member of parliament. Other factors include the MP's public prominence and party status.

Factions also control much of the use of infrastructure. The individual members of parliament are obliged to arrange their work procedures with their respective factions. Before the "Mitarbeitergesetz" (Cooperators Act) of 1992, members of parliament were not expected to organize office work on their own, instead relying on their factions to provide them with a staff and material. Now members of parliament have a budget with which they can hire an assistant or a secretary. Members of the same faction usually share office space as well as assistants and secretaries.

The "Mitarbeitergesetz" has been a step toward the independence of individual members of parliament from their party, that is, from their faction. This development fits into the overall pattern of the decline of the party state and of the increase of individualistic perceptions of politics.

An additional structural element of the National Council is the Presidential Conference, which comprises the three National Council presidents and the chairpersons of the factions. The task of the Presidential Conference is to ensure that the factions involved arrive at a consensus on all questions of parliamentary procedure: dates for plenaries and committees, quotas for speaking times, and conflicts of procedure. It is a kind of "steering committee" responsible for parliamentary routine. The Presidential Conference usually meets two or three times per month (Fischer 1997: 105). The Presidential Conference tries to reach unanimous decisions; if this cannot be achieved, the final decision regarding controversial questions of procedure lies with the First President of the National Council.

The power the First President has was demonstrated in 1993, when a group of five FPÖ members of parliament broke away from their faction to found the LIF. The constitution and the National Council's Procedural Act ("Nationalrats-Geschäftsordnung") are ambiguous about such a development. The issue at stake was whether the five dissidents would remain "wild" members of parliament, with none of the rights that only membership in a faction would entitle them, particularly the rights to be provided with office space and a staff and to sit on the committees. For understandable reasons, the FPÖ wanted to deny the Liberals these rights. When no unanimous decision could be reached, the First President, Heinz Fischer (SPÖ), decided in favor of the LIF.

As is normally the case in parliamentary systems, the execution of the National Council's various functions depends primarily on whether a representative belongs to one of the ruling factions or to the opposition. The control function is primarily the task of the opposition. From the viewpoint of the opposition, the control instruments are not sufficient. For this reason, minority (opposition) parties have constantly demanded an expansion of their control rights. Various reforms have expanded these rights. According to the reforms of procedures enacted in 1989 and 1996, the opposition has the following control rights: written interpellation, urgent inquiries (of a minimum of five representatives), oral questions during the "Question Hour" or the "Topic Hour" ("Aktuelle Stunde"), and special investigations by the General Accounting Office (Rechnungshof). Minority reports are possible in investigative committees that are formed by majority decision. The right to appoint investigative committees (law of official investigations—Art. 53 B-VG) is supplemented by the right to carry out parliamentary investigations. But the increased number of control rights that can be used by the minority in the National Council does not change the majority's prerogative to decide about the installation of investigative committees. Urgent inquiries, the instrument used most extensively by the opposition, are the strongest indicator of the deconcentration of the party system and the concomitant increase of factions in parliament.

The National Council has two special agencies for control (Widder 1997):

- The General Accounting Office (Rechnungshof) is an auxiliary agency of the National Council. It checks the legal and economic records of the federal administration and presents a "federal balance" to the National Council.
- The People's Attorneyship (Volksanwaltschaft) oversees the administration in response to individual claims of citizens.

Both agencies are heavily politicized and integrated into the party state. There is always fierce competition between the parties for the presidency of the General Accounting Office, a position considered equivalent to that of cabinet post. The People's Attorneyship is headed by a triumvirate that reflects the power structure of the 1970s and the strategic interests of the SPÖ in the Kreisky era, during which the "Volksanwaltschaft" was established. Its top three positions are reserved for nominees of the three largest factions in the National Council.

Austria's membership in the European Union has greatly increased the importance of the Main Committee (Hauptausschuss) of the National Council. This permanent committee, which is not restricted to any specific range of issues, is responsible for dealing with decisions that are to be made in the EU Council. Austria's representatives in the EU Council are bound to represent the decisions made in the Main Committee. This gives the National Council a new and rather unique role: On the EU level, the members of cabinet who represent Austria in the EU Council of Ministers are not free to negotiate solely according to the wishes of the cabinet. They are restricted by decisions of the Main Committee.

The political culture of consociational democracy, which in Austria parliamentarism is expressed by the dominant governmental formation of the "grand coalition" (from 1945–1947 to 1966 and from 1986–1987 onward), is responsible for a special type of "limited opposition." The representatives of one governmental party act in quasi-oppositional manner toward the government members of the other governmental party—for instance, by asking a minister questions in a critical rather than supportive manner.

The level of activity in the National Council has substantially increased. The number of parties grew from the traditional three to four in 1986, when the Greens were elected to parliament, and to five in 1993, when the Liberal Forum split away from the Freedom Party of Austria (FPÖ). The Liberal Forum's status as parliamentary party was confirmed in the 1994 and 1995 elections. Minority rights are exercised more intensively. Breeches of voting discipline within the factions are still rare but have been occurring more frequently. Attendance at National Council meetings is increasing, as is its importance in political communication. The National Council (and as a consequence, Austrian parliamentarism) is developing a stronger life of its own. This is reflected in the proportional composition of its representatives:

- The number of National Council representatives from economic associations is decreasing, not only in general but also within the factions of the SPÖ and ÖVP, which have long been connected with each other by the tradition of social partnership (Karlhofer and Tálos 1996: 45).
- The proportion of women in the National Council has been increasing steadily since 1979, although the 20 percent level in 1995 indicates that the female electorate is vastly underrepresented (Nick and Pelinka 1996: 50).
- Representatives are tending to serve fewer terms, and it is very difficult to predict whether a representative will be reelected because there have been much greater fluctuations in electoral results since 1986.

This development also signals a process of professionalization, one example of which is the above-mentioned "Mitarbeitergesetz." The legislative period between 1990 and 1994 marked the first time that the individual representatives, regardless of their party affiliation, were given the opportunity to appoint their own parliamentary staff, thus gaining more independence from faction and party.

The four-year legislative period of the National Council can be terminated prematurely by a decision of the National Council or the federal president, thus calling for early new elections. Corresponding to the de facto parliamentary character of the political system, the premature termination of legislative periods in the Second Republic has always been based on National Council decisions. The federal president has never used his right to dissolve the National Council (Art. 29 B-VG). The most frequent reasons for a National Council dissolution, which requires a simple majority decision, and thus premature new elections of a National Council (most recently in October 1995) were conflicts within a coalition government. A dissolution of the National Council is meant to prevent the governmental parties from rendering each other powerless.

The premature dissolution of the National Council is used quite frequently, whereas the power to overthrow the federal government by means of a vote of no-confidence has never been used. This is due to the discipline that still exists within the factions and the predictability of majority building in parliament. As long as the majority parties continue to command sufficient discipline among their own ranks, a motion for a vote of no-confidence has no chance of being carried. And as long as the constitutional framework follows the pattern of parliamentary democracy, the constellation of the cabinet will always be based on a majority in the National Council.

In principle, the representatives of both the National Council and the Federal Council are remunerated according to a pay scale similar to the one of civil servants. Basically, representatives receive compensation commensurate with that of a top civil servant. Members of the federal government earn about twice this amount. Both the MPs and the cabinet members receive various additional payments.

Because its structure of factions parallels the structure of the National Council, the Federal Council is closely connected with the National Council. By virtue of their party affiliation, the representatives of the Federal Council belong to the parliamentary clubs, which are dominated by the representatives of the National Council. This in turn further weakens the relative power of the Federal Council. The composition of the Federal Council is determined by a weak senate principle: The state with the smallest number of inhabitants has three seats; the most populous state has twelve seats. Since the relative population of the nine states is constantly shifting, the number of representatives in the Federal Council varies. At the end of 1995 the Federal Council consisted of 64 representatives: 27 from the ÖVP, 25 from the SPÖ, and 12 from the FPÖ.

The Federal Council does not actually fulfill its official function, which is to represent the interests of the states in the legislative process on the federal level. The Federal Council's powers are insufficiently developed to do so. But it has several secondary functions that justify the continuing need for a second chamber:

- The Federal Council helps to substantiate the fiction that the states have an independent voice at the level of the federal legislature. As long as there is a Federal Council, those who want to justify the status quo can point out that there is a special chamber that exists specifically to represent the interests of the states. States' rights exist—at least according to the constitution.
- The Federal Council provides the parties with a kind of political waiting room. Politicians who have not yet risen high enough in their respective party's hierarchy to be elected to the National Council can use the Federal Council as a relatively well-paid training program.
- The Federal Council can function as a kind of opposition chamber. This was the case between 1966 and 1986, when a strong opposition was able to win the majority in the second chamber several times as a consequence of shifting majorities on the state level. When this happens, the Federal Council can use its power to annoy the governing majority of the National Council. But this tactic never amounts to more than an irritation.

These functions alone are sufficient to keep the second chamber alive. However, if the legislature is to be vitalized, the energy for it will come not from the Federal Council but from the first chamber. And vitalization is exactly what the political system is now getting from the National Council.

Never has the National Council been more dynamic than during the 1990s. The decline of the party state reduced the amount of control the two major camps had over all aspects of the political system and brought about a palpable increase in parliamentary activity. New parties, the Greens and the Liberals, and a transformed traditional party, the FPÖ, are now using parliament as their arena to challenge the coalition whose partners are no longer so dominant.

The Legislative Process

The legislative process on the federal level is characterized by a sequence of preparliamentary and parliamentary stages. The federal government, the administration, and interest groups organized according to the principles of social partnership dominate the preparliamentary level; the National Council dominates the parliamentary level. Because of the focus on parties in Austria's political system, the two levels work in close coordination. Dominating interests on the preparliamentary level are closely interconnected with those on the parliamentary level (see Figure 3.1).

It is true that, in principle, this corresponds to the legislative process of parliamentary systems in which the executive branch controls the access to and process of legislative procedures because it is accountable to the legislature. In Austria, this is reinforced by the formalization of the preparliamentary level and the strong position of economic associations in "evaluation procedures." However, in the 1990s there has been a strong tendency to move away from an extreme focus on parties and associations. This is expected to weaken the unique Austrian system of additional linkages. One indication that this is already happening is decreased party-political voting discipline in the National Council.

Long-term statistics show that significantly more than two-thirds of all legislative decisions have followed these legislative procedures (Fischer 1997: 108). Concrete drafts, the political result of lobbies, are formulated by civil servants who are employees of a particular ministry and who specialize in carrying out the legislative tasks directly assigned by the federal minister in charge. This system intensifies the interconnection of the legislative and executive branches and gives the federal bureaucracy the opportunity to shape the legislative process according to their own needs.

As required by law, the ministerial draft undergoes an evaluation process (Begutachtungsverfahren) involving the other ministries, the state governments, the economic associations organized according to the principles of social partnership, and other lobbies that can be assumed to have a direct interest (e.g., officially acknowledged religious denominations). The parliament itself, for example, as well as its committees, is not involved in the evaluation process. As part of the

FIGURE 3.1   Legislative Procedures

A. Preparliamentary Stage

1

Interests

=

2

Parties or associations articulate their interests.

=

3

The government (a minister) charges specialized civil servants of the ministry
with the task of working out a draft.

=

4

A draft is worked out.

=

5

Evaluation procedures: Once more, interest groups have a direct influence.

=

6

The Council of Ministers votes on the draft to make it a governmental draft.

B. Parliamentary Stage

1

National Council: Factions and committees

=

2

Plenary session of the National Council: The law is passed.

=

3

The Federal Council agrees (if not, insisting vote by the National Council
guarantees the passing).

=

4

The federal president and the federal government fulfill
all remaining formal requirements.

SOURCE: Nick and Pelinka 1996: 52.

evaluation process, the groups and individuals involved are asked to formulate
their consent, criticism, or rejection of the draft within a specified period. The results of the evaluation process are then—again at the request of the federal minister, who determines the general political guidelines for the draft—more or less
taken into account in terms of governmental policy; that is, they are integrated
(or not) into the future law.

The evaluation process is rather significant in Austrian legislation because it involves all the major organized interests. The participation of economic interest groups is especially effective in synchronizing corporatism with government. The social partners are invited to represent their interests in the legislative procedure even before parliament itself becomes involved. This also applies to the officially acknowledged religious denominations: The law provides for the churches' interests to be integrated into legislation, which is completely antithetical to the principle of separation between church and state, religion and politics.

The draft is then passed on to the Council of Ministers, which either passes it unanimously—in which case it becomes a "governmental draft" (Regierungsvorlage)—or postpones the decision on the draft, which happens only in coalition governments when the governing partners still have conflicting opinions that must be clarified. In one-party cabinets, dissent would have been dealt with in an earlier stage.

Next, the governmental draft is discussed on the parliamentary level, first by the appropriate National Council committee and then by the plenary session of the National Council. Because of the parliamentary principle and the still-pronounced focus on parties and party discipline, the committee frequently changes the draft but in most cases not significantly. The reason for the committee's caution is the linkage between government and majority in parliament. In the reasoning of parliamentary rule, the cabinet and the majority in parliament are expected to cooperate. As soon as the government, which is identical to the leadership of the governing parties, has made up its mind concerning the draft, the interests of the governing parties have already been taken into account. Therefore, the National Council committees rarely have to make any significant changes in such a draft. The majority in the committee uses its power to pass the draft over any opposition.

Once the text of the draft has been worked out this way, the majority of the National Council is sure to give its consent following plenary discussion. The plenary sessions are opportunities for the parties to announce in public the decisions they have already made. The factions declare what their positions are. As in other parliaments, the plenary discussion is more an exercise in public debate than in lawmaking. Plenary discussions have a theatrical flavor: What a speaker says is not as important as how he or she says it. Insiders know what is coming before the speaker even takes the floor, and legislation is finalized before plenary discussion even begins. The real function of the plenary sessions is to provide politicians with a permanent campaign trail.

Both the party state and the close interconnection between preparliamentary and parliamentary levels are slowly disintegrating as evidenced by fewer unanimous decisions and less voting discipline in the National Council (see Table 3.1). The first of these two indicators expresses the deconcentration of the party system and thus the increased competition between the parties. The second indicator hints at a gradual emancipation of the parliament from the government and of individual parliamentarians from their party.

TABLE 3.1 Voting Behavior in the National Council in the 18th Legislative Period (1990–1994)

	Total	Unanimous	SPÖ ÖVP	SPÖ ÖVP FPÖ	SPÖ ÖVP Greens	SPÖ ÖVP LIF	SPÖ ÖVP FPÖ Greens	SPÖ ÖVP FPÖ LIF	SPÖ ÖVP Greens LIF	SPÖ ÖVP FPÖ Greens LIF	Diverging Voting Behavior[a]
			*Passed with a Majority of*								
Laws	632	173	162	118	41	41	25	42	24	6	55
State treaties	172	91	9	28	0	16	8	15	4	1	15
Governmental reports[b]	113	17	52	21	8	7	3	4	1	0	10

[a]One (or several) factions did not vote uniformly.

[b]The agreement or disagreement regarding governmental reports dealing with certain issues (e.g., "The Social Report") has only a declamatory character.

SOURCE: Data provided by the parliamentary head office.

The bill is subsequently sent to the Federal Council. The consent of this body is almost certain when the government also has a majority in this chamber, which was not always the case in the years with no grand coalition (1966–1986). However, a veto on the part of the Federal Council only sends the bill back to the National Council, which can then, by virtue of a simple majority, pass an "insisting vote" (Beharrungsbeschluss) to complete the legislative process.

The signatures required at this point—from the federal president, the federal chancellor, and the federal ministers—have no political relevance since they entail no veto right. A signature can only be withheld when, for instance, the federal president has doubts as to the constitutionality of the procedures leading to the law. In contrast to presidential systems, the presidential elements in the Austrian constitution do not give the president the power to veto legislature.

The normal legislative process based on a governmental initiative is supplemented by the following exceptions:

- Legislative initiatives from parliament itself: A minimum of eight representatives of the National Council ("parliamentary initiative"), a National Council committee, or the Federal Council can initiate the legislative process. A draft initiated this way is then treated by parliament (i.e., first the National Council) in much the same way as a governmental initiative or a popular initiative. In the reality of Austrian parliamentarism, a parliamentary initiative is important only when it is backed by a parliamentary majority. Opposition initiatives aimed at attracting publicity have practically no chance of success. Parliamentary initiatives based on the activities of representatives from the governmental parties are used to avoid the time-intensive evaluation phase (which is binding for governmental initiatives). The committees of the National and Federal Councils almost never use their right to initiate the legislative process. Only a small number of laws are based on parliamentary initiatives.
- Legislative initiative through popular initiative ("Volksbegehren"): This plebiscitary initiative requires that after introductory procedures, a minimum of 100,000 eligible voters sign the text of a draft. In this case the National Council must deal with it—without being bound to the content of the draft—as if it were a governmental draft. The frequency of popular initiatives in the Second Republic shows that this instrument has become a tool the parliamentary opposition uses in attempts to attract more attention (see Table 3.2). This is the reason why popular initiatives are almost invariably rejected by the ruling majority in the National Council.

Popular initiatives exemplify the trends in Austrian democracy. Any proposition that claims to have the direct backing of "the people" receives more public and media attention than propositions by parties and interest groups. Any party in parliament can start any legislative initiative in parliament itself, but the glam-

TABLE 3.2   Popular Initiatives in Austria

Year	Initiative	Supportive Signatures Absolute Figures	% of Qualified Voters	Politically Successful
1964	Reform of the Austrian broadcasting system	822,353	17.3	yes
1969	Law pertaining to working hours	889,659	17.7	yes
1969	Suspension of the 13th school year	339,307	6.8	yes
1975	Protection of human life ("Pro-Life")	896,579	17.9	no
1980	Suspension of atomic nonproliferation law	421,282	8.0	no
1980	Stricter atomic nonproliferation law	147,016	2.8	no
1982	Cancellation of Conference Center	1,361,561	25.7	no[a]
1985	Konrad Lorenz initiative	353,906	6.6	no
1985	Prolonging alternative military service	196,376	3.6	no
1985	Initiative regarding interceptor jets	121,182	2.2	no
1985	Anti-interceptor jet initiative	244,254	4.5	no
1987	FPÖ initiative against privileges	250,697	4.6	no
1989	Lowering number of children per classroom	219,127	3.0	no
1989	Initiative to secure broadcast freedom in Austria	109,197	2.0	no
1991	Initiative for a plebiscite on European Economic Area (EEA) membership	126,834	2.3	no
1993	Initiative "Austria First" ("Anti-Foreigners")	416,531	7.4	no
1996	Animal protection	459,096	8.0	open[b]
1996	Neutrality preservation	358,156	6.2	no
1997	Gene technology	1,225,790	21.2	open[b]
1997	Women's demands	644,665	11.2	open[b]

[a]Not successful in terms of the issue but the mobilization effect aimed at by the ÖVP was achieved.
[b]Not yet decided by parliament in July 1997.
SOURCE: Data provided by the parliamentary head office.

our of plebiscitarian movements has a universal appeal, which attracts attention and makes these movements ideal instruments for opposition parties.

An example is the initiative "Austria first," which was started by the FPÖ at the beginning of 1993 (Bailer and Neugebauer 1994: 450–456). This initiative was highly publicized because it was seen as the latest expression of the FPÖ's newest xenophobic wave. The initiative was the last straw for five FPÖ representatives who left the party to found the LIF. "Austria first," better known as the "antiforeigner" initiative, was an emotional clash between the FPÖ and an informal center-left alliance consisting of Catholics and Marxists, Social Democrats and Greens, and most of the politicians from parties outside the FPÖ.

The degree of this polarization made it obvious that the initiative would be voted down by the majority in parliament, and that is exactly what happened. But from the outset, the FPÖ's strategy had not been to get parliament to pass the legislative text signed by more than 400,000 voters. The party's strategy was exactly to create that emotional polarization. The FPÖ wanted to be perceived as the only party that cared more about Austrians than about foreigners.

Indications like the FPÖ initiative to the contrary, the importance of the parliamentary stage is increasing. Parliament is emerging as the constitutional winner of the latest developments. The proof lies in the parties' loss of control over individual members as indicated by the number of deviant votes from individual deputies and by the professionalization of parliament.

The Federal President

The federal president is elected directly to a six-year term of office by an absolute majority of voters. If none of the candidates has an absolute majority, there is a second ballot in which the two candidates with the highest number of votes face a runoff. This system of direct election was first implemented in 1951. Prior to that, even after the 1929 amendment, contingency laws had stipulated that the federal president be elected by parliament. In three cases—in 1951, 1986, and 1992—a second ballot was necessary. Each time, the winner was a candidate associated with one of the two major parties. Two of the federal presidents, Rudolf Kirchschläger and Kurt Waldheim, were nominated by the SPÖ and ÖVP respectively but were not members of these parties (see Table 3.3).

The major parties are the gatekeepers of the highest office in Austria. Anyone who wishes to become head of state has to have the backing of one of the major parties. Without party support, there is no access to the presidency.

The behavior of the federal presidents has been characterized by a "renunciation" of their powers (Welan 1992). Although the constitution does not expressly state that the federal president has to follow majority conditions in parliament when appointing the federal chancellor and the other members of the federal government, federal presidents have always turned over the task of forming a government to the candidates for chancellorship of the strongest party in parliament and, following the presentation of a cabinet, appointed them federal chancellors. Additionally, none of the federal presidents has ever used his right to dismiss the federal government on his own initiative. Thus, without any direct pressure from the constitutional system, the federal presidents respect the parliamentary character (albeit limited) of the political system and the unwritten rule that the federal government is formed always after the election of the National Council and not after the election of the federal president. The federal government reflects the majority interests of the National Council and not the wishes of the federal president.

This reduces also the importance of presidential elections. Formally, the two direct elections on the federal level provided for in the constitution—the election of the federal president and the election of the National Council—are equally important. But because the formation of the government and the naming of the fed-

TABLE 3.3   The Federal Presidents of the Second Republic

Election Year	Federal President	Party Affiliation	Votes
1945	Karl Renner	SPÖ	Unanimous[a]
1951	Theodor Körner	SPÖ	51.1% in the second ballot[b]
1957	Adolf Schärf	SPÖ	51.1%
1963	Adolf Schärf	SPÖ	Reelected with 55.4%
1965	Franz Jonas	SPÖ	50.7%
1971	Franz Jonas	SPÖ	Reelected with 52.8%
1974	Rudolf Kirchschläger	none	51.7%[c]
1980	Rudolf Kirchschläger	none	Reelected with 79.9%[d]
1986	Kurt Waldheim	none	53.9% in the second ballot[e]
1992	Thomas Klestil	ÖVP	56.9% in the second ballot

[a]The elections of December 20, 1945, were carried out by the Federal Assembly (National Council and Federal Council).
[b]1951 saw the first direct election of an Austrian federal president.
[c]Supported by the SPÖ.
[d]The ÖVP did not nominate a candidate.
[e]Supported by the ÖVP.
SOURCE: Compiled according to Khol 1992: 1052 f.

eral chancellor depend on the result of parliamentary elections, the presidential elections are of secondary importance.

The president's "renunciation of power" in terms of the formation of the federal government depends, however, on clear majority conditions in the National Council. If these conditions do not exist, it is quite possible or even likely that the federal president will be called upon to exercise his constitutional rights and make independent decisions regarding the formation of the government.

Although the federal constitution gives the federal president the right to represent the Republic of Austria abroad, this power lies de facto with the federal government. Most recently, this situation gave rise to a dispute over who was to represent Austria in the European Council. Following the model of the president of the French Republic, Thomas Klestil insisted on his right to represent Austria at European Union (EU) summit conferences. However, after he himself had signed Austria's EU membership agreement at the Corfu summit in June 1994, he renounced his right to participate in the following meetings of the European Council. At these summits, Austria was represented by the federal chancellor.

By law, the federal president is not politically accountable to anyone. The federal constitution does, however, foresee the possibility of the federal president's removal from office by a plebiscite following a resolution of the National Council passed by a minimum of two-thirds of its members. This obstacle prevents the deposition of the federal president on political grounds. The federal president does, however, have legal accountability. The constitutional court has the right to remove the federal president from office if he violates the federal constitution (Adamovich and Funk 1985: 262).

No federal president has ever been impeached according to this legal (not political) responsibility. Presidents have always been much "above" politics. Political conflicts did not reach their office precisely because the presidency was merely ceremonial. Until the Waldheim presidency, the head of state was never involved in party politics. According to Walter Bagehot's famous dictum, he was one of the "dignified" rather than the "efficient" parts of the constitution. The task of being "efficient" was left to the federal chancellor.

The Waldheim presidency had a strong impact on both the office itself and the public perception of it. Waldheim was a very controversial president. This was not the result of his policies as president. He did not in any significant way change the mostly ceremonial character of the president's role established by his predecessors. But circumstances prevented him from being an integrative factor. His presidential campaign was—at least in its final stages—completely dominated by the discussion of Waldheim's past. Had he been a member of the SA, the NSDAP's militia? Was he in any way guilty of war crimes? What had he omitted from his biographical data and why? Waldheim had little opportunity to develop an understanding of his office. He was too busy defending his record not as president but as an officer of the Greater German Wehrmacht (Mitten 1992).

Waldheim was the first president to be the subject of such international and domestic controversy. A highly symbolic head of state who abstains from party politics should be someone who has the ability to mobilize consensus. Because Waldheim was not able to do this, he changed the role of the president by politicizing it—against his will. No other president had ever been the target of such constant and open criticism from important segments of the Austrian public; no other president had ever been so divisive. In that sense, the Waldheim presidency marked the end of the nonpolitical character of the office. Waldheim was too controversial to be merely one of the dignified parts of the constitution as his predecessors had been.

This politicization of the office goes hand in hand with the current tendency to expect more from the president. During their campaigns, both Kurt Waldheim and Thomas Klestil emphasized their willingness to be "strong presidents." Waldheim's tenure was completely overshadowed by the discussion of his past, so he never really had the opportunity to prove that his intention to be a "strong president" was more than campaign rhetoric. Klestil is in a much better position to test an expanded understanding of his role. His insistence on being more engaged on an international level, which he demonstrated at the EU summit in Corfu, is one example of this. Another one is his more arbitrary handling of the chancellor's appointment.

After the elections of the National Council in October 1994 and again in December 1995, Klestil deviated slightly from the traditional behavior of previous presidents. He did not immediately turn the task of nominating a new cabinet over to the leading candidate from the strongest party in the National Council. Instead, he first consulted with the leaders of all five parties in parliament. Only then was Franz Vranitzky, the strongest party's candidate for the chancellorship, nominated. In a clear demonstration of the president's constitutional powers, Klestil used his discretion to decide who should form the government.

But the president's increased influence is not only the result of personal factors. The majority in parliament has become less clear than in the past. Not only is it no longer reasonable to expect overall majorities of one party, but the number of parties has also increased. The possibility of different majorities in the National Council is greater than ever. But as the parliament has become less predictable, the president has become more of a player. The deconcentration of the party system has increased the president's options.

Several factors are working together to politicize the president's role. They include the disintegrative consequences of Waldheim's presidency, Klestil's demonstration of his intentions on the international and domestic level, both men's campaign promise to be a "strong" president, and especially the deconcentration of the party system and the decline of predictability in parliament. The role of past federal presidents was to reign but not to rule. Future presidents may be expected to do both.

This will of course result in conflicts. In the Second Republic, ruling has always been the role of the federal chancellor. Any increase in the president's importance means a decrease in the chancellor's, and the future relationship between the head of state and the head of government will be significantly more challenging than it used to be. If future presidents manage to shed their merely "dignified" roles, the two political leaders will end up competing for the most "efficient" role.

Cabinet and Administration

The federal government (Bundesregierung) consists of the federal chancellor (Bundeskanzler), the vice chancellor (Vizekanzler), the federal ministers (Bundesminister), and the undersecretaries of state (Staatssekretäre) who are under the direct control of federal ministers. When the federal government acts as one body, it congregates as the Council of Ministers (Ministerrat), where the chancellor, the vice-chancellor, and the ministers have a vote, but the undersecretaries of state do not.

The federal government is a collective body. The federal chancellor as the head of government is, in principle, only a primus inter pares. This is expressed, among other things, by his lack of direct authority over the federal ministers and his only very generally formulated power to determine governmental policy. The absence of a clearly defined legal authority of the head of government is most evident in the principle of unanimity of the Council of Ministers: If the federal chancellor is opposed by even a single minister, he cannot implement his ideas even if he controls a vast majority of the votes in the council (Müller 1997: 127–132).

TABLE 3.4   Federal Chancellors and Governments in the Second Republic

Term	Federal Chancellor	Composition of Cabinet
1945	Karl Renner (SPÖ)	Provisional government
1945–1947	Leopold Figl (ÖVP)	All-party ÖVP/SPÖ/KPÖ government
1947–1953	Leopold Figl (ÖVP)	Grand coalition ÖVP/SPÖ
1953–1961	Julius Raab (ÖVP)	Grand coalition ÖVP/SPÖ
1961–1964	Alfons Gorbach (ÖVP)	Grand coalition ÖVP/SPÖ
1964–1966	Josef Klaus (ÖVP)	Grand coalition ÖVP/SPÖ
1966–1970	Josef Klaus (ÖVP)	ÖVP majority government
1970–1971	Bruno Kreisky (SPÖ)	SPÖ minority government
1971–1983	Bruno Kreisky (SPÖ)	SPÖ majority government
1983–1986	Fred Sinowatz (SPÖ)	Small coalition SPÖ/FPÖ
1986–1987	Franz Vranitzky (SPÖ)	Small coalition SPÖ/FPÖ
1987–1997	Franz Vranitzky (SPÖ)	Grand coalition SPÖ/ÖVP
Since 1997	Viktor Klima (SPÖ)	Grand coalition SPÖ/ÖVP

Constitutionally, the Austrian federal chancellor has significantly less power than either the U.S. president or the British prime minister. In reality, however, his position is much more important than his formal "first among equals" status implies. This is reflected in the public perception of his role. The career goal of party leaders is always to become chancellor, and elections of the National Council are always decisions about the person of the chancellor. Public interest focuses on the chancellor because he is considered to be the person who wields the greatest political power and is at the center of political decisionmaking. This perception is based on political reality.

The importance of the federal chancellor in the constitutional reality of Austria is a result of Austria being a party state ("Parteienstaat"). Since 1945, the federal chancellor has always been the candidate for the chancellorship (in most cases the chairman) of the strongest party in the National Council, the party with the greatest number of seats (see Table 3.4). Thus his authority within his party has accorded him a measure of power that is not formulated in the constitution, especially power with regard to the government members of his own party.

That explains why the most powerful chancellors were those who headed a one-party cabinet, backed by an overall majority of their own party in the National Council. Only two chancellors have ever been in this position: Josef Klaus in his one term from 1966 to 1970 and Bruno Kreisky in his three terms from 1971 to 1983. The electoral results that enabled Klaus and Kreisky to form a stable cabinet consisting only of persons of their choosing are the preconditions for maximizing the chancellor's power.

A coalition government (in the Second Republic, 1945–1966 and from 1983 to the present) places definite limitations on the chancellor's power. Government members who do not belong to the chancellor's party consider the vice-chancellor (the leader of their party), not the chancellor, to be their boss. This separation is already evident during the formation of the government. The candidate for the chancellorship charged by the federal president with the task of forming a government can, if his party does not hold an absolute majority in the National Council, only form a government in cooperation with a partner. Based on past experience with the formation of coalition governments, the negotiating parties or party leaders have full autonomy over their governmental staff, which is to say the federal chancellor has no influence on the members of the government nominated by the coalition partner. The background of this coalition power is the political responsibility of the federal government to the National Council. The latter can—with a simple majority—cast a vote of no-confidence with regard to the federal government or its individual members, upon which the federal president must dismiss the government (or individual members).

In the Second Republic there has never been a successful vote of no-confidence. It is true that the opposition regularly uses no-confidence votes in the National Council to attract publicity; however, on an equally regular basis these attempts fail to get the necessary majority. As the most powerful weapon of the National Council against the federal government, the no-confidence vote is thus significant only in its anticipative, indirect effect; in this respect, however, it is very effective. In order to avoid a vote of no-confidence, the federal government needs the support of the majority in the National Council right from the beginning. This was also true in the only case (since 1945) of a minority government: In 1970–1971, the Bruno Kreisky government was backed by only a minority of SPÖ representatives. It could, however, be sure that any ÖVP no-confidence vote would fail to get a majority because of an agreement with the FPÖ (Pelinka 1993: 18).

With regard to coalition governments, a complex pattern of informal and formal compromises has been the standard procedure. Before the weekly meeting of the Council of Ministers, members of the government meet the most important functionaries (e.g., the chairpersons of parliamentary factions) in a round of preparatory ministerial discussion organized according to party affiliations in order to harmonize the party line for the Council of Ministers. This is followed by discussions in contact committees, where the individual positions are harmonized. If necessary, the chairpersons of the parties (i.e., federal chancellor and vice-chancellor) can meet for a summit. Subsequently, there is a joint preparatory session for the Council of Ministers where the final details are worked out; this is then followed by the correspondingly short and formal Council of Ministers headed by the federal chancellor.

This complex system of mutual discussion and harmonization was developed in the course of the 1983–1986 SPÖ/FPÖ coalition (Pelinka 1993: 63–68). The next coalition (SPÖ/ÖVP), which was formed in January 1987 after the National Council elections, continued this system. In principle, it corresponds to the working committee that the "old" grand coalition (until 1966) used to find compromises within the coalition. It must be said, however, that the growing self-confidence of the parliamentarians and the comparably larger and more heterogeneous opposition forces have made it harder to work out details between the coalition partners. The complexity of structure designed explicitly to facilitate compromise is part of consociational democracy Austrian-style. It is typical of the elitist style of this kind of political culture: If the elites of the different camps are empowered to bargain behind closed doors, they will be able to reach optimal compromises. In official institutions such as the Council of Ministers or the National Council, elitist negotiation sessions could not be kept private. That is the reason for the different informal preparatory meetings.

The position of the federal chancellor is therefore dependent on two main factors:

- First and foremost, he (or she) must be able to win elections. Parties choose only candidates who they are sure can win elections. Winning elections is crucial: In all the years of the Second Republic, the chancellor has always been the leader of the winning party.
- Second, the chancellor must be able to cultivate the different power brokers and interest groups and traditional wings of his or her own party. But of course, nothing feeds the chancellor's intraparty authority better than success at the ballot box.

There is constant tension between the position of the chancellor according to constitutional law (primus inter pares) and his position in constitutional reality (head of government by virtue of his party leadership). This tension is increased by the federal chancellor's lack of power to appoint personnel: It is not the chancellor but the individual ministers who decide on the administrative personnel of the government (Müller 1997: 132–134). The chancellor has only the authority to appoint the personnel of the federal chancellery, which is seen as a ministry among others.

As a consequence, certain party-political patterns have become firmly established in the individual ministries. For instance, the Ministry for Agriculture—which from 1945 to 1970 and then again since early 1987 has been headed by an ÖVP minister—is an ÖVP domain. The Ministry for Labor and Social Affairs—headed by social-democratic ministers except between 1966 and 1970—is, correspondingly, a domain of the SPÖ.

Despite the general dominance of professional civil servants, Austria has political civil servants as well. Any federal ministry has established ministerial offices (also called "ministerial cabinets") consisting of persons especially chosen by the minister for personal and political reasons. The ministerial offices form an independent hierarchy of their own, in direct competition with the formal hierarchy of the professional civil servants. These ministerial offices comprise up to five persons; only the staff (cabinet) of the federal chancellor is somewhat larger. These persons, who enjoy the political and personal trust of the chancellor, the vice-chancellor, or the minister, find themselves in a structurally created field of tension with regard to the professional civil servants in the ministries (heads of departments, groups, sections). In contrast to professional civil servants, the careers of the members of these cabinets depend on the career of the respective minister (or chancellor). Holding such an office is, however, in many cases the stepping stone to a top-level political career.

This is part of the closed circle of political clientelism. Cabinet members use their hiring power to recruit persons of their confidence, usually through the channels of their respective camps. The hiring of a personal staff is only one part of a minister's member-recruiting activities. Hiring practices for other attractive administrative positions outside the minister's (or chancellor's) personal staff are also based on political affiliations. The careers of those admitted to this circle follow the logic of the spiral: If they don't violate important rules, they will automatically stay within the circle and move higher through the automatism of generational change.

This is also an aspect of the lack of any real separation between the legislature and the executive. Many members of parliament formerly held positions in the executive branch, and most cabinet members formerly served in parliament. The administration therefore does not see its task as merely to "administer" or to "implement" what others have decided. Instead, the administration is part of the political decisionmaking process. This is most obvious in the preparliamentary stages of the legislative procedure.

The Judiciary

In Austria, jurisdiction is the exclusive power of the federal level. There are no courts by virtue of state laws, and no courts are embedded in the subfederal level of the political system. All the judiciary is federal, including the recruitment of judges (Adamovich and Funk 1985: 309–317).

The courts of the ordinary jurisdiction (civil and criminal law) are organized into a four-level hierarchy:

- district courts (Bezirksgerichte),
- state courts (Landesgerichte),
- high courts (Oberlandesgerichte—total of four: Vienna, Graz, Linz, Innsbruck), and
- the Supreme Court.

In the ordinary judiciary, the principle of peer recruitment prevails: Judges determine who will be judges. It is true that the federal minister of justice selects the candidates for judgeship from the proposals of the personnel committees of the high courts and that the federal president signs the formal appointment document. In practice, however, the judges themselves have full authority in terms of recruiting. On the one hand, this strengthens their independence; on the other hand, peer recruitment tends to bring about social and political isolation.

The Austrian legal system is different from the tradition of the Anglo-American case law system. It is based less on precedent decisions and more on the legal texts passed by parliament. This reduces the authority of judges but still leaves ample room for the interpretation of law. The appointment of judges is thus a politically sensitive issue.

The independence of the judges has never been in dispute in the Second Republic. The full independence of the judiciary—aside from their obligation to follow the law—is part of the general consensus upon which the Second Republic is built.

This independence also applies to the extraordinary jurisdiction, which consists of two further superior courts (Adamovich and Funk 1985: 324–351):

- The Administrative Court (Verwaltungsgerichtshof) is the highest court for administrative cases.
- The Constitutional Court (Verfassungsgerichtshof) is the highest court for all conflicts that require constitutional interpretation.

The federal government has a significant influence on the appointment of the president and vice-president of the administrative court. They are appointed by the federal president, who acts in accordance with a government proposal drawn up with no direct influence from other judges. This kind of political influence does not fit into the pattern of peer recruitment.

In the case of the constitutional court, the recruitment of the total of fourteen members and six substitute members is clearly political: according to the wording of the constitution, the federal president follows the proposal of the federal government (or the National Council and the Federal Council) in appointing the court's president, vice-president, twelve other members, and six substitute members. Functionaries of political parties are expressly excluded from being appointed. The members of the constitutional court must have a law degree and a professional legal background.

In the consociational political culture of the Second Republic, the formal procedure focused on party-political independence has been replaced by a de facto recruitment that gives the two major parties balanced access to and control of the constitutional court. Since 1945, coalition or majority governments of the SPÖ and/or ÖVP has dominated the federal government, the National Council, and the Federal Council. The two parties therefore informally agreed on a proportional representation of judges in the constitutional court along party-political lines. A judge proposed by the SPÖ was to be succeeded by another SPÖ judge, and a judge with ÖVP affiliations should be replaced by another candidate from the People's Party. In this way, SPÖ and ÖVP judges' benches were created.

The consequence of party-political recruitment is, however, a tendency for the constitutional court to become depoliticized in its jurisdiction and to maintain a noninterventionist position on politically sensitive issues. The court's constitutional interpretations are correspondingly cautious. A prime example is the constitutional court's refusal to acknowledge the question of abortion as part of its jurisdiction. The Austrian court's position is a sharp contrast to that of both the U.S. Supreme Court, which is highly sensitized on this issue, and the German Federal Constitutional Court. Independent of this pattern of "depoliticization through politicization," the members of the constitutional court have traditionally been highly qualified in jurisdiction. Since 1945, the presidents have normally been professors of constitutional law, while the other members and substitute members have been either academic experts or experienced practitioners in the field of law.

The constitutional court is an exceptional product of consociational democracy and the party state. The two major parties have respected the letter and the spirit of the constitution. The court is highly professional, and its independence has never been in doubt. But at the same time the SPÖ and the ÖVP developed a technique to control the access to the court without violating the rules. By doing so, they have created a court that hesitates to be too interventionist. The court's legal philosophy is to leave politics to the other constitutional institutions and to the politicians. Its tendency to abstain from intervening in sensitive political matters suits the interests of the parties perfectly.

Some of these status quo conditions are likely to change. It is doubtful that any new coalition partner will respect the unwritten rule that balances SPÖ and ÖVP judges. It is doubtful that a younger generation of constitutional experts will continue the tradition of self-restraint and of abstaining from opinions seen as too interventionist, too political. It is doubtful that public opinion, in its tendency to find new things to criticize—especially the overlapping of party interests and constitutional rules—will continue to accept the informal division along party lines.

Despite its professional qualities, the constitutional court has always given the traditional elites as much liberty as possible to shape the constitution according to their interests. The fact that there has not been a constitutional crisis since 1945—with the exception of one incident in 1963 (Mommsen-Reindl 1976)—may justify the court's ambivalence between politicization and depoliticization. But as the traditional political elites' ability to control the general political process erodes, so does their traditional control over access to the constitutional court. And once this control is lost, the judicial restraint will be over.

States and Municipalities

The States

According to the constitution, federalism in Austria is relatively underdeveloped (Esterbauer 1995: 72–86; Adamovich, Funk, and Holzinger 1997: 158–168). The nine states have no jurisdiction of their own—even all major financial decisions are made at the federal level. Federal constitutional law expressly gives the prevailing power in terms of legislation and execution to the federal and not the state level. Still, the states wield significant influence. The high degree of autonomy that the state organizations of the parties and chambers (not the ÖGB) have indirectly strengthens the autonomy of the constitutional organs of the states as well.

The actual weight of the states is, among other things, determined by a regional consciousness that has developed over centuries. With the exception of Burgenland, which was granted to Austria as the sum of the western Hungarian areas with a German-speaking majority by the Trianon Treaty of 1920, each of the states has its own centuries-old regional history. "Subnational" identities have strengthened the de facto autonomy of the states. Austrian national identity has had to compete not so much with a traditional pan-German or a new pan-European identification as with strong local allegiances. Many Austrians identify more strongly with their state and/or city or village. The importance of the subnational political level can therefore be seen not only in the vertical separation of power between the federal, the state, and the local levels but also in the regional and local identities (Breuss, Liebhart, and Pribersky 1995; Bruckmüller 1996: 67).

This creates a cleavage that is frequently exploited, especially on the state level. It is rather easy to criticize "Vienna," which stands for big government. Again and again the states have managed to use certain anticentralist emotions as instruments of political mobilization and thus gain support for action against the federal administration. These anticentralist emotions are also fueled by party-political factors: In six of the nine states (exceptions are Vienna, Burgenland, and Carinthia) ÖVP state governors have been in power continuously since 1945. They have been able to maintain the approval ratings because of resistance to "red Vienna" ("red" in a double sense: as the seat of the federal government—since 1970 either social democratic governments or governments dominated by the SPÖ—and as a city/state traditionally dominated by social democrats).

The states also take advantage of the anti-Vienna sentiment to further their common purposes. Their main instrument is the Governors' Conference (Landeshauptleute-Konferenz), the institutionalized lobby they use to present their states' rights agenda. The states constantly lobby for more rights, especially with respect to the distribution of finances.

As it can be seen in Table 3.5, the states differ not only along party lines. The referendum of June 12, 1994, showed a cleavage that had almost nothing to do with party lines (Pelinka 1994). In Tyrol and Vorarlberg, the states with the strongest ÖVP majorities, the results of the EU plebiscite differed significantly: Tyrol was the state with by far the smallest majority in favor of Austria's EU membership, while Vorarlberg voted exactly like Austria as a whole. In the FPÖ's stronghold of Carinthia, voters cast significantly more "yes" ballots than Austria in general, despite the FPÖ's outspoken "no" position. Each state influenced the election independently.

The nine Austrian states are organized according to the principles of democratic systems. A directly elected state diet (in the state of Vienna simultaneously

TABLE 3.5   Voting, by State, in the EU Plebiscite on June 12, 1994

	Yes (%)	No (%)
Burgenland	74.7	25.3
Carinthia	68.2	31.8
Lower Austria	67.9	32.1
Upper Austria	65.5	34.5
Salzburg	65.1	34.9
Styria	68.9	31.1
Tyrol	56.7	43.3
Vorarlberg	66.6	33.4
Vienna	66.1	33.9
AUSTRIA	66.6	33.4

SOURCE: Official results.

the city council) appoints the governor ("Landeshauptmann," head of the government) and the other members of the state government, the state counselors ("Landesräte"). They are politically accountable to the state diets. In seven of nine states (exceptions are Vienna and Vorarlberg) the state constitutions require that the composition of the state governments reflect the proportional strength of the parties represented in the state diet ("system of proportional government") (Marko and Poier 1997: 823–826). As a consequence, in many states all the parties represented in the state diet are represented in the state government as well—in other words, there is no opposition in parliament.

This deficit of opposition is a consequence of a twofold situation:

- Proportional government as it exists in seven of the nine states is part of the general pattern of consociational democracy. State constitutions mandate what has long existed on the federal level by virtue of political decision rather than constitutional necessity: "grand coalitions," according to Arend Lijphart one of the central instruments of consociational democracy (Lijphart 1977: 25–31).
- Proportional government diffuses the functions parties want to fulfill. In 1994, for example, the Greens were obliged to nominate a candidate for the Tyrolean government because they had the electoral strength and therefore the necessary number of seats in the Tyrolean diet. No one asked the Greens if they really wanted to join the government, and no one asked the Tyrolean People's Party, which still had an overall majority in the diet, if they wanted the Greens to join.

The role of state governors takes on special significance for several reasons. First, the state governments operate on the majority principle (in contrast to the federal government, where the principle of unanimity applies). Because the state governor is normally the top candidate of the strongest party, which frequently also has an absolute majority in the state government, the governor's position is further strengthened. In addition, the power to hire personnel rests not with individual members of the state government, the state counselors ("Landesräte"), but with a specially appointed member of the state government, in most cases the governor.

Because members of the state government lack the power to hire and fire, there is less incentive for a smaller party to participate in state government as a minor coalition partner. There is significantly more incentive on the federal level, where any member of the cabinet (federal government) can use his or her veto to block any cabinet decision. Each federal minister is responsible for hiring the civil servants in his or her ministry. A state counselor has no comparable power. He or she can be voted down by a majority in the state government. And against the will of the majority, he or she cannot hire state employees. The obligation to join a state government is therefore increasingly seen as entailing all the disadvantages of a minor coalition partner without any of the advantages.

In the 1990s, several states (Tyrol, Salzburg, Upper Austria, Styria) began to take a critical look at proportional governments. It was an effort to predict which new constellations might result from the decline of the SPÖ and ÖVP. The FPÖ, for instance, has become a party that is represented in almost all the state governments. This again can be seen as an opportunity to integrate parties that would otherwise be in permanent opposition—or as the neglect of the functions the opposition should fulfill in any democracy.

On January 1, 1997, only three of the nine states, Upper Austria, Carinthia, and Burgenland, had three parties in the state parliament; in all the other states, four or five parties were represented. Thus, it is clear that deconcentration of the party system has also been taking place in the states. The fact that most of the state constitutions ensure a proportional government is increasingly regarded as a way of avoiding parliamentary opposition. The disadvantages of proportional governments are beginning to outweigh the advantages. The principle of proportional government is the target of growing criticism. This is another expression of the erosion of the political culture embodied by consociational democracy, a system with a basic pattern of mutual guarantees of power sharing that perfectly accommodates the principle of proportional government.

Below the state level there is, first of all, the level of political districts. They are pure administrative entities in which no democratic elements exist. The district governor ("Bezirkshauptmann") who heads the district administration is a state official directly subordinated to the state government. The lack of any democratic representation on the district level is one of the unfulfilled promises of the constitution. There have been many concepts and proposals to give this pure administrative level democratic quality, but interest in democratizing the district level has never been strong enough. One reason is that for a country of Austria's size, three democratic levels (federal, state, local) seem to be enough. Another is that the democratic autonomy of the political districts would reduce the power of the state governments. The informal alliance of the states thus prevents the districts from becoming democratically autonomous (Adamovich and Funk 1985: 284–286).

The one exception to this principle is a group of mostly larger cities with a status of their own ("Städte mit eigenem Statut" or "Statutarstädte"). They are not integrated into a political district and have all the powers of both a municipality and a political district. The cities with this special status enjoy the constitutional liberty to maximize the autonomy of a municipality—at the cost of state power. There is no district governor to stand between the mayor of such a city and the state government. The mayor has all the administrative authorities the district governor usually has but with the democratic legitimation all mayors enjoy.

It is interesting that the only state that does not have a city with special status is Vorarlberg. (Vienna is both state and city and is therefore an exception in itself.) Vorarlberg is usually very active in defending states' rights and demanding increased state powers. But its interest in decentralizing power is limited to the federal-state relationship. Vorarlberg has no interest in transferring state power to the municipalities by giving some of the cities special status. The state rights movement, of which Vorarlberg has always been a vanguard, naturally has its own self-interests (Kreisky 1981; Barnay 1983; Luther 1997).

The political mobility expressed in electoral mobility increases the states' political weight. "Vertical" electoral mobility implies that for more and more voters, the election level determines their party preference. The party they vote for on the state level is not necessarily the same party they vote for on the federal level. Voters can use this tactic to stress their home state's unique identity, either by casting their ballot against "big government" in Vienna, especially if the voter's own party is not part of the central government; or by voting so as to distinguish the state party from its federal organization, should the voter's own party be in power in Vienna.

This works against the internal unity that characterized the major Austrian parties. There is a constant temptation, especially within the ÖVP, to forget the party's federal links. There is suddenly a "Styrian" or a "Tyrolean" People's Party that pretends to have nothing to do with a party called the "Austrian" People's Party. Internal differentiation within the political parties is the product of the increasing independence the political process has on the state level, and that independence is in turn strengthened by internal differentiation.

Municipalities and Local Politics

In principle, municipalities are also organized according to the parliamentary system. The federal constitution overrides territorial autonomy by determining the structure of local politics. The basic rules defined by federal constitutional law apply to all municipalities in all eight states, with the notable exception of Vienna (because it is both a municipality and a state) and the cities with special status discussed above. All other municipalities are treated equally according to the principle of the "uniform municipality" (Einheitsgemeinde) (Adamovich and Funk 1985: 291–303).

The municipalities are autonomous within the framework of the federal constitution and the constitution of their state. They have both a delegated and an autonomous sphere of responsibility: In the former, they act as the arms of the federal or state government; in the second, they act independently. This means that the financial situation of the municipalities depends in part on the federal and state governments' distribution of funds.

In some states, mayors are being elected by direct vote. This indicates that the personality-oriented (quasi-presidential) factor has been strengthened at the cost of parliamentarism. This trend of the 1990s gives the local level a flavor different from the more parliamentary orientation on federal and state levels. In the municipalities of seven of the nine states, the principle of "proportional government" prevails. In the municipal governments, the parties are represented according to their strength in the city council (city parliament). Still, even the states where the mayors are not (yet) elected by a direct vote, mayoral elections by the city council do not follow the proportional system, but rather require a majority decision of the city council. The result is that even representatives from smaller parties can become mayors as well.

For this reason, there are frequent attempts on the municipal level to establish alternative majority formations, which differ from majority formations on the federal level. The FPÖ has been notably successful on the municipal level more than once since the 1970s. The FPÖ used the election of mayors to break out of the isolated position in domestic politics it had before 1983 and then again from 1986 onward. Examples of this include the cities of Graz, Klagenfurt, and Bregenz. Thus, the municipal level also functions as a kind of political test lab.

Every Austrian municipality belongs to at least one of two associations that serve as lobbies for their common interests: The Federation of Austrian Municipalities (Österreichischer Gemeindebund) represents the smaller municipalities, which are traditional ÖVP strongholds. The Federation of Austrian Cities (Österreichischer Städtebund) represents the larger municipalities, in which the SPÖ is usually the strongest party.

The municipalities are trying to use the political mobility generated in the 1980s and 1990s for their special interest: strengthening territorial autonomy, especially concerning financial aspects (Neuhofer 1997). Recent developments appear to be favorable. The municipalities are following populist trends, most notably by introducing the direct elections of mayors. It is a trend that weakens the consistency of local parliamentary rule but strengthens the position of mayors by giving them greater legitimacy.

The test lab quality also works in favor of the local level. Social movements are by their very definition designed to succeed in local politics (Gottweis 1997). It is no longer easy for a federal party apparatus to exercise centralized control over the municipalities. The local level profits from the general tendency toward "subsidiarity." Although this concept may be ambiguous on the European level, its implication for Austria is clear: The smallest unit should be given more power. And the smallest unit is the municipality.

Conclusion

The Austrian constitution has long been overshadowed by the reality of political parties. The techniques of consociationalism created a constitutional flexibility that made unwritten rules more important that many of the rules in the constitution. As the parties have gradually lost the ability to control society, their power to control the constitution has also weakened. Consequently, some of the constitutional agencies have begun to show indications of a new independence.

Like Sleeping Beauty, constitutional agencies are awakening, using their growing independence to become acquainted with their relatively new importance. Parliament is becoming increasingly active and controversial. The changing role of the federal president, traditionally a rather ceremonial office, is largely the result of the Kurt Waldheim controversy. The constitutional court has started to play a new role as an active arbiter in matters that have a decisive political impact.

Does the constitution matter politically? Since 1945, the answer has been neither a simple no or a definite yes. Now, however, the yes is becoming clearer.

4

POLITICAL PARTIES, ELECTIONS, AND INTEREST GROUPS

In Austria, more than in other liberal democracies, politics has been dominated by political parties and the interest groups affiliated with them. The major traditional parties (the SPÖ and the ÖVP) were responsible for determining the rules of the game—those of the constitution and especially those of the political culture, which is based more on loyalty to ideological camps than on loyalty to the republic or its constitution.

The Second Republic has always been a densely organized "party state" in that there were few areas of politics not clearly defined by the major political parties. At the same time, the "party state" gave birth to its own Siamese twin: the "corporate state," consisting of economic interest groups closely interrelated with major parties. Decisionmaking in Austria became a highly developed performance art. Political elites chose the theater in which they preferred to perform: either the "party state," which controls all the constitutional agencies including parliament, or the "corporate state," which dominates the sphere of economic and social policies.

Political Parties and Elections

The Development of Parties

Austria is a party state developed to the extreme, a political system in which parties tend to become identical with the constitutional government and to dominate all of society. The political parties and the institutions established by the constitution are virtually identical. Austrian parties have much greater control over the government than parties in other democracies. The parties that founded the republic and framed its constitution created contemporary Austria.

This is, among other things, the consequence of a long tradition. The party system with its three traditional parties goes back to the 1880s, when, as a consequence of modernization movements in society, three "camps" and three corresponding parties evolved (Pelinka and Plasser 1989):

- The socialist camp was politically organized as the Social Democratic Workers Party, which renamed itself the Socialist Party of Austria (SPÖ) and, from 1991 on, the Social-Democratic Party of Austria.
- The Christian-conservative (or Catholic-conservative) camp was politically organized as the Christian Social Party, renaming itself the Austrian People's Party (ÖVP) in 1945.
- The pan-German camp, the third, significantly smaller camp, was first organized as several smaller parties. In 1949 (Second Republic), it was called the League of Independents (VDU), and in 1956 it was renamed the Freedom Party of Austria (FPÖ).

The development of this traditional party system was the result of specific cleavages. Austrian society at the end of the nineteenth and the beginning of the twentieth century was influenced by the adherence to one of three dichotomous perspectives:

- Class. Society was seen as divided into two segments: the working class and the bourgeoisie. All the other divisive factors were considered secondary to this dominant cleavage, according to the socialist camp.
- Religion. This perspective also interpreted the society as fragmented into two groups: those who followed the Catholic doctrine and the others. This Christian-conservative view logically evolved into political Catholicism.
- Ethnicity. The overall dominant conflict, according to the third camp, was between the Germans and the others. The pan-German camp rallied all who considered themselves German and pitted them against the others.

This background of the Austrian party system correlated with a marked absence of national loyalty toward the existing state, Habsburg Austria. Incapable of inspiring the degree of patriotism felt in other countries, pre-1918 Austria suffered from a deficit in emotional support. These specifically Austrian conditions became responsible for two of the unique characteristics the Austrian party system had from its very beginning:

- The three camps and the parties at the camps' centers aroused much more emotion than parties usually do under different conditions. For many Austrians, their party became their real fatherland. This was the beginning of the "subcultures" that were so important for the developments that led to civil war at the end of the First Republic. But it was also the beginning of an elitist structure that made Austrian-style consociational democracy possible after 1945. The Austrian masses had no great inclination to follow national leaders: The moderate Habsburg-oriented patriotism that existed was a far cry from nationalistic fever sweeping other countries defined as "nation states." The masses' greater willingness to follow their party leaders resulted in political mobilization as well as political control by party elites. The party state was born out of this kind of fragmentation.

- The pan-German camp and its parties distinguished Austria from other European countries. The Social Democratic Workers' Party and the Christian Social Party reflected a degree of normality: All across Europe, social democratic parties were being established at the same time, and in most Catholic countries, parties like the Austrian Christian Socials were founded. But the pan-German camp and its parties were a deviant case. It included a national party that claimed to speak for the national interests not of an underprivileged minority but of the dominant ethnic group of a country it considered its own. The very existence of the pan-German camp was proof of the lack of Austrian patriotism. Nationalism in Austria was not Austrian but German. The official goal of the national party was the "Anschluss"; the ultimate perspective of nationalism in Austria was the liquidation of Austria. And that was the most striking of all the Austrian peculiarities.

The parties in the tradition of those three camps dominated the First Republic. The general pattern of government was the "bourgeois" coalition ("Bürgerblock") of the Christian Socials and the two small parties of the pan-German camp, with the social democrats as a principal opposition. The authoritarian regime between 1934 and 1938 was also based on this camp system: It was the rule of one camp, of political Catholicism, over the two others. And the Austrian Nazi movement came out of the pan-German camp.

In contrast, the Austrian Communist Party (KPÖ) has never been able to achieve any degree of relevance. With the exception of the early years of the Second Republic, when the KPÖ was identified with the Soviet occupational power, it has never had any real influence on Austrian politics.

Outside the camps there has been no way to successfully organize a party. But the emergence of the Greens in the 1980s and the LIF's successful bid for recognition in the 1994 and 1995 elections are indications of the changes taking place. The camps are no longer able to control the party system. New parties have already been established, and there are likely to be further developments. The proportional representation called for in the constitution (Art. 26 B-VG) is especially being interpreted as an invitation to establish new parties, which will contribute to a further deconcentration. Now that the camps have lost their ability to control new developments, deconcentration is the logical consequence in the 1990s.

The strong influence the parties had on Austrian society and politics—the party state—also explains why a clarification of the parties' legal status was relatively late in coming. It was not until 1975 that the law on parties finally anchored the parties in the legal system and, in part, in the constitution as well. The parties were considered to have a preconstitutional existence. As a consequence of their status in 1918 and 1945, there had never been a need for the constitution to include a legal definition of a political party. The party law was occasioned by the wish for the government to regulate public party financing.

Since 1975, a party is founded legally when the party statutes are deposited with the Ministry of the Interior. According to Austrian law, the ministry can prevent the foundation of the party only if it violates the law pertaining to renewed Nazi activities ("Verbotsgesetz"), in which case the party can appeal to the administrative and constitutional court.

Party System

The main characteristic of these parties as camps was that they did not restrict their activities to the usual functions of a party, that is, recruitment of political personnel for parliament and governments on the state and federal levels and the corresponding integration and legitimation functions. Like subsocieties, the Austrian parties organized (and organize) a comprehensive structure of social activities with the party at the center. For this reason, they were densely organized parties, which originally perceived politics in principle as external conflicts. The militancy of interparty conflicts in 1934 led to two civil wars and brought about a deep social fragmentation (Lehmbruch 1967; Powell 1970: 118–137). In February 1934, the "authoritarian" government formed by the Christian Socials used arms to win over the Social Democrats. In July 1934, the government warded off a violent coup d'état attempt by the Austrian National Socialists.

Political parties in Austria used to be more than just parties. Their substitute functions as subsidiary fatherlands had a disruptive effect for the First Republic because the elites were not able to find a way to bridge the deep cleavages. The parties were not up to the task of integrating a fragmented society.

The foundation of the Second Republic in 1945 (a procedure that in part paralleled the founding of the First Republic in 1918) meant a "peace settlement" between the ÖVP and SPÖ. The party state and proportional representation, characteristic features of the first years and decades of the Second Republic, were thus features of the Austrian variation of consociational democracy (Lijphart 1977). The extreme party focus (party state) in the Second Republic is expressed by the following features:

- A high degree of concentration in the party system: At the height of this concentration process in 1975, 93 out of 100 voters cast their vote for one of the two major parties in an election with a voter turnout of more than 90 percent. No other liberal democracy in Western Europe has ever had such a high degree of concentration. Despite proportional representation, no fourth party outside the camp system was successful.
- A significant organizational density of the party system, especially of the two large parties: In the 1970s, approximately 30 percent of the (adult) Austrian population consisted of party members. The two major political parties thus controlled not only the political process but also most other aspects of society. This traditional clientele system was a formal way of creating a method to politicize the society.
- A party recruitment function comprising all of society and extending far beyond the political sphere in the narrower sense: The parties—especially the SPÖ and ÖVP—controlled access to management positions in banking and industry (made possible by the nationalization laws of 1946 and 1947) as well as access to teaching and administrative positions in schools (indirectly legitimized through the school laws of 1962).

Until the 1980s, the Austrian party system was the model of a two-and-a-half-party system. The two large parties—the SPÖ and ÖVP—and the relatively small third party—the FPÖ—had no serious competition from a fourth or fifth party (see Table 4.1). But in the 1980s, new political mobility and the concurrent erosion of the extreme party state significantly changed the party system and transformed the features that had characterized the Austrian party state for so long:

- The Greens emerged as a fourth party in 1986, when the National Council elections gave them access to parliament. Since then the Greens' position has been stabilized.
- The FPÖ repositioned itself as a "right-wing populist" party (Plasser and Ulram 1995), a move that has increased its influence at the cost of the two major parties since 1986.
- The Liberal Forum split from the FPÖ in protest over the latter's right-wing populist tendencies. This led to the establishment of the Liberals as a fifth party in the National Council in 1993.

A special feature of this development is the absence of alternative majority formations. Although the changes in the party system would seem to work against the idea of a grand coalition between the SPÖ and ÖVP, they have in fact strengthened it—despite the force of recent developments. The reason for this is the FPÖ's right-wing extremist tendency since 1986, which makes it impossible or nearly impossible for the Freedom Party to find coalition partners. The FPÖ thus finds itself in a paradoxical situation: On the one hand, it profits from outdated governmental structures; on the other hand, it perpetuates these same structures because its "right-wing populist," xenophobic attitude largely makes it undesirable as a coalition partner (Dokumentationsarchiv 1994; Plasser and Ulram 1995; see also Chapter 9). As a consequence, one of the expected effects of a deconcentration of the party system, that is, the generation of different, competing patterns of majority formation, has yet to appear.

Because of the FPÖ's isolation, the SPÖ and ÖVP seem to be more bound together than ever at the end of the 1990s. But this could change very quickly; any new development may break up the grand coalition. Any further deconcentration that does not work exclusively in favor of the FPÖ would increase the possibilities of majorities without either the SPÖ or the ÖVP, despite the FPÖ's isolation.

The grand coalition of the 1990s is the result of a lack of alternatives. Most of the coalition's goals are reached: Austrian democracy is stabilized, Austrian society is Westernized, and Austria is a member of the European Union. Ending neutrality may be the last purpose this coalition has. But this would not be enough to hold the coalition together. At the first real opportunity, one of the coalition partners will be ready to try an alternative. This is also Westernization and normalization.

The deconcentration tendencies that primarily effect the SPÖ and ÖVP are polarizing the party system. The parties that benefit from this tendency—the FPÖ on the one hand and the Liberals and Greens on the other—are clearly on opposite sides of the political fence from one another, especially with regard to issues typical of the right-wing populism of the FPÖ. Conversely, the formerly large parties, as governmental parties and representatives of a middle ground, seem to have no clear profile.

The SPÖ and ÖVP are rather lame ducks sitting in the middle of a highly mobile and dynamic situation. Because they represent especially the interests of the older generation, the SPÖ and the ÖVP appear to be on a downhill course. The SPÖ and ÖVP may still be able to stabilize their positions—but not as dominant major parties, only as the biggest parties of medium size among others.

Electoral System and Voting Behavior

Federal constitutional law calls for proportional representation in the National Council and in the state and municipal legislatures (Art. 26 B-VG). At the federal level, that is, the National Council, an election law passed in 1992 supplements the principle of proportional representation by introducing elements of a personalized election law (Müller 1996: 251–264).

For the election of the National Council, each of the nine federal states is a constituency. Each constituency is subdivided into 43 regional constituencies. The 183 members of the National Council are elected on the regional, the state, and the federal level according to the principle of proportional representation. The regional constituencies' small size initially produces distortions in terms of proportional representation, but these distortions are rectified by the distribution of seats on the other two levels.

TABLE 4.1 Election Results of National Council Elections in the First and Second Republics

First Republic	Soc.[a]		Chr.[b]		GN[c]		LB[d]		HB[e]		NSDAP	
	%	Seats	%	Seats	%	Seats	%	Seats	%	Seats	%	Seats
1919	40.8	72	35.9	69	18.4	27	—	—	—	—	—	—
1920	35.9	69	42.3	85	16.7	28	—	—	—	—	—	—
1923	39.6	68	45.0	82	12.6	15	6.3	9	—	—	—	—
1927	42.3	71	48.4	73	—	12	—	—	6.2	8	—	—
1930	41.1	72	35.7	66	11.6	19	—	—	—	—	3.0	—

Second Republic	ÖVP		SPÖ		FPÖ		KPÖ		ALÖ		VGÖ		LIF	
	%	Seats	%	Seats	%	Seats	%	Seats	%	Seats	%	Seats	%	Seats
1945	49.8	85	44.6	76	—	—	5.4	4	—	—	—	—	—	—
1949	44.0	77	38.7	67	11.7	16	5.1	5	—	—	—	—	—	—
1953	41.3	74	42.1	73	11.0	14	5.3	4	—	—	—	—	—	—
1956	46.0	82	43.0	74	6.5	6	4.4	3	—	—	—	—	—	—
1959	44.2	79	44.8	78	7.7	8	3.3	—	—	—	—	—	—	—
1962	45.4	81	44.0	76	7.1	8	3.0	—	—	—	—	—	—	—
1966[g]	48.3	85	42.6	74	5.4	6	—[h]	—	—	—	—	—	—	—
1970	44.7	78	48.4	81	5.5	6	1.0	—	—	—	—	—	—	—
1971	43.1	80	50.0	93	5.5	10	1.4	—	—	—	—	—	—	—
1975	43.0	80	50.4	93	5.4	10	1.2	—	—	—	—	—	—	—
1979	41.9	77	51.0	95	6.1	11	1.0	—	—	—	—	—	—	—
1983	43.2	81	47.6	90	5.0	12	0.7	—	1.4	—	2.0	—	—	—
1986	41.3	77	43.1	80	9.7	18	0.7	—	4.8[i]	8	—	—	—	—

(continues)

TABLE 4.1 (continued)

Second Republic	ÖVP		SPÖ		FPÖ		KPÖ		ALÖ		VGÖ		LIF	
	%	Seats	%	Seats	%	Seats	%	Seats	%	Seats	%	Seats	%	Seats
1990	32.1	60	42.8	80	16.6	33	0.5	—	4.8[j]	10	2.0	—	—	—
1994	27.7	52	34.9	65	22.5	42	0.3	—	7.3[k]	13	0.1	—	6.0	11
1995[l]	28.3	53	38.1	71	21.9	40	0.3	—	4.8[k]	9	—	—	5.5	10

[a] Social Democrats

[b] Christian Socials

[c] German Nationalist parties

[d] Landbund. In 1927, one of the two German-nationalist parties, the Pan-German People's Party (Großdeutsche Volkspartei), ran together with the Christian-Socials Party, while the Landbund remained independent.

[e] Heimatbund

[f] In 1945 and 1953, the predecessor of the FPÖ, the Electoral Party of the Independents (Wahlpartei der Unabhängigen—WdU) ran in the elections.

[g] In these elections the DFP (Franz Olah) gained 3.28% of all votes.

[h] The KPÖ did not run nationwide.

[i] In 1983 ALÖ (Alternative List of Austria) and VGÖ (United Greens of Austria) ran on a separate platform, whereas in 1986 they ran together under the name "The Green Alternative" (Die Grüne Alternative).

[j] Later the VGÖ split again from the "Green Alternative." The party that ran in 1990 as "Green Alternative" and entered the National Council can thus no longer be regarded a combination of ALÖ and VGÖ. In 1993 this party officially assumed the name "The Greens" (Die Grünen).

[k] Official list "The Greens"

[l] Tentative final results including votes cast by absentee ballot cards; data from Dec. 27, 1995.

SOURCE: Official election results.

The first element is the prerequisite that in order for a party to participate in the distribution of National Council seats, it must either receive a minimum of 4 percent of all the votes cast in the election ("4 percent clause") or already hold a seat at the regional level. As the elections of 1994 and 1995 proved, it is much easier for smaller parties such as the Greens and the LIF to get the minimum 4 percent vote than to get a seat directly. The smaller parties usually get their seats either on the state or the federal level. The larger the party is, the more seats it can win directly.

The 1992 election law also supplements proportional representation by introducing a personal element to the voting process. Although voters still have to vote a straight party ticket, they can express their personal preferences by voting for a certain candidate, provided that the name appears on that same party list. Ballots may not split between parties. An alternative discussed at some length was the double ballot system used in Germany, whereby the first ballot is cast for a candidate of any party and the second for a party that must not be the party of the candidate who got the first ballot. This system would have given Austrian voters a wider range of choice, but it was never implemented. Experience in Germany had shown that ballot splitting benefited the smaller and medium-sized parties to the detriment of larger parties—an effect the SPÖ and ÖVP wanted to avoid.

The electoral law of 1992 also provides a possible incentive for regional parties. Its emphasis on regional constituencies with their comparatively small size ultimately works against parties without special regional flavor. In providing for strong regional interests, the law works to the advantage of locally prominent candidates who can motivate the regional electorate. If a regional party gets about 25,000 votes in its own regional constituency, it will have one seat. By winning the same number of votes in a neighboring constituency, the party wins a second seat. This can even lead to an overproportional effect: A regional party could have more seats in the National Council than the rule of proportional representation would allow. In the long run, the regionalization and personalization of election laws contributes to further deconcentration (Müller 1996: 254 f.).

On the one hand, the development of voting behavior shows an erosion of the features that characterize the traditional party system, specifically the factor of profession. For instance, the relatively uniform block of blue-collar votes for the SPÖ shows clear signs of crumbling. On the other hand, factors such as age, education, and gender increasingly determine voting behavior.

This development also means that in the future there are likely to be fewer "traditional voters" and more "personality voters" and "negative voters," that is, voters who react more strongly to short-term than to long-term factors (see Table 4.2). This is the result, among other things, of increasing mobility in society, which has decreased the importance of the milieus that historically determined the camps and cleavages (social class for the SPÖ; religion for the ÖVP). This means that the element most significant in the Second Republic, its extreme focus on parties, is diminishing.

Voting has become much more flexible. The disregard for traditional loyalties, especially among the younger generation, is indicated by lower voter turnouts, switching party preferences, and the phenomenon of "late deciders": As a conse-

TABLE 4.2 Determining Factors of Voting Behavior

Percent of Voter-types on October 9, 1994[a]	*SPÖ*	*ÖVP*	*FPÖ*	*Greens*	*LIF*
Personality voters (candidate-oriented voters = 38% of all voters)	49	10	23	9	8
Traditional voters (interest- or milieu-oriented voters = 49% of all voters)	42	38	16	5	0
Negative voters (Voters casting their vote for "the lesser evil" = 19% of all voters)	33	33	21	7	7

[a]Classification of voter types based on motive questions on the exit poll
SOURCE: Fessel+GFK 1995: Exit Poll 1994.

quence of the increased flexibility, a surprisingly high percentage of voters remain undecided about how to vote until the last hours or even minutes.

But this volatility cannot be interpreted as complete individualization of voting. Independent variables still influence voting decisions, and individual voters are still very much under pressure from their social environment. Greater voter flexibility does not result in the total independence of the individual voter but in a more complex and especially more crosscutting dependence. Class and religion, the traditional determinant factors of electoral behavior in Austria, now have to compete much more with other factors that have become stronger: generation, education, gender, and region.

According to the concept of "cross-pressures," this mix of factors has certain consequences on voting (Lazarsfeld, Berelson, and Gaudet 1944). Generally, mobility is growing. In concrete terms, the increase of conflicting influences on electoral behavior has several consequences:

- The number of voters who switch their party preference from election to election is on the rise. More Austrians than ever before are voting for different parties vertically as well as horizontally: vertically according to the different levels of elections (federal, state, local); horizontally on the same level, but changing their preference from one election to the next.
- The number of voters who abstain is also rising. The increase of "cross-pressures" provokes more voters to escape the conflicts between different loyalties—to spouses, peers, and traditions. The electoral turnout is declining.
- The importance of election campaigns is growing. Because so many voters have not made up their minds by the time campaigning starts, the intensity of the campaigns has increased and campaign strategies and techniques are becoming more sophisticated and also more expensive.

- The political traditions will count less. The decline of traditional parties may lead to the end of one party or the other, and new parties that may appear will not just be the heirs to the same type of loyalties. There will be fewer guarantees on the political market than ever before.
- The electoral philosophy will be "anything goes." Of course, this does not mean that everything is politically doable, but there will be fewer obstacles to success—which also implies fewer obstacles to failure.

This complex "mix" creates the lack of predictability so typical of the new circumstances in which the party system finds itself. After decades of stability so extreme it approached paralysis, the electoral behavior is now in turmoil. The consequence is that almost anything is possible at the turn of the millennium. Austria's parties were successful in stabilizing society by controlling it efficiently and providing it with a strong party state. But because they were so successful, they have lost control. The stabilization of the society results in the destabilization of the party system.

Party Organization and Democracy Within Parties

Political parties in Austria are characterized by a remarkably high (though decreasing since 1980) organizational density, especially the SPÖ and ÖVP. Although both of these traditional parties are termed "member" parties, their organizational structures are extremely different. The ÖVP is characterized by a "corporate" structure in which party membership is indirect, by virtue of membership in one of the six suborganizations. The SPÖ, in contrast, is a more centralist organization that accepts only direct membership. Each member has joined the party individually. Despite strong personal and structural connections with labor unions, union membership does not include party membership, as is sometimes the case in Great Britain.

The organization of the other parties is also defined by immediate, direct, individual membership only. In 1995, the FPÖ tried to reorganize itself as a "movement" in which the term "member" was replaced by that of "card holder" with different degrees of participation. But the FPÖ has never been as densely organized as the SPÖ and the ÖVP. The Greens and the Liberals have similar weak and loose organizational structures.

Official party membership statistics can be misleading. This is especially true of figures given for the ÖVP (see Table 4.3). As a consequence of its indirect form of organization, the People's Party has no centralized membership statistics. Figures given are just based on data furnished by the party's different suborganizations.

Nevertheless, the figures indicate a clear trend: The organizational density of the Austrian party system is decreasing. The SPÖ is rapidly losing members. The ÖVP's losses are probably comparable but less evident because of the party's unusual organization. The LIF and especially the Greens, who do not count mem-

TABLE 4.3　Party Members and Degree of Organization (in thousands)

Party	Members 1979	Members 1990	Members 1994	Degree of Organization[b]
SPÖ	721	675	513	32%
ÖVP[a]	560	488	433	34%
FPÖ	37	37	44	4%

[a]"Consolidated" membership numbers: Only full dues-paying members of the party suborganizations for workers and employees, farmers, and entrepreneurs are taken into account. Because of the indirect organizational structure, figures can only be estimated.

[b]The year of reference for the degree of organization is 1994.

SOURCE: Karl Ucakar. *Die sozialdemokratische Partei Österreichs;* Wolfgang C. Müller. *Die österreichische Volkspartei;* Karl Richard Luther. *Die Freiheitliche Partei Österreichs,* in Dachs et al. 1997: 259, 272, 293.

bers at all, represent the antithesis of the traditional Austrian pattern of densely organized party organizations.

But the most remarkable phenomenon is that of the FPÖ's membership. In a little more than a decade, the FPÖ has managed to more than quadruple its share of votes in national elections, from just 5 percent in 1983 to more than 20 percent three elections later. But during the same period, there was no significant change in its membership figures. The "new" FPÖ is even less well organized than it used to be. It is a party almost without a clientele bound to the party by membership. The FPÖ's attraction lies with other factors. The voters that the FPÖ has been able to attract since 1986—overproportionally young, male, less educated—are willing to vote for the FPÖ but not to join it.

All these factors combined must be interpreted as a dramatic break with an Austrian peculiarity. Voters no longer consider political parties their "home." This applies to the FPÖ, the LIF, and the Greens, and increasingly also to the SPÖ and the ÖVP as well. The relationship between the Austrians and their political parties has already changed and is changing even more. It is a much more sober and at the same time short-term relationship. Younger Austrians especially don't see the party of their choice as a closed ideological group whose members cannot easily leave. The parties have already lost most of their former presecular appeal and are well on their way toward secularization.

This is one factor that is dismantling the party state. If fewer and fewer Austrians are interested in "belonging" to a party, ideally for a lifetime, then the parties cannot maintain their control over society. And if they no longer control Austrian society, they no longer control the access to positions, a power that motivated many people to join a party. The parties are less attractive because they are less powerful, a circle that must seem vicious to the SPÖ and the ÖVP.

Despite the decline of the party state, the two major parties are still traditional in that they retain many of their traditional features. One of these is the phenomenon of subparties. Within the SPÖ and even more so within the ÖVP, certain subgroupings are extremely important. In the SPÖ this is true especially of the nine state organizations, the women's organization and Organization of Social-Democratic Unionists (FSG), which forms a link between the Federation of Austrian Trade Unions (ÖGB) and the SPÖ. In the ÖVP, the nine state organizations plus the following six suborganizations are of importance:

Austrian League of Workers and Employees (ÖAAB)
Austrian Farmers' League (ÖBB)
Austrian Business League (ÖWB)
Austrian Women's Movement
Austrian Senior Citizens' League
Young People's Party

The first three of these suborganizations, like the FSG and the women's organization in the SPÖ, have traditional rights or quotas for filling certain positions, for instance the candidates for federal and state elections. The 1990s have seen increasing tendencies—within the ÖVP as well as within the SPÖ and the Greens—to use intraparty primaries, which significantly loosen these traditional patterns of distribution. Yet the dense albeit decreasing organization of the SPÖ and the ÖVP continues to influence the nomination process: The traditional claims of suborganizations—of sections and of women's and union groupings—are based on the division of the traditional large parties. This orientation conflicts both with the trend toward primary elections and with the focus of election campaigns on the top candidates.

Primaries do not follow a uniform pattern; they vary from party to party and even within the parties, between the individual regional organizations. The top party executives, in turn, try to increase the influence they have on the federal nomination lists in order to counterbalance the anticentralist aspects of regional tendencies. The degree of influence that party headquarters (chairpersons, federal party chairpersons, etc.) can exercise varies. The headquarters of a party in power doesn't have much independence from the government because the chancellor (or vice-chancellor) is usually the party chairman. Opposition parties, in turn, tend to make their chairperson the leader of the party (or of the party's faction) in the National Council. The FPÖ has regularly done so since 1991; the Greens, between 1994 and 1995; the LIF, since 1994.

Of the three traditional parties, the ÖVP has experimented most extensively with primaries. In 1994, the ÖVP used an open primary system to recruit its candidates for the general elections. The ÖVP organizations on the state level had the opportunity to invite nonparty members to participate, and the results were binding for the regional level. But the competitive element—even though it was officially accepted—did not have much impact. The candidates on the final list were almost all those who would have been nominated without primaries. The

innovative effect of this experiment with open, binding, and competitive primaries was rather minor. There was no change in the balance among the three
subparties, the ÖAAB, ÖWB, and ÖBB (Nick 1995: 84–101).

Compared with the ÖVP, the SPÖ has been more cautious from the beginning.
Despite positive signs such as increased voter turnout, the results of the 1994 primaries did not differ at all from those of the traditional recruiting methods the
party had used in the past: The balance among regional organizations, quotas for
representatives from the FSG and from the women's organization, and seniority
were all maintained. The FPÖ chose a completely different method: Candidates
are nominated by the chairman, who then turns his attention to getting maximum exposure in the mass media (Nick 1995: 71–83, 101–106).

In all cases, intraparty democracy is seen as a function of interparty democracy.
Interparty democracy is responsible for unmasking the failure of the SPÖ and the
ÖVP to learn from their experiences in 1994. For the premature elections in 1995,
neither of the parties had time to repeat its experiments with primaries. Intraparty
democracy was handled in the traditional way, and candidates were recruited without any pretext of maximum participation. Thus the return to the old pattern was
the direct result of the 1994 elections. The experiment with new methods of intraparty democracy had not paid off, so the experiment was called off.

For the Greens and the Liberals, the situation is completely different. As new
parties with a loose membership organization, they can afford to develop their
own methods. The Greens have adopted certain rules they strictly enforce. The
most effective one calls for a one-to-one ratio of men and women. Within these
rules, the Greens' state organizations are free to choose their own candidates. The
federal organization uses its authority at the third and final level to ensure that
the candidates elected to parliament are experts in certain fields. The LIF has a
more traditional approach: Their rather elitist recruiting system is based on the
predominance of the party's founder and chairperson, Heide Schmidt (Nick
1995: 106–115).

The party system's dense organization used to have strong financial ramifications: More members meant more income from membership fees. But for a long
time now, party expenses have grown much faster than income from membership
fees. This, in connection with shrinking party membership since 1980, means that
members are no longer critically important for party finances. Parties and their
campaigns are increasingly financed by the federal government, the states, and the
municipalities. In the 1990s, direct and indirect forms of public party financing
have contributed nearly half of the parties' budgets. If one includes the Austrian
party tax, dues politicians (in the wider sense of the word) pay to their parties as
compensation for the position they have received through the party, more than 50
percent of all the money parties currently receive is public money (Sickinger 1995).

In comparison, donations to parties play a relatively small role. A direct and legal large contributor is the Association of Austrian Industrialists (VÖI), which
regularly donates money to the ÖVP. Additionally, parties indirectly receive

money from the party's suborganizations, the Confederation of Austrian Trade Unions and the large chamber organizations (Chamber of Labor, Chamber of Commerce, and Chamber of Agriculture).

The financial links between public money and party financing give the term "party state" a special meaning. Governments on all levels—federal, state and local—help finance parties. But in Austria, more than in other liberal democracies, governments and parties are virtually one and the same. The interests within the governments and parliaments that influence decisions about party financing are the parties themselves. This connection could potentially provoke a negative interpretation of the financial interdependence between parties and governments (Sickinger 1997: 327–372).

The dynamism of the late 1990s makes the problem more urgent. The camps are no longer able to finance the parties, largely because of declining membership. The parties are looking for new sources of income, and the best source seems to be the government. But there is a growing negative resentment over the parties' absolute control of government party financing. The party state feeds its critics.

Interest Groups, Corporatism, and Media

Economic Interest Groups

Another characteristic of Austria's political system is a pronounced structure of economic associations (or interest groups). After 1945, the parties developed a second political decisionmaking system of highly organized economic associations. They in turn created their own political decisionmaking level, the system of social partnership. The elites of the major camps were thus able to control two levels of decisionmaking: the party system and social partnership. From its beginning, this second level had the function of a "paracoalition"—a coalition in addition to the coalition (Steiner 1972: 311–318), and it has the advantage of being relatively immune to the volatility of the political market.

The economic interest groups assumed such a degree of importance that the Second Republic must be defined as a democratic system whose liberal features are limited by this corporatist structure. There is an Austrian corporate state, but its intention has always been to complement rather than replace the party state. The parallel existence of two stabilized and synchronized levels of central political decisionmaking is the main characteristic of the Second Republic's political culture, of consociational democracy.

The Austrian corporate state has three main features:

- a close interconnection of parties and economic associations, ensuring that on a political level details can be harmonized between party-political parliamentarism and the system of social partnership determined by the associations;

- a dense organization of economic associations expressed by a degree of union membership density that is above the EU average, in combination with a system of chambers with legal, that is, obligatory membership;
- a comprehensive system of co-decisionmaking powers within the system of social partnership based on the large economic interest groups, which puts Austria at the top of the international list of comparable structures of corporatism (Lehmbruch and Schmitter 1982).

The most important "free" economic interest groups (i.e., without compulsory membership) are the Federation of Austrian Trade Unions (ÖGB) and the Association of Austrian Industrialists (VÖI). In addition, there are the three large chamber organizations, namely the Chamber of Labor, the Chamber of Commerce, and the Chamber of Agriculture. There are also several smaller chambers for specific professional groups (physicians, lawyers, pharmacists, engineers, architects, etc.).

The ÖGB was founded in 1945 by the proponents of the tradition of social-democratic and Christian unions in cooperation with the Communists, who played an important role for a short period. It is a relatively centralist umbrella organization with fourteen smaller individual trade unions. The ÖGB has a factual monopoly: There are no unions outside of the ÖGB. Approximately 50 percent of all people employed in Austria are members of the ÖGB.

The ÖGB is structured according to industrial groupings, with one exception: the separate Union for Private Employees, the largest of the fourteen individual unions, consists only of white-collar workers. The principle of industrial groupings ("Industriegruppenprinzip") is intended to integrate different groups of employees into a small number of unions to minimize the traditional differences between white-collar and blue-collar workers. The labor movement, in Austria as elsewhere traditionally a blue-collar movement, has always striven to put an end to separate organizations for different status groups.

Another principle that guides the ÖGB and its politics is its centralist structure. It is the ÖGB, not the fourteen unions, that represents the employees' interests in all corporatist networks. It is the ÖGB, not the unions, that controls union finances, including the strike funds. It is also the ÖGB that, as the central employer, controls all the personnel employed by both the federation and the unions—and not the unions themselves.

The largest of the fourteen unions are the Union of Private Employees, the Union of Public Employees, the Metal, Mining, Energy Union, the Construction Union, and the Union of Municipal Employees. All the unions and the ÖGB itself are politically organized according to factions: The largest is the FSG (Faction of Social Democratic Unionists), a suborganization of the SPÖ. The second largest is the Faction of Christian Unionists, which is closely linked to the ÖVP. There are also weaker smaller factions, including the FPÖ faction, a faction indirectly linked to the Greens ("Gewerkschaftliche Einheit"), and a tiny Communist faction ("Gewerkschaftlicher Linksblock").

The strength of the factions is not the result of union elections but of elections in which the employees choose their legal representatives in the shop committees. This reflects a dual structure that is typical of the Austrian unions: The unions want to be dealt with independently from constitutionally based legal organizations such as the Chamber of Labor or the shop committees (Betriebsräte, Personalvertretungen). But in reality, the relationship is so close as to be nearly identical.

In 1995, the ÖGB had 1,583,365 members, a figure about 50,000 below the 1991 level (*Taschenbuch* 1997: 315). This drop is neither dramatic nor nearly as significant as the decline in party membership, but it fits into the general pattern of an increasing distance between the social and the political system. The ÖGB is facing the same problematic trend as the political parties are: Austrians today are less inclined to join political organizations than they were 20, 30, or 40 years ago.

The most important feature of the Association of Austrian Industrialists (VÖI) is not its large number of members but its relative financial power. All the important Austrian industrial enterprises are members of the VÖI—with the exception of the nationalized industries, whose importance has declined continually since the mid-1980s. One of the VÖI's most important functions is party financing: It provides regular support for the ÖVP and, until 1993, supported the FPÖ as well. Because of the FPÖ's anti-EU position, the flow of financial support—at least on the federal level—was redirected from the FPÖ to the newly founded Liberal Forum (Pelinka 1993: 86 f.; Sickinger 1995: 268 f.; Sickinger 1997: 250–252).

The Chambers of Labor are, like all large chamber organizations, present in every one of the nine states. They are organizations with compulsory membership of all employees with the exception of civil servants and employees in agriculture and forestry. The Chambers of Labor and their nationwide umbrella organization, the Federal Chamber of Labor, are closely affiliated with the ÖGB. Politically, the ÖGB's role is more offensive because it involves sensitive issues such as determining wage policies, whereas the Chambers of Labor have a protective function that includes legal advice and consumer protection.

Each of the Chambers of Commerce is divided into six sections: trade, crafts, industry, traffic, tourism, and a section for banking and insurance. The chambers are the legal representatives of all the self-employed persons in these six sections. Their umbrella organization, the Austrian Chamber of Business (Wirtschaftskammer Österreich, the former Federal Chamber of Commerce), is the official counterpart of the ÖGB (in terms of social partnership) in the areas of cooperation and confrontation, for example, in wage negotiations. The Austrian Chamber of Business organizes Austria's trade delegations all over the world and appoints the trade delegates responsible for promoting Austrian exports.

The Chambers of Agriculture are the legal representatives of agricultural interests. Their membership consists of farmers. Their federal organization, the Presidents' Conference of the Chambers of Agriculture, represents agricultural interests at the various levels of social partnership.

The three large chamber organizations are legally required to conduct elections at regular five-year intervals. These elections are organized by the factions that correspond to the parties—for example, the ÖVP leagues whose candidates run for office in the three chambers (the ÖAAB in the Chambers of Labor, the ÖBB in the Chambers for Agriculture, and the ÖWB in the Chambers of Commerce) or the Organization of Christian Unionists (FCG), which is affiliated with the ÖVP, in the ÖGB. The ÖGB has no corresponding direct elections; instead of direct union elections, the ÖGB uses the results of the shop committee elections (employees' council or, in the public service sector, employees' representatives) to define the relative strength of the intra-union factions. Most of these shop committee elections are organized by the various competing factions, such as the Organization of Social-Democratic Unionists (FSG) and the Organization of Christian Unionists (FCG). This formation of factions results in a mutual penetration of parties and economic associations (see Table 4.4). In each of the four strongest associations (in terms of members), one of the traditional large parties dominates, while the other large party holds a controlling minority position. In addition, there is a smaller but growing FPÖ proportion, and in the Chamber of Labor, the Greens are taking hold as well.

The chambers are facing a loss of support, which is reflected in decreasing voter turnout. This is especially true of the Chambers of Labor. These chambers, which represent the vast majority of working Austrians, are bearing the brunt of the general mood of growing dissatisfaction with political organizations in Austria. In 1994, for the first time ever, voter turnout for elections in the Chambers of Labor was below 40 percent. Along with this disinterest, there were several "scandals" that raised questions about the chambers as such. The FPÖ was especially outspoken in its charges that obligatory membership creates privileges for top officials who would not be obliged to act in the interests of their members.

In the aftermath of this criticism, the federal government asked the chambers to ask their members whether they were interested in having the chambers as their legal representatives. The chambers conducted those polls in 1995 and 1996, and the results were favorable for the chambers. It was especially surprising that the Chambers of Labor were so successful in mobilizing a voter turnout that significantly exceeded that of the 1994 elections. During the first half of 1996, about two-thirds of all members participated in the poll; of those, about 90 percent said "yes" to Chambers of Labor (Pelinka and Smekal 1996).

This procedure touched on some of the basic concepts of the Second Republic. Without obligatory membership, the chambers would not be distinguishable from organizations such as the ÖGB or the VÖI. The Austrian system of economic association would lose one of its most unique characteristics. In 1996, this first attack was successfully repulsed, but there are no guarantees: neither that the siege is over nor that the Austrian system will prevail next time.

Corporatism and Social Partnership

The social partnership institutions were formed by the economic associations in cooperation with the parties and the government to fulfill a large number of

TABLE 4.4   Survey of the Most Important Economic Associations and Their Links
with Parties

	SPÖ	*ÖVP*	*FPÖ*
ÖGB[a]	Majority	Minority	Small proportion
Chambers of Labor	Majority	Minority	Medium proportion
Chambers of Commerce	Minority	Majority	Medium proportion
Chambers of Agriculture	Minority	Majority	Small proportion

[a]There is a significant proportion of shop stewards (employee representatives in the employees' council) who are not affiliated with a party.
SOURCE: Data provided by the economic associations.

functions (Tálos 1993). There are several important examples of this type of (neo)corporate participation:

- The Joint Commission on Wages and Prices, founded in 1957, issues policies on wage and price control. These decisions are not legally binding, and adherence to them is voluntary.
- The various advisory boards and committees founded by the federal and state governments serve to politically integrate the economic associations.
- Economic interest groups participate in the legislative process on the preparliamentary level (evaluation stage).
- Economic associations have legal control over social security institutions. This control gives the interest groups power in decisions concerning health, old age, and accident insurance.

Social partnership, as the Austrian version of corporatism, is open to multiple interpretations. Social partnership can be defined in a variety of different ways, and everybody is free to choose the definition that best suits his or her purpose. For Social Democrats, corporatism is an important part of industrial democracy, designed to democratize capitalism and the market economy. For Christian Democrats, it is the fulfillment of the popes' doctrine of a third alternative somewhere between capitalism and socialism. For capitalists, it is the best way to integrate labor unions and prevent class warfare. For unionists, it is the opportunity to participate in decisions from which they would be otherwise excluded. And for Austria, it is a policy that guarantees social peace and domestic security, the domestic equivalent of neutrality, which guarantees peace and security on the international level.

But for the Austrian elites, corporatism is the arena that was missing in the First Republic. An exact definition of the Second Republic is parliamentary rule plus corporatism. The centrifugal democracy of the First Republic did not bring about the ideal combination of liberty and security that democracy is expected to achieve. The Second Republic did, at least in the eyes of most Austrians. They believe that social partnership made the difference.

Social partnership is the most peculiar institution created by and developed in the Second Republic. It has been criticized for a variety of reasons (Pelinka 1981: 69–79). Its voluntary control of market mechanisms such as the price policy authority of the Joint Commission must be anathema to those who believe in the free market without any reservation. But its institutionalized balance between labor and business must also be anathema to orthodox Marxists. And its extraconstitutional status can never be acceptable to those who believe that the constitution should be the Bible for political decisionmaking.

Corporatism Austrian-style has been always identified with different "general theories." There have been different approaches to how social partnership should be perceived from an academic viewpoint. The scholarly interpretations of Austro-corporatism have followed certain trends or fashions that can be defined as a change of paradigms (Prisching 1996: 15–46). These interpretations include the following: consensus between the main political and economic organizations; pluralism as an arrangement between major articulated interests; conspiracy of a sinister elite using social partnership as a sophisticated instrument of power; disempowerment of government by virtue of shifting responsibilities from the constitutional to the extraconstitutional level; stabilization as a general concept for surviving the cycle of crises that seem to plague capitalism; sclerosis as the inevitable result of corporatism's lack of adaptability; symbiosis as the fusion between government and interest groups.

But in the end, which paradigm is chosen or which interpretation of the peculiar Austrian institutions of social partnership seems to prevail is a moot point. In 1992, the Joint Commission was reinterpreted, its price control authority was declared obsolete, and a new subcommittee was established to deal with "international questions." It was the death knell—not for social partnership in general but for the specifically Austrian version of it. The farewell to Austro-corporatism had begun.

The Position of Churches and Religious Organizations

The Austrian political system has no stringent separation of church and state. In the Second Republic, a system of mutual recognition between the government and the most important religious organizations developed, based on the historically dominant position of the Catholic Church ("political Catholicism"). The "officially recognized denominations" are groups endowed with certain privileges, specifically, the right to organize religious education in the schools according to the doctrines of the individual religious organization. The expenses for religious education are paid for by the state. Additionally, the officially recognized denominations have the right to levy taxes ("church tax") from their members, which can, if necessary, be collected by state authorities (Zulehner 1995b).

The Catholic Church, to which a significant majority of Austrians still belong, has additional rights based on the 1960 version of the Concordat of 1933. Among these is the exclusive right of the bishops of the diocese to both grant and rescind permission to teach in theological faculties of the universities in Vienna, Graz, Innsbruck, and Salzburg. The officially recognized denominations are involved at the evaluation level of the legislative process (preparliamentary stage) in all issues that concern them.

The relationship between church and state in Austria is based on Josephinism, the system created by emperor Joseph II in the late eighteenth century. It states that the government must be tolerant and show a moderate interest in the well-being of the Catholic Church and the other recognized denominations. The churches enjoy the privileges that this close relationship provides. This status is the antithesis of the separation of church and state, which exists in different ways in France and the United States. It confirms the continued existence of a still formal tradition of mutual instrumentalization.

Under the Austrian political system, the recognized denominations are treated on an equal basis with economic associations. They are invited to participate in the legislative process—like the ÖGB, the VÖI and the chambers. They enjoy a high degree of autonomy and fulfill certain functions closely linked with the government, such as providing religious instructions in public schools or serving as army chaplains with the rank of commissioned officers. In that respect, the position and the functions of the churches are part of a culture of corporatism that goes beyond economic interests.

But the government grants the internal structures of the denominations more autonomy than it allows the economic interest groups. There are no legal regulations that the churches have to follow in their internal decisionmaking. It is up to the denominations whether to have internal democracy: Most Protestant denominations and the Jewish community do; the Catholic Church does not. The kind of control the government has over the chambers through their obligatory internal elections does not exist with respect to the churches. Despite some similarities between Austro-corporatism and the system of recognizing religious denominations, there is a significant difference: The churches have a higher degree of autonomy than the economic interest groups, especially the chambers.

The quasi-corporatist relationship between government and churches strengthens the position of the Catholic bishops. As the representatives of a denomination that does not follow the principle of internal democracy, they speak for the by far largest denomination without democratic legitimacy. The bishops and their conference speak on behalf of the Catholic Church when the Church is asked for an opinion concerning legislature. The bishops, not a conference of elected or delegated laypersons, are invited to exploit the options that the dense church-state relationship provides.

This implies certain problems of synchronization. The bishops are not dependent, at least not directly, on the demands of the active Catholic segment of Austrian society. The greater the discrepancy between Catholic interests as defined by the bishops and the interests of active Catholics, the less chance there is that the bishops' politically integrated statements will voice the dynamic tendencies within the Catholic segment.

This is the ambiguity of contemporary Josephinism: It guarantees optimal conditions for cooperation between church and state by seeing it as cooperation among equals. But it also has a petrifying effect. In accordance with the overall legal framework, the Catholic Church must be treated as if it were a static entity. And this indeed is the case. This perception ignores the dynamism within the church, an omission that can only result in various forms of alienation.

The quasi-corporatist form of the church-state relationship has had a stabilizing effect on the whole political system. It has helped to quell the potentially explosive ideological conflicts that destabilized the First Republic. Since 1945, questions concerning the influence the church (any denomination) should have on schools and universities, the legitimacy of divorce, and even the legality of abortion have not caused much disruption. But because the relationship has a quasi-corporatist structure, it has to deal with the threat of advancing sclerosis. It may be too institutionalized, too static, and too elitist oriented to adapt to a new mobility led not by an elite such as the Catholic bishops but against them.

New dynamic developments cannot be easily integrated into the existing structure of officially recognized denominations. The appeal of Eastern religions, the growth of American-style evangelical Christian groups, and the increasing pluralism within the Catholic Church—these are relatively new developments that an affiliation built on the assumption of the existence of internally accepted hierarchies is poorly equipped to handle.

The Second Republic may be the last period in which Josephinism will flourish. But the church-state relationship, like the philosophy of the enlightened emperor Joseph, wants to give the people everything—except the right to participate.

Mass Media

The main characteristics of the Austrian mass media are, on the one hand, a high a degree of concentration and, on the other hand, a high degree of dependence on foreign countries (Plasser 1997). In the field of print media, the Second Republic has an increase in the degree of concentration predominantly at the expense of the traditional party newspapers. By the 1990s, the three largest newspapers (*Neue Kronen Zeitung, Kurier, Kleine Zeitung*) were reaching approximately two-thirds of the entire Austrian market. Regional (quasi) monopolies and supraregional "quality newspapers" (*Standard, Salzburger Nachrichten, Presse*) shared the rest of the market. The fact that many Austrian newspapers are linked with each other and with foreign (German) capital is a characteristic of the entire media situation. For instance, the *Neue Kronen Zeitung* and *Kurier* are linked by the partial ownership of a German media group. The same is true of the *Tiroler Tageszeitung* and was true for the *Standard*. The weekly magazine *News* is also affiliated with a German media group.

Concentration in the field of electronic media is expressed by the broadcasting monopoly of the state-owned ORF (Austrian Broadcasting Corporation). In compliance with a federal law, a board of trustees, a kind of supervisory board, makes all the basic decisions regarding the ORF. This board of trustees is staffed by the political parties, which is to say that broadcasting policy within the ORF is an expression of party-political constellations. The strength of the parties on the federal level and their ability to form coalitions determine the outcome of key decisions made in the ORF, in particular the (secret) election of the general director who heads the ORF for a period of four years. The board of trustees is composed according to party-political patterns. The ORF monopoly of radio stations will end in the late 1990s, and similar developments are expected in television. Increasing numbers of foreign programs reach Austria via cable and satellite so that the broadcasting monopoly has long since ceased to be a monopoly on the receiving end.

The media system is, more than any other subsystem, the product of developments the party and the corporate state were no longer able to control. The hegemony that the daily papers owned by political parties had enjoyed for decades was crumbling in the 1970s. Papers backed by economic interest groups have more or less lost their base of support. Examples include the *Neue Kronen Zeitung,* founded with money from social democratic labor unions and the *Presse,* which for decades was indirectly owned by the Chamber of Business. The market has taken over the print media, and the result is concentration—fewer papers for more readers.

The media is also feeling the effects of international dependence. The important role German media corporations have been playing for years in Austria is merely a forecast for similar things to come in other parts of the Austrian economy and society. This dependence is even stronger in the field of electronic media, which is in the process of opening up the market. The monopoly the ORF enjoyed was a sheltered workshop. The end of this monopoly will make Austria a mere appendage of the German market.

This does not necessarily imply any particular political impact. The purpose of the German media's activity in Austria is not to promote special political interests. Those corporations are looking for financial rather than political reward. Nevertheless, this emphasizes the lack of equality between Germany and Austria. Austria may have about the same per capita income as Germany, but because Germany is so much larger, the two countries have a relationship that is sometimes compared that of the United States and Canada. It is a big brother–little brother relationship characterized by an oversensitivity on the part of the little brother and a lack of sensitivity on the part of the big brother (Riekhoff and Neuhold 1993; Holzer 1995).

Internationalization has not come about as a consequence of Austria's EU membership. The influence of the German media on the Austrian market started much earlier. But the general trend points to a certain logic behind this development: The Austrian political system is losing control over Austrian media.

This implies that Austria has moved away from the status quo of the post-1945 era, when consociational democracy was seen as a way to distribute media shares among the members of the elitist cartel. First, the political parties—the ÖVP and the SPÖ—had the say. They had their newspapers and direct control of the electronic media. After the decline of party papers, the market took over more and more of the print media. And now the parties are losing control of the electronic media.

This can be seen as the depoliticization of the media market. But it must also be seen as the end of the Second Republic's ability to guarantee the synchronization of the political culture and the media. The media now follow different rules, which have little to do with consociationalism Austrian-style.

Conclusion

The party state and corporate state have started to lose some of their grip on the political system. The decline in membership of organized parties and labor unions, increasingly volatile electoral behavior, the challenges the chambers face, and a media system getting out of (political) control all emphasize the degree of political deconcentration.

This development is the flip side of the increasing autonomy constitutional agencies enjoy. Put into comparative perspective, this trend toward autonomy indicates the decrease in factors considered "typically Austrian." One important example is the reduction of politics to the "one plus one" formula, in which politics is the sum of the SPÖ plus the ÖVP, or labor plus business, respectively. This formula has not yet disappeared completely, but it no longer explains the whole picture. New actors have entered the political arena, and the political process has lost its predictability. Austria has become less "Austrian."

5

THE END OF
THE SUBSOCIETIES

The Austrian party system and the Austrian political culture are the products of specific cleavages. Among these cleavages, religion and class had been dominant for more than one hundred years. The conflict between Catholicism, which traditionally had a strong impact on Austrian politics, and the secularized parts of the Austrian society was the main incentive for the development of the Christian-conservative camp. The conflict between the socialist labor movement and a society dominated by the "bourgeois bloc" was the basic foundation of the socialist camp.

At the turn of the millennium, Catholicism and socialism—linked by a complex history of antagonism and cooperation—are losing their impact on the Austrian society. Austria is not a Catholic country anymore, at least not in the same sense that it used to be. And socialism changed from an ideal that was able to recruit millions of Austrians to a pale mixture of nostalgia and embarrassment. The two major subsocieties, Catholicism and socialism, which were responsible for the stabilization of the Second Republic, are in decline. Austrian society is becoming less fragmented by the traditional cleavages.

A Farewell to Catholicism

In June 1995, about a half million Austrians signed a petition directed at the bishops of the Roman Catholic Church in Austria. As the signers testified with their signature that they were members of the Church and were over age sixteen, it can be seriously assumed that about 10 percent of Austrian Catholics backed the positions expressed in this petition. Roughly 20 percent of Austrians who are officially registered as Catholics are regular participants in activities of the Church, and it can be also assumed that most of the petitioners were active Catholics—signing such a petition being an indicator of a strong interest in the Church. It follows that about 50 percent of Austrian Catholics who are active in the Church agree with the beliefs and intentions expressed in the petition.

The petition was called "Kirchenvolks-Begehren" (Zulehner 1995a), a title reminiscent of the "Volksbegehren" (popular initiative), the plebiscitarian instrument the Austrian constitution provides for legislative initiatives by the electorate. The basic constitutional philosophy is to give a qualitative minority of the voters the possibility to propose legislation, independent of political parties and parliament. The "Volksbegehren" is to be seen as a corrective to representative government— in favor of the governed. The political background of this Catholic initiative was precisely the plebiscitarian right to use democratic means to change the Church, which has had a deep impact on Austrian society for centuries.

The intention of the "Kirchenvolks-Begehren" was, for the Catholic Church, a radical one (Zulehner 1995a, 16 f.):

- to eliminate the principal differences between the clergy and laypeople;
- to establish democratic participation of the local church in the process of appointing bishops;
- to end all distinction between male and female roles in the Church, including the opening of priesthood for women;
- to overcome celibacy as a precondition for priesthood;
- to liberalize Catholic doctrines concerning sexuality, especially premarital sexual relations, homosexuality, and contraception;
- to change the policy toward remarried divorcés and married former priests who, as a consequence of their marriage, lost most of their rights within the Church.

For a Protestant who had witnessed the changes most Protestant churches went through after 1945, these demands must sound familiar. All the points made in the Catholic petition of June 1995 are more or less reality in contemporary Protestantism, even in the Anglican and Episcopal churches, whose forms, rites, and traditions are most similar to those of the Roman Catholic Church.

The petition was a de facto demand for the protestantization of the Catholic Church, including the renunciation of the most important political aspect of the papal primateship, control over the appointment of bishops. The petition was the result of an already-existing protestantization of Austrian Catholicism: Before such a comparatively large segment of Austrian Catholics could sign a document calling for the reformation of their church in the tradition of Calvin and Luther against the will of their leadership, Austrian Catholicism had to have undergone a decisive process of secularization. First, the meaning of the Catholic doctrines must have lost its impact not only on the Austrian Catholics in general but also on the significant minority of Austrian Catholics who were actively participating in

TABLE 5.1   Intentions and Attitudes Toward the "Kirchenvolks-Begehren" among Party Loyalists

	Outspoken Against the Petition	*Will Sign the Petition*	*Other Attitudes*
SPÖ	23%	10%	67%
ÖVP	31%	15%	54%
FPÖ	31%	10%	59%
LIF	31%	14%	55%
Greens	22%	21%	57%

Sample: 1.000 – representative of the Austrian population.
SOURCE: Zulehner 1995a: 45, 53 f.

Church life and regularly using the Church's services. The success of the petition was only possible as a consequence of such a Catholic liberalization.

The aspect of protestantization was also evident in the political affiliations of the petitioners (see Table 5.1). The Catholics protesting the conservative structure and the teaching of their church had rather pluralistic political attitudes.

According to these results, more than a half million people should have signed the petition. This can be explained by the fact that the poll asked people whether they intended to sign and not whether they actually had signed. Evidently many of those who had the intention to sign ultimately did not do so.

The "outspoken against the petition" figures probably reflect two very different and contradictory positions: opposing the petition on the grounds of an active role within the Church and active agreement with its status quo but also total disinterest in the Church and therefore opposition to such an innovative activity coming from within. However, the respondents who claimed the intention to sign the petition had a rather clear attitude toward the Catholic Church: They were motivated by their interest in the Church and by their dissatisfaction with its present situation. Their signature must be interpreted as a form of opposition from within the Church. And within this intra-Catholic opposition, party affiliations were divided:

- There was no party whose sympathizers had a common attitude toward the petition and therefore toward the Church per se.
- The highest percentage of those who signed were Green voters, followed by ÖVP and LIF voters. SPÖ and FPÖ sympathizers showed the least inclination to sign.

This of course had also something to do with the socioeconomic and educational-cultural background of the Catholic Church in Austria: The active Catholic segment is significantly overrepresented in the educated bourgeoisie and in the agricultural sector and significantly underrepresented in the proletarian sector.

Seen in the light of these groups' historical and current voting bias—the SPÖ has traditionally a much stronger following of blue-collar workers than the ÖVP, Greens, and LIF, a position the FPÖ currently also enjoys—this correlation explains the differences in the tendencies of party sympathizers to sign the petition.

The role of the Green sympathizers in the "Kirchenvolks-Begehren" reflects the generation gap among better educated Catholics: The younger, more critical, and in that sense "leftist" element has a strong position within the Green Party, indicating the political break with the older generation of the same educational-religious background, traditionally the core group of the ÖVP. The ÖVP can no longer be considered the party of the subsociety characterized by active Catholicism. The Greens are competing with the ÖVP for younger, better-educated, active Catholics.

The traditions of Austrian politics, in which being an active Catholic has always meant accepting one's affiliation with the Church as a complex set of obligations influencing every aspect of life, should have produced a different picture. No movement should have succeeded against the will of the bishops, especially a movement whose intentions were in direct opposition to the pope; no such movement should have been able to mobilize such an important segment of the subsociety of active Catholics; no such movement should have succeeded in bringing together activists with such diverse political orientations—either as friends or as foes. The confrontational style and politically pluralistic platform of the "Kirchenvolks-Begehren" also represented a break with traditional perceptions of Austrian Catholicism.

The impact of Catholicism on Austrian politics and society has become diffuse and inconsistent. Members of the active Catholic subsociety are no longer relegated to one of two distinct groups: those who are "in" and those who are "out." Both the inclusiveness and exclusiveness of Catholicism have lost their significance, first and foremost in respect to politics. But that means that the Catholic subsociety has ceased to exist because such a subsociety is defined by its very nature as including and excluding according to undisputed patterns.

Catholicism no longer represents a political cleavage. The Church has lost its ability to implement its—or any—political message on society. But what has this message been?

In the late nineteenth century, the message was clear. The Church tried to reconcile its social existence with the democratic tendencies that had reached Austria. After the constitution of 1867, a parliament had to be elected and political parties came into existence. The Church, especially under Pope Leo XIII, wanted to become more involved in democratic procedures, so it started to accept politics according to the rules of parliamentarism. But the Catholic Church was still influenced by its opposition to most of the values bourgeois revolutions—and especially the French—had championed. The Church opposed the separation of state and church, of politics and religion. The Church wanted to influence society by means of the social doctrine Leo XIII formulated in his 1891 papal encyclica, "Rerum novarum." In this letter, the pope encouraged the participation of Catholics in modern politics but demanded that this participation be organized and controlled by Catholic institutions such as Catholic parties, labor unions, and other groups, in order to distinguish the special Catholic agenda from the others.

At the end of the nineteenth century, the Catholic Church in Europe recognized that it faced two hostile political concepts: liberalism (in the sense of capitalism) and socialism (in the sense of Marxism). In an effort to compete with these concepts, the Church tried to establish Catholic parties such as the Center Party ("Zentrum") in Germany. The situation in Austria was different than in Germany, Italy, or France. In Austria, the government was considered sensitive to Catholic interests. The Habsburgs represented the strongest Catholic tradition among all the ruling families. There was no structural conflict between church and state like there was in Italy, where the pope could not forgive and forget that modern Italy was built upon the ruins of the papal state. There was no Protestant (or any other non-Catholic) majority like there was in Germany, where it was difficult to successfully represent Catholic interests. And there was no republican, laicist, anticlerical mood dominating politics like it did in France, where the Church had lost its control positions in sensitive areas such as schools and marriage.

In Austria, the Church had to overcome another problem: Catholics were not used to participating in politics. The delay of the constitution had a particular effect on the Catholic mainstream, traditionally linked to the Habsburgs and therefore not used to organizing themselves into political parties and interest groups. Recognizing that Catholic interests were not being represented because there were too few Catholic laymen in politics, the clergy stepped in. It was especially the young generation of Catholic priests, the low-ranking clergy, who in the 1880s started to organize political groups in order to give Catholics a voice in politics. Together with Catholic intellectuals such as Karl von Vogelsang and aristocrats such as Prince Alois Liechtenstein, clergymen such as Franz M. Schindler became the midwives of political Catholicism in Austria (Boyer 1981: esp. 70–72, 223).

This was the case in the Vienna area, where this new breed of Catholic politicians, accepting the rules of the parliamentary game, had to rely heavily on the small bourgeoisie as their constituents. The labor segment was already more or less lost to the socialists. For the agricultural areas, the situation was not so different: Farmers, especially in the alpine regions, were politically organized by priests such as Aemilian Schöpfer in alliance with reform-minded aristocrats and especially active farmers such as Jodok Fink (Boyer 1995: esp. 78, 94 f.).

In both urban and rural areas, the fledgling Christian Social Party had to deal with the hostility of some bishops and old conservatives toward a movement that was willing and able to overcome the deep gap separating the Catholic tradition from modern politics. The young movement, thanks to the involvement of the clergy, was able to win the approval of its supreme authority, Pope Leo XIII. The pope, realizing that the Austrian Christian Socials were exactly the type of party he had in mind, backed their movement and quieted their more conservative critics within the Church by publicly giving the Christian Socials his blessing (Boyer 1981: 345).

The pope had backed a party that was both clerical and progressive: clerical by virtue of accepting priests in leading functions and by defining its agenda as the implementation of the pope's social doctrine; progressive by virtue of opposing rather than defending the existing social order. The backing of the pope was decisive for the structures that the party was able to develop, structures characterized by the alliance between the Church and the party. The rectory became the local party headquarters; Catholic organizations became identical with party organizations. The Christian Social Party was not distinguishable from the Catholic Church, neither in its social outlook, nor in its political programs. The party was the Church in politics.

This was the birth of the Christian-conservative camp. A closed milieu consisting of various clerical organizations used for political purposes among others, it was also a set of beliefs rationalized as the indisputable consequences of Catholicism and a clear-cut combination of autostereotypes—as well as heterostereotypes. The latter consisted of the others, the enemies who were also in the process of organizing their parties and organizations in approximately the same style, camps with respective closed milieus: the socialist camp and the pan-German camp.

The person who most successfully represented the Christian Socials in the first years of their existence and who became the integrative, heroic figure political Catholicism needed was Karl Lueger. Lueger, a lawyer and a politician who had already tried his luck with some less-organized "liberal" bourgeois groups, was the charismatic figure Christian Socials were identified with—and with whom they themselves were eager to identify.

Lueger was mayor of Vienna from 1897 until his death in 1910. He was important for his political techniques and his political programs. He was able to develop extraparliamentary instruments, "the politics of the rowdy and the mob," and "transformed an ideology of the Old Right—Austrian political Catholicism— into an ideology of a New Left, Christian Socialism"(Schorske 1980: 133). Lueger transformed traditional political Catholicism into its present-day form by giving Christian Socials their "leftist," interventionist, (comparatively) egalitarian profile, a profile that theoretically oriented persons like Vogelsang had already prepared. But it took the pragmatic Lueger to popularize this new image of political Catholicism. And it took Lueger's "radicalism," which was more a radicalism in style and less in substance (Boyer 1981: 184–246).

Lueger had many admirers, the most prominent of whom was Adolf Hitler, who claimed to have been influenced especially by two Austrians. The first was Georg von Schönerer, the passionate leader of racist anti-Semitism and representative of the anti-Catholic, anti-Habsburg wing of pan-Germanism (Schorske 1980: 120–133). The second was Karl Lueger, who may have been less consistent in his racist justification of anti-Semitism but whose populistic techniques and the ability to inflame the emotions of the masses impressed Hitler.

Lueger was a democrat in the sense that his style was populistic and anti-elitist and that he adapted his policies to suit the moods of those electoral segments he needed to win in the next elections. Lueger was a pragmatist, and this pragmatism foreshadowed the pragmatism his successors in the Christian-conservative camp would demonstrate later. One such pragmatist was Ignaz Seipel, who was a monarchist until 1918 but a republican beginning with the fall of the very same year. Seipel managed to strike a bargain with the Social Democrat Otto Bauer regarding the constitution of 1920 but became more and more of a radical antisocialist, going so far as to adopt some elements of prefascist thinking (Gulick 1948: vol. 2, esp. 775–819; Diamant 1960; Klemperer 1972). This pragmatism was also typical of Engelbert Dollfuss, the founder of the authoritarian regime and its first dictator in 1934, who mixed Catholic traditions, Austrian patriotism, pan-German sentiments, and Italian fascism to create a very inconsistent system (Tálos and Neugebauer 1988; Hanisch 1994: 310–323). This pragmatism was also responsible for the very successful catch-all party concept of the ÖVP after 1945.

Lueger was a pragmatist even in his anti-Semitism (Pulzer 1988: 198–201). He used existing anti-Semitic prejudices to stir up emotions for his constant campaigning. Although he used "the Jews" as scapegoats, as whipping boys, he did not create Catholic, Christian anti-Semitism. Anti-Semitism had of course already existed as a Christian, European phenomenon for centuries. Lueger can perhaps be called the first democratic anti-Semite in the sense that he proved the usefulness of anti-Semitic rhetoric in election strategies. But his most prominent admirer proved to be superior to him in that respect.

The Christian-conservative camp existed as a milieu centered around its two focal points, the Christian Social Party and the Catholic Church. In the 1930s, the alliance between the party and the Church became more delicate. The authoritarian government claimed to be the legitimate expression of the newest social doctrines of the Church as defined by Pius XI in his 1932 encyclica, "Quadragesimo anno." Neither the pope nor the Austrian bishops corrected this interpretation. On the contrary, the Church backed the regime's claim (Hanisch 1994). But the regime was weak; it had spilled the blood of Social Democrats, who had tried to save the republic and the republican constitution in February 1934. The regime was especially challenged by Nazism, from both inside and outside, from the Austrian Nazis and from Nazi Germany. And when, as a result of military blackmail and internal upheaval, Schuschnigg resigned on March 11, 1938, the Catholic bishops tried to appease the new men in power, Hitler first and foremost.

This appeasement must be seen also as the abandonment of a regime that had every reason to believe it was acting in agreement with the Church. While the bishops were trying to reach a compromise with Hitler, the leading representatives of the authoritarian regime, who also represented political Catholicism and the Christian-conservative camp, were already imprisoned in Dachau or elsewhere (Botz 1978: 117–128; Dokumentationsarchiv 1988: 430–435, 527–541).

In 1945, the Church and the party did not reestablish their association. It was not a divorce, at least not an unfriendly one, but the politicians coming from the old Christian Social Party wanted a more secularized profile. For that reason, they opted for a name that would not include the term "Christian" and renamed the old Christian Social Party "Österreichische Volkspartei" (Austrian People's Party). The Church, represented by the bishops, wanted to establish a more neutral attitude toward politics—especially after their experience with a "Christian" dictatorship between 1934 and 1938 and the disastrous results of their attempts to appease the Nazi regime.

This dissociation had more to do with structure than with substance, at least at the beginning of the Second Republic. The ÖVP had to establish the intraparty structures the Christian Socials were able to waive because the Church had these structures ready for the party, too. So the ÖVP had to establish organizations for youth, women, and other groups, parallel to still existing or reestablished Catholic organizations.

But the relationship between the party and the Church was not in the least hostile. The milieu that connected Church and party still existed, as did the Christian-conservative camp. The difference between the First and the Second Republic in regard to the relationship between Catholic Church and political parties was very much limited to the very formal, very top level. The bishops no longer directly intervened in party politics: There was no official episcopal recommendation on how to vote, and the bishops also took pains to withdraw one very visible clerical element from politics by forbidding clergymen to enter politics. Priests in politics, most prominently Ignaz Seipel, were a thing of the past, and political responsibility was shifted completely to Catholic laypersons (Zulehner 1995b: 526).

This was a first step—but just a step—toward secularization. The liaison between Church and party, the Christian-conservative camp and the special milieu of political Catholicism still existed. It could be seen on the electoral level, where most active Catholics still voted for the ÖVP. It could also be seen in the recruiting patterns the ÖVP was using, patterns more or less the same as before 1938. Most persons starting their political career in the ÖVP came from organizations that still exhibited the close connection between Church and party; in other words, they were recruited from the still existing milieu. Two types of Catholic organizations were (and still are) of special recruiting importance for the ÖVP:

- Catholic organizations directly under the control of the bishops, bound together through the Catholic Action, the formal lay organization of the Church. One especially important was and still is the Catholic Students' Organization ("Katholische Hochschuljugend"). The ÖVP's last three chairpersons, Josef Riegler (1989–1991), Erhard Busek (1991–1995), and Wolfgang Schüssel (since 1995), all came from this recruiting base.
- Catholic organizations that are autonomous from the bishops but that have a long tradition of numerous links to the milieu of the Christian-conservative camp. Most important are the Catholic students' fraternities of the Austrian Cartel-Verband (CV). Almost all of the other ÖVP party chairpersons not mentioned above came from the CV, as did the ÖVP

chancellors Leopold Figl (1945–1953), Julius Raab (1953–1961), Alfons
Gorbach (1961–1964), and Josef Klaus (1964–1970).

The ÖVP represented the "camp mentality," the thinking typical of the Catholic
milieu: Being a Catholic—in the sense of an active Catholic, defined by regular
church attendance—was virtually the same as being a member of the ÖVP. The
ÖVP was still considered the political arm of the Catholic Church in Austria.

After 1945, the relationship between Austrian society and Austrian Catholicism
and between Austrian politics and the Catholic Church was defined by the dissociation agreed upon by the Christian-conservative camp and the Church. The
logical consequence of this dissociation was the modus vivendi the Church and
the SPÖ had to develop. The SPÖ, together with the ÖVP, represented the political power of the Second Republic, and the Catholic Church wanted to come to an
understanding with all the elements of the Austrian power structure, including
the Socialist Party. On the other side, the SPÖ was tempted to challenge the de
facto monopoly of the ÖVP in the Catholic milieu. Catholic voters were also attractive to Social Democrats.

The main obstacle for such an arrangement between the SPÖ and the Church
was the question of the concordat that was responsible for defining all aspects of
the relationship between the state and the Catholic Church. In 1933, the Austrian
government had signed a concordat with the Holy See. But Chancellor Engelbert
Dollfuss, already on his authoritarian course, had abolished the National Council,
so this concordat never received the parliamentary ratification required by the
constitution of 1920. Instead, the concordat was implemented by the authoritarian state until the Anschluss. In 1945, the pope, the Austrian bishops, and the
ÖVP all insisted that the concordat was valid by virtue of the signatures from
1933. But the SPÖ insisted that the document's lack of parliamentary ratification
made it invalid.

The real reason for this conflict was not procedural but substantial. The con-
cordat included two regulations that the SPÖ was especially unhappy about: first,
Austria had to accept the Catholic marriage laws regarding members of the
Catholic Church, which meant no divorces or remarriages for the majority of the
Austrian population; second, Austria had to guarantee the equal treatment of
Catholic and state-run schools. Both regulations were against the social demo-
cratic tradition deeply rooted in the liberal principle of separation between
church and state (Steger 1982: 37–61).

In the late 1950s, a generational change made a breakthrough possible. In 1958,
Pope John XXIII followed Pius XII, who had identified his policy with the style and
substance of the concordats so typical of his era. Two years previously, Franz König
had been appointed as Vienna's new archbishop. König tried to overcome some of
the blockades from the past with which his predecessor, Theodor Innitzer, who had
been archbishop in 1934 and 1938 and thus a symbol of traditional political
Catholicism, had been identified. In the SPÖ, Adolf Schärf, party chairman and

vice-chancellor, was elected federal president in 1957. His departure from the party leadership made changes within the SPÖ possible. The new leadership, consisting of Bruno Pittermann, Bruno Kreisky, Franz Olah, Felix Slavik, and Christian Broda, displayed much more flexibility and pragmatism than the old leadership had.

One result was the new party program the SPÖ passed in 1958. Using some parts of a declaration formulated by the Socialist International, the SPÖ manifesto expressed the following principles for the relationship between socialism and religion: "Socialism and religion are not contradictions. Any religious person can be a Socialist at the same time" (Steger 1982: 81).

This was one indication among others. The new Church and the new SPÖ leadership were now able to compromise on the concordat: The SPÖ had to give in with respect to the school dispute and the Church had to give up its right to define the marriage laws for Austrian Catholics. The result was a supplementary concordat signed in 1960 that changed some of the agreements from 1933. The Church accepted Austria's right to define all legal aspects of marriage for all persons under Austrian jurisdiction regardless of their religious beliefs, and the Republic of Austria guaranteed the existence of private (especially Catholic) schools, including the payment of teachers.

The compromise eased the traditional tensions between the Catholic Church and the socialist camp. The Church gained wider acceptance as a moral factor in society, even by Social Democrats. The Cardinal Archbishop of Vienna, Franz König, was seen as the key person in the Church who had accepted political pluralism. He was widely regarded as the guarantor of the Church's neutrality in matters of party competition, the man who would prevent a return to the old days of the 1920s and 1930s, when priests used the pulpit and bishops their episcopal letters to encourage their flock to vote for the right party, the Christian Socials (Diamant 1960).

But this compromise was an elitist one. The bishops, Franz König first and foremost, had an agreement with the SPÖ leadership. Their respective followers were not much impressed—at least not immediately and not with respect to their political behavior. SPÖ activists still considered the Catholic Church an alien institution and part of the bourgeoisie whose power the SPÖ had promised to break. And active Catholics in Austria could not stop seeing the SPÖ as the party that they had to fight politically. The fierceness of this conflict may have changed, but the conflict still existed. The religious cleavage was still there.

Some tried to bridge the gap. A minority of active Catholics officially declared their political affiliation with the SPÖ, a move still considered rather strange in the 1950s and 1960s (Steger 1982: 177–274). Not until 1970, when the Kreisky era started, did the tensions between the Catholic milieu and the SPÖ take on a new quality. This new quality had some specific aspects:

- For the first time in the history of the republic, there was an Austrian government without representatives from the Christian-conservative camp. The politically sensitive element among active Catholics no longer felt represented on the federal level.

• Some delicate decisions had to be made regarding the relationship between Church and state, particularly the decision on the legal consequences of abortion.

In 1973, the Austrian parliament passed the new criminal code, which included a rather liberal solution for abortion: During the first three months of pregnancy, women were free to decide. This "pro-choice" decision was strongly opposed by the ÖVP in parliament and by the bishops. Supported by all bishops, Catholic circles started a "pro-life" movement called "Aktion Leben" (Action Life), which organized a popular initiative ("Volksbegehren") signed by almost one million voters in 1976. But the SPÖ, which at that time controlled the National Council with its overall majority, voted this petition down (Steger 1982: 97–102).

Surprisingly, this decision against the "pro-life" movement all the bishops had unreservedly backed had no significant impact, neither on the relationship between the bishops and the SPÖ nor on electoral behavior along religious lines. The relationship between the Catholic Church and Austrian social democracy was already stable enough to survive the embarrassment the SPÖ's "pro-choice" decision must have been for the bishops. The relationship between the Church and social democracy had proved itself flexible.

But even this new flexibility in the relationship between the SPÖ and the Church did not significantly change the preference of most active Catholics for the ÖVP. After so many years of mutual adaption, the inroads the SPÖ was able to make into the milieu of active Catholicism were comparatively minor, especially compared with the more intensive links the Greens had established with that milieu.

These profiles reiterate some of the factors emphasized by the "Kirchenvolks-Begehren": The ÖVP is still the political party with which most practicing Catholics are affiliated. In relative terms, the Greens are the second most attractive party for active Catholics. The religious profiles of the SPÖ and the FPÖ are rather similar (see Table 5.2).

But these profiles do not correspond with the data on formal church membership. The differences in the party affiliations that separate Catholics from non-Catholics are much less significant. In 1994, 72 percent of all SPÖ voters were members of the Roman Catholic Church, compared with 94 percent of ÖVP, 77 percent of FPÖ, 72 percent of Liberal, and 80 percent of Green voters. Of significance is the much stronger position Austrian Protestants have within the SPÖ and FPÖ electorate (8 percent and 6 percent, respectively) than among the ÖVP voters (2 percent) (Zulehner 1995b: 536). The Protestant bias is the continuation of an old pattern: For Austrian Protestants, the Christian-conservative camp was just the old alliance between the Catholic Church and the dominant political powers—until 1918 the monarchy and after 1918 the Christian Social Party. This alliance, responsible for the Counter Reformation several centuries ago and for the

TABLE 5.2   Religious Profile of Voters

1994	SPÖ	ÖVP	FPÖ	LIF	Greens
Regular church attendants	13%	53%	18%	8%	22%
Other religious attitudes	56%	36%	58%	62%	58%
Nonreligious	31%	12%	23%	30%	21%
Sum	100%	101%	99%	100%	100%

SOURCE: Zulehner 1995b: 533. Under "regular church attendants" Zulehner combines two categories he terms "Kirchliche" ans "Kulturkirchliche" Austrians, the latter to a lesser degree affiliated with the church than the first. Therefore the overall number of "regular church attendants" may be a little expanded, although Zulehner stresses the fact that "Kulturkirchliche" are also regularly attending church.

authoritarian regime in the 1930s, had and even today has an alienating effect for Protestants. Protestants therefore significantly preferred Social Democrats or pan-Germans in the past, and they still prefer the SPÖ and the FPÖ.

There is a rather stable pattern behind this development. Practicing Catholics, more and more a minority among a tolerant but indifferent pro forma Catholic majority, are still linked with the ÖVP—not as the result of any official policy the bishops follow, but due to milieu and tradition. This pattern is jeopardized by the existence of the Greens who are able to attract some of the young generation of the Catholic milieu. The old conflicts over the cleavage between religion and politics, which were so important in the past, no longer mobilize significant numbers of people for or against any issue. Austria seems to be a rather secularized country despite the still existing ties between the party of historical political Catholicism and the active segments of the Church. The Church itself, as demonstrated in the "Kirchenvolks-Begehren," is not immune to criticism from within.

But does than mean that Austria has ceased to be a Catholic country? Is the tradition evident in so many cathedrals and monasteries and the proverbial Catholic "character" of Austrian society a thing of the past?

The Austrian Catholic Church is, in many respects, divided. There is a horizontal division between bishops and laypersons. And there is a vertical division between Catholics who define the consequences of their church affiliation in very different ways. There is the bishops' church, and there is the people's church, the latter divided into many de-facto denominations consisting of many different de facto beliefs, all of them coexisting in a pluralistic situation.

The bishops' church draws its strength from the global and centralized character the Catholic Church still enjoys. The acceptance of the pope's primacy is the main characteristic that distinguishes the Catholic Church from other Christian churches, and this strong organizational and dogmatic bond provides the Catholic bishops with a formal unity other churches are missing. The bishops' church in Austria is also strengthened by the church-state relationship that the concordat and the corporatist character of the Second Republic established. It is the bishops' conference that is treated as the official representation of the Catholic Church in concordat matters or when the interests of the Catholic Church are to be integrated into the legislative process on the preparliamentary level. The bishops' conference is the partner of the government. And the bishops still feel the necessity to demonstrate unity, thereby reflecting the global church's centralized structures.

The scandal that was the immediate motive for the "Kirchenvolks-Begehren" in 1995 demonstrated both the intensity and the limits of this unity within the bishops' church. The scandal broke when a former (male) Catholic student accused the Cardinal-Archbishop of Vienna Hermann Groer of having sexually abused him years before Groer became archbishop (Zulehner 1995a: 23–28). First, all the bishops reacted unanimously by defending their colleague, who in 1995—the year of the scandal—was also chairman of the bishops' conference. But because Groer himself did not deny the allegation and public opinion seemed to favor the accuser, some of the bishops became more and more cautious in their defense of Cardinal Groer. It became obvious that there was not much unanimity left among the bishops, although the bishops' conference continued to present a united front. Only after Groer had resigned first as chairman of the bishops' conference and then as archbishop, could the bishops' conference return to normalcy, back to its behavior as a closed elite.

According to public opinion, there is little belief in the unanimity of the bishops, and the different groups and wings within the Church's active segment claim different bishops as their respective guardians. It is obvious that behind the official facade of unity, even the bishops are sharply divided into at least two wings, one more conservative and the other more progressive. The active lay element is using this pluralism to justify their rejection of central doctrines. The "Kirchenvolks-Begehren" was proof of the degree to which many Catholics have already distanced themselves from doctrines supported by the pope and the especially outspoken conservative wing of the Austrian bishops.

Significantly, the doctrines and papal teaching that antagonize many groups of active laypersons do not touch politics in the traditional sense. The conflicts are about the Church and not the state, about democracy within the Church and not within the state. It is celibacy and gender and participation within the Church rather than questions raised decades ago by popes such as Leo XIII and Pius XI that incite so many active Catholics.

The contradictions and conflicts among Austrian Catholics do not primarily concern party politics or aspects of general political orientation. In principle, active Austrian Catholics are overproportionally inclined to accept demands for more solidarity between the privileged and the underprivileged, between the winners and the losers of modernization (Zulehner et al. 1996: 214–217). But this egalitarian outlook correlates with education: Because better-educated Austrians are at least rhetorically in favor of a higher degree of solidarity, and because active Catholics (as well as ÖVP, and Green and Liberal voters) are overproportionally better educated, it is not possible to say that Austrian Catholics have such an egalitarian orientation in politics because they are Catholics.

The contradiction and conflicts among Austrian Catholics do not primarily concern aspects of individual ethics either. Especially when it comes to questions of sexuality, most Austrian Catholics, including the active segment, behave as if papal teaching has nothing to do with their personal lives. Austrians believe in general sexual freedom in a way that fits almost perfectly into the beliefs demonstrated in other Western European countries, with the significant exception of Ireland (Zulehner and Denz 1993: vol. 2, 141). With respect to sensitive, much disputed topics such as abortion, Austrian opinion does not differ significantly from the prevalent opinion in traditionally Protestant countries such as Great Britain or the Scandinavian countries, but it again differs significantly from that of Ireland (Zulehner and Denz 1993: vol. 2, 139).

The explanation is not protestantization in a traditional sense. Only insignificant numbers of Austrians change denominations. Some nontraditional Protestant denominations that Austrians consider sects and not churches (for example, Jehovah's Witnesses) are growing but are still a rather tiny minority phenomenon. And even the losses shown by the official membership statistics of the Catholic Church are of quantitatively minor importance.

The explanation is secularization. The Catholic Church has lost much of its ability to define and control the lives of Austrians. The result is that being a Catholic in Austria at the end of the century has little meaning. A Catholic can be very active— or completely passive. A Catholic can favor one party or the other—even among practicing Catholics, the predominant tendency is no longer to one particular party only, but to two parties, the ÖVP and the Greens. A Catholic can defend celibacy and the exclusion of women from priesthood—or can participate in movements such as the "Kirchenvolks-Begehren," which is outspoken in its opposition to the papal doctrines. A Catholic can apply those doctrines to his or her sexual life, limiting it to strict monogamy—or ignore that pattern as hopelessly outdated.

A comparative study done in 1990 described the Austrian population as still having a strong religious autostereotype. Among sixteen West European countries, the population's self-perception as being religious was stronger only in Ireland, Northern Ireland, Italy, and Iceland. More than two-thirds of Austrians considered themselves to be religious (Zulehner and Denz 1993: vol. 2, 3). The majority of Austrians still believe they believe, but this religious expression is not matched by behavior, if "religious" is interpreted according to the Catholic Church's definition.

It is a self-perception that has little to do with the concrete obligations demanded by the Church. Only about 20 percent of Austrian Catholics regularly attend mass, but about 70 percent of them consider themselves religious. This is a dissonance that needs an explanation.

It is interesting to note that Ireland and Italy are among the countries that have an even stronger self-perception of being "religious." These are the two countries in Western Europe that have two things in common with Austria: a traditional dominance of Catholicism and a complex relationship between Church and state.

These connections have been weakened only recently. Aspects of concordats and issues such as marriage law, Catholic schools, and the penal code were the subject of heated debate in all three of these countries after 1945. In all cases, the connections between Church and state have become less and less intense. The alliance between Church and state is no longer strong enough to guarantee a Catholic society and Catholic dominance over values and behavior.

In Austria, the explosive conflict between "clericalism" and "anticlericalism" is dead. Secularization has not come about through an almost revolutionary break between Church and state as it did in France during the Third Republic. Secularization is coming through the back door. Austrian society is not dominated by hostility toward the Church; on the contrary, the traditionally hostile Social Democrats are happy with the pragmatic modus vivendi the Second Republic has achieved. But neither is Austrian society dominated by a strong religious attitude beyond formal church membership and general claims of being "religious." Most Austrians are simply no longer moved by the Church—neither for nor against it.

The Catholic milieu is practically dead—or rather, it is fragmented into different mini-milieus that do not have much in common. The Christian-conservative camp, which had such an impact on shaping contemporary Austria, exists primarily for historians and in museums, where the relics of this camp can be studied. And it exists as a recruitment pattern enabling the ÖVP to get most of its elite out of a still rather coherent group. But even this group, this milieu, exists in a state of contradiction as expressed in the "Kirchenvolks-Begehren."

Austrian society still seems to be Catholic. Three out of four Austrians still claim to be Catholic. The Catholic Church enjoys a variety of privileges other churches in other countries can only dream of. There is no strong movement in the country against the principles of this arrangement between Church and state. After the reconciliation with its former most powerful opponent, the socialist labor movement, the Church and its bishops are broadly accepted as representatives not only of a legitimate denomination but of an important part of Austria's past and present. Even if not everybody loves the Church, nobody seems to hate it anymore.

But the Church is crumbling. There is deterioration from within. Secularization Austrian-style has not so much challenged the privileges that the state guarantees the Church. Secularization Austrian-style has eroded the former closed Catholic milieu by transforming it into diverging milieus. The Church as a unified force exists only on the surface. Beneath that surface, the Church seems to consist of many different churches.

The Protestant Reformation has not been unsuccessful in Austria. The decomposition of the Catholic milieu as a closed subsociety is the final triumph of the Reformation over the Counter Reformation.

A Farewell to Socialism

Contemporary Austria is still full of monuments and other memorials that stress the socialist character of important parts of its society. The most impressive housing project of Vienna's interwar period is still called "Karl Marx-Hof." In cities such as Linz or Bruck and der Mur, there are monuments of the heroic battles between the socialist militia ("Republikanischer Schutzbund," Republican Defense Federation) and the Austrian army and police forces in February, 1934. In the late 1990s, the Viennese Social Democrats are one of the last party organizations in Western Europe to still celebrate May 1st as the international holiday of labor with traditional mass marches through the city. Many organizations active in fields as diverse as sports or child care are ideologically bound to socialist traditions. Socialism might be out of favor in many parts of Europe, but not in Austria, at least not on the surface.

No other social democratic party—with the possible exception of Sweden's—has enjoyed as much success as the SPÖ. The Austrian Social Democrats have a great ideological tradition represented by Austromarxism, the most leftist, most Marxist wing of democratic socialism after the Russian Revolution. And the Austrian Social Democrats have an almost unique history of electoral success. No other Western European party has ever won an overall majority among voters three times in succession; no other social democratic party—with the exception of the Swiss, where the party is a permanent part of the government under the Swiss rule of perpetual four-party cabinets—has been in government for forty-six years within five decades.

The Austrian Social Democrats represent a special claim, promoting an alternative "third way" (Sully 1982), by pursuing the political concept of building a society neither Communist nor capitalist. During the interwar period, this specific profile was characterized by the Austromarxists' intention to bridge the gap between the Communist Party family, organized in the "Third International," and the social democratic "Socialist Workers International." The international socialist movement had been broken up due to the experiences of World War I and the Russian Revolution, and first attempts to reunite it failed. The Austrian party then participated in the "Second International," the social democratic. But it always considered itself part of the Second International's left wing, interested in fulfilling Marxist expectations within the framework of a democratic constitution (Rabinbach 1983). This was exemplified especially by the party manifesto that Austrian Social Democrats passed at their 1926 conference in Linz. In this program, the most significant document of Austromarxist strategies and intentions, all the different wings and traditions within the party were united by the goal of building socialism through democracy (Gulick 1948: vol. 1, 468, 699, 766–769).

The "third way" intention became even clearer and more outspoken when the Social Democrats had to go underground. After the civil war of February 1934, the authoritarian regime outlawed the Social Democrats—the party as well as the trade unions. The party leadership went into exile, and an illegal organization ("Revolutionäre Sozialisten," Revolutionary Socialists) was established in Austria. During this period, Otto Bauer, the leading theoretical figure of Austromarxism, philosophized about the possibility of "integral socialism," uniting social democracracy and communism again. It was the dream of an immobilized, exiled elite group, but it signified the tradition of Austromarxism, eager to find a way to reunite all socialist traditions in one international organization despite outspoken criticism of the "despotic socialism" the Soviet Union represented (Gulick 1948: vol. 2, 1397–1400).

When Austrian democracy was reestablished after World War II, the Social Democrats still were fighting for their third way. Experience with Soviet presence in Austria between 1945 and 1955 and in neighboring Central European countries such as Czechoslovakia and Hungary ended any hope that the party might have had of democratizing Communist power. But it still claimed to be neither Communist nor capitalist and to represent a general formula between the two options—between capitalism, anathema to democratic socialism for reasons of economic exploitation, and communism, anathema to democratic socialism for reasons of political dictatorship (Stauber 1987: 333–366).

Perhaps the most striking aspect of the Austromarxists' refusal to be forced to take sides in the great dichotomous struggle between West and East was the success the Austrian Social Democratic Party had with Austrian voters. Despite their programmatic complexity (or because of it), the Social Democrats did extremely well during all periods of Austrian history in which free elections were held: during the last years of Habsburg Austria, during the First Republic, and especially since 1945. The SPÖ also succeeded in spite of (or because of) the general anti-Communist mood, prevalent among Austrian voters during the First and again during the Second Republic. The KPÖ (Communist Party of Austria) was never a serious competitor for the SPÖ on the left of the political spectrum—after 1945 especially, due to the party's dependence on the USSR (Gärtner 1979).

The Austrian Social Democrats have a history of success. Founded in 1889 under the auspices of multinational Habsburg Austria, the Social Democratic Workers' Party ("Sozialdemokratische Arbeiterpartei," SDAP)—in close alliance with social democratic labor unions ("Freie Gewerkschaften," Free Trade Unions)— soon became a dominant factor in the Austrian parliament. In 1911, the SDAP won a plurality of votes and seats in the last parliamentary elections for Habsburg Austria's Lower House ("Abgeordnetenhaus," Chamber of Deputies) before World War I, and Austria's defeat put an end to the peculiar combination of imperial rule and parliamentary rhetoric.

The SDAP was the best-organized "power reserve" the Austrian parliament was able to create. The major political parties, the SDAP and the Christian Socials, were already perfectly organized mass parties before 1914, but the constitution prevented parliamentary and party politics from having any real impact on the power structure. Real authority was still with the traditional elites, their power preserved by the prerogative of the emperor to appoint the prime minister and his cabinet, who were not responsible to parliament.

The major parties—first and foremost the SDAP—were like the British "fleet in being": of no immediate instrumental value, but a possibility for any future conflict (Kennedy 1976). The "fleet in being" was important because of its mere existence and not because of any battles it actually fought. And when the Habsburg rule collapsed, the SDAP was there to fill the power vacuum together with the parties of the two other camps, the Christian Socials and the pan-Germans.

The SDAP ruled in the days of the so-called revolution of late 1918 and early 1919, when an extreme supply crisis, a deep sense of dissatisfaction over the military defeat, and myths about the events in Russia created not a revolution but a revolutionary atmosphere. Nothing else was better able to prevent a revolution Russian-style than social democracy (Gulick 1948: vol. 1, 69–83). It was precisely because the SDAP, and especially its left wing, led by Friedrich Adler, had such great credibility with groups inclined to follow the Leninist example, that the Leninist faction could be contained by peaceful means. In contrast to Germany, where the Spartakists' unrest was brutally oppressed, the Austrian revolutionaries were integrated or isolated and rendered more or less harmless by the Social Democrats.

Karl Renner, the leading pragmatist of the SDAP's right wing, was provisional chancellor from 1918 and 1920—a role that included responsibility for the treaty of St. Germain in 1919 and for accepting the Anschluss prohibition, thereby waiving the claim of unification with republican Germany. The Renner government also accepted the responsibility for using political means to fight the revolutionary unrest stirred up by the far left of the political spectrum, the Communists. By paying lip service to the revolution, the SDAP (and Renner as well as Otto Bauer and especially Friedrich Adler) fed revolutionary expectations, but by accepting the rule of compromise, the SDAP stabilized a system that Marxists regarded as a "bourgeois" republic.

This was the birth of the model for which Austrian social democracy stands: for the discrepancy between leftist theory and centrist politics. The SDAP spoke about revolution but did nothing to implement it. On the contrary, the SDAP did everything in its power to ensure that there was no revolution. This was also the beginning of a credibility gap, which any consideration of democratic socialism had to deal with. Austromarxism's "third way," which claimed to be more democratic than the Russian model and more socialist than the concepts of other social democratic parties such as the German SPD or the British Labour Party, was not reflected in the pragmatic compromise orientation that characterized the first social democratic power experiment.

But this credibility gap never surfaced during the First Republic. After the constitution was worked out and agreed on by Social Democrats and Christian Socials, the SDAP left the cabinet and took over the role of parliamentary opposition, facing the majority of an alliance between the Christian Socials and the smaller parties of the pan-German camp ("Bürgerblock," bourgeois bloc). The SDAP expected to come to power by means of the ballot and did well in the elections, especially in 1930, when it again became the strongest party in parliament by winning a significant plurality but not an overall majority of votes and seats.

Even after that success, the SDAP stayed in opposition, hoping that the next elections would bring the decisive breakthrough. But before this democratic strategy could succeed, the European wave of fascism reached Austria. Democracy was abandoned and the Social Democrats repressed.

It was the "waiting for power" during the First Republic that allowed the SDAP to philosophize about socialism without having to act on it. The party could retain its special Austromarxist profile without being forced to implement its party program. Otto Bauer was the centrist figure between Karl Renner on the right and Friedrich Adler and Max Adler on the left, who dominated this double strategy. The first part consisted of the party following the path of constitutional struggle, hoping for one electoral victory after another until it achieved a majority in parliament and socialism could start, and abstaining from any participation in power beyond its role as opposition in parliament. The second part was to keep the faith alive by exploring all the aspects of democratic socialism—in theory, on paper. Reality and the credibility gap could not shake the faith in the "third way" because the party was allowed—largely because of the politics of the right—to abstain from power (Leser 1968).

There has been one significant exception to the SDAP's exclusion from government: The Social Democrats ruled Vienna, the capital and the most populous state of Austria. Called "red Vienna" by both proud Socialists and the critics from the right who wanted to give it a negative hallmark, it became the showcase of Austromarxism. Viennese politics between 1919 and 1934 was a worldwide exhibition for the innovative spirit that the combination of socialism as a goal and democracy as means could create (Rabinbach 1983). Vienna's housing projects, the educational facilities and experiments, and health policies were designed to identify the Social Democrats not only with manifestos but also with the "real thing" of politics, with government and power and "Realpolitik."

In Vienna, the SDAP could always rely on a significant majority in City Hall. The city and its proletarian districts, plus the Jewish element—about 10 percent of Vienna's population—provided the party with a solid power basis. "Red Vienna" demonstrated electoral strength and political reforms. It was not until the end of the First Republic that the working-class electorate started to erode—in favor of the NSDAP (Nazi Party).

It was obvious that within the federal system of Austria, socialism could not be established in only one of the states. Nobody took "red Vienna" as a sign that socialism was already in place; it was, perhaps, one step in that direction. But because expectations—both hopeful and fearful—were necessarily modest, "red Vienna" did not have to face the challenge that capitalism was still around, that the various innovative projects had to be financed by tax revenues from a still-capitalist economy. "Red Vienna" was not socialism; it was reformed capitalism; it was a kind of New Deal exemplified in one big city.

It was not until 1945 that the credibility gap started to become effective—and even then only slowly. Only when the SDAP, now transformed into the SPÖ, became a governing party on the federal level again could its claims be compared with the political reality that any governing party must explain and be responsible for. The SPÖ had learned from the past, and at the beginning of the Second Republic, it did not repeat its mistake of leaving power too soon. The SPÖ stayed in the coalition with the Christian Socials, now transformed into the ÖVP, despite being only the number two party. It took twenty-five years for the SPÖ to become the strongest party in parliament—first in 1970, with only a plurality of seats; then in 1971, 1975, and 1979, with a majority of votes and seats.

The SPÖ's electoral success made it a virtually permanently governing party. With the exception of the years 1966–1970, the SPÖ has been part of the federal government since the end of World War II. From 1945 to 1966, it was the coalition partner of the ÖVP; from 1970 to 1983 it was the sole governing party; then it became a coalition partner again, but this time as the strongest and most visible party, the party that decided the chancellorship. The history of Austrian social democracy as "the" governing party of the Second Republic made it impossible for the party to criticize society from the outside, as if social conditions had nothing to do with its own politics. The SPÖ became the leading party of Austria—therefore Austrian politics and Austrian society had to be seen as the SPÖ's responsibility.

Social democracy was in charge of the Second Republic. Of course, as a consequence of consociational democracy, political power was always divided. Even in the years of the Kreisky era, when the SPÖ ruled without a coalition partner, the party was not always able to make decisions alone (Secher 1993; Fischer 1993; Bischof and Pelinka 1994). The Kreisky cabinet was interested in keeping certain balances, such as social partnership, alive. The result was a power structure much more complex than the existence of a one-party cabinet for thirteen years might have suggested.

But from the outside, the SPÖ was "the" government, and the government was social democratic. The SPÖ was understood to control political decisions regarding all policies in every important field. And even after the Kreisky era, after the return of coalition cabinets, this high visibility of social democratic power did not change significantly because Social Democrats (Fred Sinowatz 1983–1986, Franz Vranitzky 1986–1997, Viktor Klima since 1997) still held the top positions in government.

After so many years of social democratic dominance, the Austrian political system and Austrian society came to be seen as a model for social democratic policies. Already in 1980, the governing power of the SPÖ was the longest and most intensive of all non-Scandinavian social democratic parties in Europe (Pelinka 1983: 80). As in all Scandinavian countries, even Sweden, social democratic parties had to go through long periods of opposition in the 1980s and 1990s; the Scandinavian social democratic parties would have fallen back in this ranking. In the mid-1990s Austrian social democracy ranked first in governing power—the social democratic party in Europe with the longest experience with government and as government after 1945. If social democracy has something to do with socialism, this ranking of the SPÖ should have some impact on society. Was or is Austrian society more "socialist" than other postwar societies governed according to the rules of liberal democracy?

There was an understandable tendency to identify Austria—especially the Austria of the late 1970s and the early 1980s—with social democracy as such. A party that had been outlawed by an authoritarian and a totalitarian regime for eleven years not so long before had made a triumphant return. Widely accepted by the electorate, it was governing Austria almost permanently. Such a political party must have been very special, and the outcome of the party's hegemonial role must have been something special, too. But how special, in a socialist sense, was the SPÖ's Austria, how was it interpretable as the purest result of social democratic experiments, as the implementation of social democratic visions?

One indicator, which rather early demonstrated that social democracy in power is not the same as social democracy in opposition was the transformation of the party structure. In the First Republic, the SDAP was considered an excellent example of a mass membership class party with undisputed inclusions and exclusions. But soon after 1945 the SPÖ became increasingly a catchall party (Shell 1969). There was a noticeable decline in the degree of ideological distinctiveness. As the champion of different electorates—former members of the NSDAP, for instance, but also certain progressive elements among active Catholics—the exclusiveness had to be watered down. The SPÖ did not succeed because Austromarxism was accepted more and more by Austrian voters; the SPÖ grew because Austromarxism was seen less and less as the decisive guidebook that provided the party and the society with perfect formulas for political decisionmaking.

The party was transformed from a highly ideological, quasi-religious, closed subsystem with clear pictures of friend and foe to a party that welcomed almost everybody. This was the result of a double process:

- The modernization of Austrian society and economy changed the profile of its working population: Fewer workers were proletarians, especially in their own eyes; more and more of them became part of a new middle-class sector. There was a significant shift from blue-collar to white-collar workers. The consequence was that the Austrian labor movement—precisely because it was successful, but successful in an evolutionary way—gradually lost its traditional base. The SPÖ reflected these changes: Its electorate and membership became less and less proletarian.
- The SPÖ as the party in government was no longer able to act from a position of principal opposition to the status quo. The SPÖ had increasingly to defend more aspects of the social, economic, and political reality. As a party almost permanently in government, the SPÖ had to become more and more conservative—conservative in the sense of a party of the status quo. The SPÖ could not have avoided being identified with this status.

On the one hand, that cost the party dearly: Its image as the party of the suppressed, the outcasts, and the underprivileged became less and less credible. On the other hand, the party profited from the situation: Social democratic governments calmed the fear of nonsocialists that the SPÖ was bolshevism in disguise. This negative stereotype was nullified by social democratic governments.

Three major trends significantly changed Austrian social democracy. In 1954, these trends were just beginning, but despite the early warning, the party was not able to reverse them. Two of the tendencies already clearly visible in 1954—the tendency to attract more older rather than younger voters and the tendency to become a party of and for public employees—indicated that the SPÖ's socialist character might be in danger (see Table 5.3). Decades later, the SPÖ was almost totally transformed as a consequence of these trends, which had been visible only nine years after the restoration of democracy:

- The Vienna party organization was not able to regain its old strength: Compared with the First Republic, the membership figures for the first decade of the Second Republic showed a decline of more than 100,000 members. This was balanced by increased membership figures in the other parts of Austria. Austrian social democracy, formerly seen as a Viennese party, became more and more an all-Austrian party. One of the dominant conflicts from the past—"red" Vienna against the rest of Austria—was considerably reduced.
- The importance of blue-collar workers declined—not so much in favor of white-collar employees of the private sector but of civil servants. The SPÖ as a party in government had the ability to recruit a great number of public employees, and this patronage created a kind of clientelism new to the social democrats who had been in the opposition so long. The SPÖ had become a party that attracted many Austrians by its power—apart from its ideology and programmatic traditions.
- Aging party membership was already evident: The number of retired had tripled. The generation gap, which would have such a dramatic impact on the SPÖ in the 1980s and 1990s, was soon visible: In the early years of the Second Republic, many people already regarded the SPÖ as the party of the older generation. The party designed to change the very nature of society had to rely more and more on the older generation because it was losing its attractiveness for the young.

More than three decades later, after the peak of its electoral success from 1970 to 1983, the party's tendencies to age and to be identified with government were significantly more visible. In 1987, the SPÖ's membership figures continued to reflect the consequences of tendencies developed during the postwar period: The

TABLE 5.3   SPÖ Membership in Vienna, First and Second Republics

	1929		1954	
	Number	*%*	*Number*	*%*
Blue-collar employees				
Private	197,156	47.49	107,031	36.87
Public sector	15,501	3.73	—	—
White-collar employees	49,170	11.84	33,608	11.52
Private				
Public sector	35,558	8.57	41,973	14.42
Free professions	7,319	1.52	5,886	2.02
Employers	17,875	4.31	8,524	2.92
Retired	9,272	2.23	30,218	10.36
Housewives	66,693	16.06	58,640	20.15
Others	17,626	4.25	5,068	1.74
Sum	416,170	100.00	290,948	100.00

SOURCE: Shell 1969: 61.

membership figures for the Viennese party organization stood at 214,559, a loss of more than 75,000 members since 1954 and of more than 200,000 since 1929. This decline in Vienna happened in spite of the stabilization of the overall membership the SPÖ was still able to claim: In 1987, the SPÖ had a total of 659,239 members in all nine states, slightly more than in 1954 (Cap 1989: 50). Although the dramatic decline in membership outside Vienna had already begun in the 1980s, the consequences of this decline, which had started much earlier in Vienna, were not really evident until the 1990s. In 1995, official data provided by the SPÖ showed 417,587 members—a record low for the party. Since 1987, the party had lost about a quarter of a million members—and this time the decline was not only a Viennese phenomenon (Nick and Pelinka 1996: 75).

The structural changes in the SPÖ's rank and file also applied to age and profession. In 1987, 26 percent of the SPÖ's members were sixty-one or older—above the average Austrian retirement age (Cap 1989: 51). The generation gap was to become the most decisive factor for the social democratic decline on the electoral level in the 1990s, when the SPÖ lost the majority of "leftist," post-1968 Marxist-influenced, better-educated, younger voters to the Greens and its majority position among the young working-class generation to the FPÖ. This dramatic loss was predictable—membership changes during the 1950s, 1960s, 1970s, and 1980s had given early warning of the trend.

By 1987, the SPÖ's plurality had shifted: White-collar workers from both the private and public sectors already accounted for 37.1 percent of party membership, while the percentage of blue-collar party members stood at 34.8 percent (Cap 1989: 51). Thus at the end of its most successful period, the SPÖ, still the biggest party in Austria and the leading party in government, had lost its proletarian outlook—and its youthfulness.

It may come as a surprise that even after these structural changes, indicated by a decline in the party's attractiveness, the SPÖ was still able to maintain its position of governmental power. Even after the loss of its majority in parliament in 1983, the SPÖ kept its plurality in 1983, 1986, 1990, 1994, and 1995. This ability to stay in power despite a decline in electoral consent and in membership numbers must be seen as the consequence of two factors: one the consequence of policy and the other the consequence of structure.

- The policy factor: The SPÖ was able to sail with the wind of the international megatrend that started in Great Britain with Margaret Thatcher's conservative success in 1979 and in the United States with Ronald Reagan's presidency. The reversal of leftist interventionism, "big government," and welfare optimism in favor of welfare state skepticism and a general antisocialist mood did not turn against the Austrian Social Democrats as was the case with the British Labour Party, the German SPD, and U.S. Democrats. The SPÖ was able to control this reversal by changing its policies. The SPÖ became more market oriented and started to back deregulation and privatization. In 1992, SPÖ party chairman and chancellor Franz Vranitzky declared it in the party's best interests to deregulate the economy despite objections coming from special interest groups on the political right (Vranitzky 1992: 145). The SPÖ itself was the leading force of "Austrian-style Thatcherism," insisting on the necessity to adapt to international, especially economic, trends and to moderate this wave of "pure capitalism." The SPÖ was "New Labour" years prior to Tony Blair.
- The structural factor: The Austrian party system, which up to the beginning of the 1980s had been a near-perfect two-party system, started to deconcentrate at the very same time the SPÖ's decline began. Therefore, the logical switch of roles between the party in government and the party in opposition—logical for a two-party system—could not happen because the ÖVP, the logical heir to the SPÖ's role in government, was the victim of the same declining tendency. The parties that profited—the FPÖ and the Greens, and later also the Liberals—were too polarized and still too small to create an alternative to the SPÖ. The FPÖ's extreme right-wing image prevented a theoretically possible coalition between ÖVP and FPÖ. So the SPÖ had to stay in power, perpetuating its image as the "natural" party of government, as the party responsible for the status of Austrian society. The outlook of the SPÖ became even more conservative, in the sense of representing the status quo.

The SPÖ is a structurally conservative party. This is not the impact of any willful or intentional change from Austromarxist to conservative attitudes; it is the unavoidable consequence of being in power for such a long time. The SPÖ governs and governs and governs—and therefore must be seen as the "Staatspartei," the party almost identical with government (Pelinka and Steger 1988). This is, of course, not the same identity as in the case of the Soviet-type one-party systems. It is more similar to that of the Japanese government, which for decades was identified with the Liberal Democratic Party, or to the Italian government and the Democrazia Cristiana for about the same length of time. The consequence of being the leading party in government for such a long time must be seen on different levels:

- As "Staatspartei," the SPÖ had to deal with the phenomenon of clientelism. As the party responsible for so many commissions so many people were interested in, and as the party responsible for recruiting so many public servants, the SPÖ became linked with interests that in some cases tended toward corruption. Most of the political scandals of the 1970s and 1980s had to do with Social Democrats; and political corruption, which probably occurs in Austria no more or less often than in other countries, had a social democratic flavor. This has nothing to do with any specific tendency Austrian social democracy had toward corruption—it was just the result of being in power so long (Gehler and Sickinger 1995: esp. 532–591 and 679–743). Anyone who wanted to promote his or her own interests through government channels had to deal with the SPÖ, the party in government, and not all these interests and the instruments they used were within the legal framework. The SPÖ was in charge of almost everything the federal government could provide; the consequence was a constant temptation to occasionally disregard some of the rules and the regularities.
- The SPÖ as "Staatspartei" is identified with (almost) everything that characterizes the Austrian political system and Austria as such. If there is the feeling that the Austrian economy is in good shape, that society is developing well and that the world envies the Austrian way of life, then credit is given to the social democratic government. But if unemployment is rising, migration provokes already existing xenophobic attitudes, and social entitlements no longer seem so secure, then it will also be seen as the fault of the party in power. The SPÖ is—automatically—on the defense, always inclined to justify the status quo, to argue that the present situation is the best possible one.

Both aspects are extremely difficult to combine with a strategy aimed at a very different society. Clientelism and the responsibility for the status quo make innovative policies almost impossible, so democratic socialism becomes the pragmatic dealing with bread-and-butter issues. The "third way," the grand perspective of the new society adding social justice to political freedom and creating the "new man," tends to be relegated to the annals of the history of the labor movement.

Austromarxism is no longer a political strategy or a political doctrine but rather the research area of historians—not despite, but because the party of the Austro-marxist heritage is in power.

The transformation of democratic socialism from a goal to self-justifying means can and must be evaluated by analyzing the direction Austrian society is taking at the end of the twentieth century. Is there anything in Austrian society that can be defined as distinctly socialist? Is there anything a social democratic party can claim as its distinct impact on society and history? Has the SPÖ promoted anything that demonstrates the difference between, for instance, Christian democratic or conservative political dominance on one hand and social democratic dominance on the other?

Democratic socialism claims to promote a more egalitarian society within the framework of liberal democracy (Pelinka 1983: 128–157). This claim distinguishes social democracy from conservative or Christian democratic parties and traditions by virtue of its egalitarian orientation. Egalité, the second principle of the French Revolution, is the socialist promise par excellence. The egalitarian orientation has different aspects, but without the aspect of economic equality it would not make sense at all. But social democracy insists on another principle: democracy in the sense of a pluralistic and competitive multiparty system. This insistence distinguishes democratic socialism from the Leninist version of Marxism, from communism.

The second of the two distinctions did not create any difficulty for the SPÖ. Beginning in 1945, the SPÖ leadership always stressed the principal difference between its interpretation of socialism and the Communist line. The days of illegal opposition to authoritarianism and totalitarianism were over, as was Otto Bauer theorizing about "integral socialism." The presence of the Red Army and the general anti-Communist mood in Austria made it rather easy to draw distinctions between the Soviet and the SPÖ's versions of socialism. Those within the party apparatus who had a different attitude toward communism and the KPÖ were purged: In 1947, the leader of this Communist-leaning wing, Erwin Scharf, lost his position as party secretary; in 1948 he was expelled from the party (Shell 1969: 122–127).

The basic differences from communism were again stressed in the official party manifesto of 1958 and in the "Eisenstädter Erklärung" (Declaration of Eisenstadt) in 1969. In this declaration, the SPÖ distanced itself from any recommendation the KPÖ could possibly give to back the SPÖ in its competition with the ÖVP. In 1966, the SPÖ had not clearly rejected a similar recommendation from the Communists. Bruno Kreisky, who became party chairman in 1967 as a consequence of his party's defeat in 1966, was eager to emphasize his party's anti-Communist orientation. In Eisenstadt, in 1969, Kreisky saw to it that the SPÖ rejected any help from the discredited Communists (Kreisky 1988: 405 f.).

The SPÖ had no problems proving the difference between itself and the Communists, but it was and still is difficult for the SPÖ to distinguish itself from the other democratic parties, especially the ÖVP, the traditional "bourgeois" party in

Austria. According to its programmatic intentions, the social democratic impact on Austrian society and politics should be seen in the degree of social equality. Has the SPÖ's leading role in Austrian politics since 1945 made a significant difference when it comes to equality? How egalitarian is Austrian society as a result of the SPÖ's fifty years of political dominance ? Is Austria a laboratory for democratic socialism, a country whose features are characteristically socialist?

The egalitarian effect of democratic socialism should be created by democratic government. Democratic socialism means using government to implement a policy of justice in society. The size of government can be measured as a first indicator for measuring the degree of socialism in Austria.

In 1992, Austria ranked ninth among the twenty-four OECD (Organization of Economic Cooperation and Development) members in taxation. In Austria, 43.5 percent of the domestic product was channeled to the government through taxes and other duties. Compared with Sweden, ranked first with 50.0 percent, Austria's position is not extreme, nor does it indicate any specific socialist character beyond the average tax policies other Western democracies pursue. What is striking is that the distribution of this tax burden differs significantly from the OECD average: In 1991, income tax in Austria accounted for only 26.9 percent of total taxation, while the OECD average was 38.8. The progressive character of income tax makes it a typical instrument of a redistributive policy through taxation. Austria even abolished property taxes, a form of taxation usually seen as especially suited for redistribution (WIFO 1995: 5–7).

At first glance, Austria's egalitarianism is not very impressive: Government is big but not as big as in some other countries; and redistribution through taxation is comparatively underdeveloped.

The second factor to be considered is the economic effect of politics: Who is profiting, and to what extent? In a society strongly influence by democratic socialism, there are two predictable effects: First, wage earners should benefit; and second, lower-income groups should benefit even more.

The indicator used to measure the income of wage earners in relation to the income from profits is the "wage quota." Since 1975, the Austrian wage quota ("bereinigte Lohnquote"—cleared wage quota) has declined steadily: The quota for net incomes dropped from about 57 percent (1975) to about 44 percent (1994) (WIFO 1995: 14 f.). This means that beginning with the peak of social democratic power in government, wage earners have been losing relative income in comparison with those who are making a profit on their property or business. But it also means that the degree of equality in Austria has already been decreasing for decades.

A look at the distribution of income shows a similar trend: There is increasing disparity between the lowest and the highest income groups, and the loss of equality is remarkable. In 1983, the poorest 10 percent (lowest decile) of Austria's wage earners received 3.3 percent of all the wages earned in Austria, and the richest 10 percent (highest decile) received 21.8 percent. In 1991, this had changed in favor of the latter: The lowest decile now received 3.0 percent, the highest 22.0. If this is measured and analyzed on the basis of households rather than individuals, the decline of equality is even more striking: In 1983, the ratio between the lowest decile of Austrian households and the highest was 4.6 to 20.3 percent. In 1991, this had changed to a ratio of 3.6 to 21.8 percent (WIFO 1995: 18 f.).

This is quite a significant development. Socialism defined as an egalitarian policy in favor of the poorer segments of society is on the decline even in an era when the party promising more equality was and is in power. The decline actually began during a period of optimal social democratic hegemony, when the SPÖ was in complete control of parliament and government due to its stupendous electoral success in the 1970s.

The effects of redistribution through government can also be measured in specific sectors of Austrian society. Who is profiting in those sectors? A breakdown of government spending ("transfer") for public education, family benefits, health care, and unemployment services reveals a clear picture (see Table 5.4).

This is redistribution not in favor of the have-nots, but in favor of the haves. The richer are getting richer and the poorer are getting poorer—in relative terms. As long as the economy is growing, this effect is less noticeable, but it is happening nonetheless.

Another way to compare the programmatic intentions of social democracy with social reality is to examine the equality between men and women. The SPÖ has always been a programmatic champion of more legal and economic equality between men and women. In 1994, after more than twenty years of governments led by the SPÖ, the average monthly income in Austria was ATS 21,657 for men— and ATS 14,981 for women. This ration of almost 3 to 2 has remained virtually unchanged for years (*Taschenbuch* 1997: 208 f.). The real equality between men and women, as measured by income figures, stabilized on an extremely unequal level. In the Austria of the 1990s, there is no evidence of progress in the sense of diminishing economic differences between men and women.

Even the pragmatic network of social services is not as efficient as it used to be. The Austrian welfare state was stable in the 1980s but began to deteriorate in the 1990s. Especially in 1995, 1996, and 1997, there were cutbacks of social entitlements in an effort to balance the budget. As early as 1993, the access to unemployment compensation had been made more difficult. Other services had been curtailed, especially those established to aid the most needy—another step to reduce social equality (Tálos, in Zulehner et al. 1996: 46–49). The decline of the welfare state is a European and not a specifically Austrian phenomenon, but it clearly shows the decline of social services that the SPÖ can claim to be the impact of democratic socialism.

Are there any traces of socialism in Austria? Decades of social democratic hegemony had no significant egalitarian effect on society. Of course, it can be argued that this development was not intentional and that without a strong social democracy, the decline of equality might have been even more significant. But

TABLE 5.4 Distribution of Public Funds to Employee Households among Sectors and Income Groups

Transfers for	Lower Third	Medium Third	Higher Third
Education	15.3%	35.2%	49.5%
Family benefits	18.6%	38.8%	42.6%
Health care	25.6%	34.0%	40.4%
Unemployment services	55.7%	27.6%	16.7%
Transfers together	21.7%	35.2%	43.1%
Gross household income	12.0%	28.4%	59.5%

SOURCE: WIFO 1995: 111, table 6.2.

one result cannot be disputed: Despite a politically dominant social democratic party, the quality of democratic socialism declined. Austria cannot be considered a social democratic laboratory.

The reason for the contradiction between political hegemony and socioeconomic development must be seen in the decline of political governability. It is naive to feed the belief that government is directly responsible for distributing or redistributing property and income. And it is especially naive to foster such an assumption in an era of an increasingly globalized economy. The ability of the Austrian political system to control socioeconomic megatrends is poorer than ever.

But there are domestic reasons for the lack of incentives to push harder for redistribution in favor of the most underprivileged. The SPÖ is no longer the party of the poorest segment in Austrian society. The poorest segment does not have a political voice. As a consequence of migration, immigrants are significantly overrepresented in Austria's lowest income group. Austria does not follow the model of full legal integration. Immigrants live in Austria for many years, even for decades, without receiving citizenship. The result is that they do not exist on the electoral market. Their interests are not taken into account by parties competing for votes because as noncitizens they are nonvoters. Any strict policy of redistribution for the poor would include a policy for those who are not entitled to participate in Austrian democracy. And for reasons easily understood, the SPÖ will not jeopardize its electoral opportunities for a principle that does not count in competitive democracy.

The SPÖ has become a catchall party. The party is interested in getting as many votes as possible and cannot afford to be particularly choosy about where the votes come from. This is not the consequence of treachery but of democratic logic. Because it is a democratic party, the SPÖ is neither willing nor able to sacrifice its electoral chances purely for the sake of its principles. The SPÖ has opted for liberal democracy, and that is what the party is getting. If the rules of liberal, competitive democracy present an obstacle to implementing certain principles, then the principles have to suffer. Democracy is a logic; socialism a principle.

The logic of stabilized Western democracy is that parties are converging. The result is that it makes less and less difference which party is in government. The SPÖ's dominance throughout the Second Republic has helped to stabilize Western democracy in Austria. But having become a catchall party as a consequence of this stabilization, the SPÖ has moved closer to the ÖVP, the other moderate catchall party. Before being able to make Austria a model of democratic socialism, socialist strategies already have reached the limit imposed by democracy.

What is left for Austrian socialism? It may still be able to moderate the effects of global megatrends, but no Austrian government can sail against the prevailing winds of change. If it can sail with those winds, the government may have some success in implementing an egalitarian policy.

One such implementation resulted in Austria's comparatively successful policy for dealing with growing unemployment. The overall trend is obvious: Unemployment is on the rise all over Europe. But data provided by the OECD gives Austria a rather favorable mark: Austria is among the countries least affected by unemployment. (See Chapter 6, esp. Table 6.2.)

Among the industrialized countries of the OECD, only Luxembourg and Switzerland are doing a better job of fighting unemployment. The interpretation of these data is simple: Austria cannot avoid feeling the impact of the global trend of rising unemployment, but it has been able to soften the blow.

But does this have anything to do with socialism? The relative success of Austria's employment policy must be attributed to the general consensus built in Austria from 1945 on. The consensus includes an agreement to reduce social costs as much as possible. Unemployment is seen as a social cost factor. Keeping unemployment as low as possible means reducing social and political costs and therefore, in the long run, even economic costs. This consensus is not socialism. The consensus had a name for its socioeconomic aspects: corporatism. Of course, Austrian corporatism has something to do with socialism—with the Social Democratic Party, with the labor unions and the SPÖ-dominated ÖGB. But corporatism also has something to do with the attitude of employers and their interest organizations, and of course, with the political agenda of the other major camp in Austria and its party, the ÖVP.

Socialism in Austria seems to be reduced to the corporatist arrangement established by employers and employees, capital and labor during the first two decades of the Second Republic. There may be good reasons for Social Democrats to defend these arrangements. But nobody can claim that they represent the realm of democratic socialism the SPÖ promised to fight for, an egalitarian society within a liberal democracy. The democracy is there—but where is the equality?

Socialism in Austria is a paradox. It exists on the political level, in government and parliament, and in the labor organizations. It is represented by a still unusually strong Social Democratic Party. But socialism does not seem to exist in society. Austrian society is generally like other European societies; specifically, it is no more egalitarian than most other Western European societies. A very strong socialist party does not mean a socialist society—at least not in the case of Austria. After more than fifty years of significant political power, socialism in Austria is neither a danger to democracy nor the fulfillment of the promise of a socialist society.

Conclusion

Catholicism and socialism used to be substitutes for a nation. In a society that did not follow the path of nation building according to Western European standards, Catholicism and socialism were able to stimulate, unite, and channel most of the social energies Austrian society produced. Catholicism and socialism formed a kind of social duopoly: two subsocieties fulfilled many of the functions of a nation state, which, in other countries, had a virtual monopoly on political loyalties.

The duopoly went through a stage of open confrontation, the First Republic, followed by an era of cooperation, the Second Republic. During the decades after 1945, Catholicism and socialism were successful in nation building, the very process they had substituted for. The stabilization of both the Austrian political system and economy as well as the development of an Austrian national identity filled a vacuum. It was the very same vacuum that had made the subsidiary role of the two camps possible or even necessary.

The process of ideological secularization eroded much of the dominant role Catholicism and socialism were able to play in Austrian politics and society. For decades, Austrian politics was defined as the relationship between Catholicism and socialism. This period is now over.

6

**THE ECONOMY:
SUCCESS AND
DEPENDENCE**

The Austrian economy is characterized by its successful performance since 1945, the result of a remarkable postwar recovery. At the end of World War II, the complete collapse of Greater Germany's war economy and the destruction of the industrial structures on Austrian territory left Austria a poor country. Fifty years later, Austria was able to join the European Union as a prosperous member state. Due to its wealth, Austria is a net payer within the European Union: It pays more into the European budget than it gets out of it.

But the success story of the Austrian economy also has a less positive side. Despite the prosperity most Austrians currently enjoy, the Austrian economy faces structural problems that can be summarized by the term dependency. Austria's economy, like that of the other EU members and especially the smaller European countries, is dependent on the EU market. The difference is that the Austrian economy is structurally more dependent than comparable countries such as Sweden, Denmark, the Netherlands, or (as an example of non–EU countries) Switzerland.

This fact expresses an ambiguity that goes back into history. By the late nineteenth century, Austria was already what it still is today: a country on the fringe of the European sphere of prosperity. Austria's economic performance has ranged from weak (as in the interwar period) to strong (as after 1945), but it has always been strongly influenced by a delay factor, a lag in development that created dependency. And this delay is the direct consequence of its geopolitical position.

Usually economic development happens in Western Europe first before it reaches Austria. In many respects, Austria is the easternmost country of Western Europe.

When Austria joined the European Union, it was ranked eighth among all nations with regard to its GNP per capita (see Table 6.1). Contemporary Austria is a wealthy country. After decades of economic growth, it has become a country with better economic indicators than many other countries, including Great Britain, Sweden, and Canada. Austrian inflation is traditionally below the EU inflation rate (*Taschenbuch* 1997: 13). Even unemployment, the scourge of industrialized societies, torments Austria to a lesser degree than most of the other highly industrialized nations. Among the fifteen members of the European Union, only Luxembourg has a lower unemployment rate than Austria (see Table 6.2).

These data have to be seen from a dynamic perspective. After years of overproportional economic growth, Austria's growth rate has slowed down. In 1995 and 1996, Austria's economic growth was below that of EU growth (*Taschenbuch* 1997: 12). Unemployment also seems well on its way to becoming "Europeanized": As a consequence of economic globalization, Austria cannot expect to have a significantly better employment situation than the other Western European nations.

The data also have to be seen from a historic perspective. Austria is a latecomer among the industrialized nations of Europe and is very much on the periphery of development. At the turn of the century, Habsburg Austria, in comparison with Western Europe, was economically underdeveloped. This circumstance created dependence because economic development depended on foreign investment.

Following a general West to East pattern, the modernization of the European economy reached Austria later than Western Europe. Modernization came late, in a series of waves of significant economic changes that had a social impact in Austria. This lag was responsible for delaying transitions in Austria that had taken place earlier in Western Europe, among them the transition from an agrarian to an industrialized society, from a rural to an urban society, from a secondary (industrial) to a tertiary (service) orientation, and from a society based on heritage to a society based on merit.

Habsburg Austria was a huge empire in Central Europe, consisting mostly of economically backward regions. Industrialization came late and only to certain parts of Austria: Bohemia, Styria, and Vienna. In these regions, the consequences of industrialization were the same as in other European countries: mass migration from the countryside to urban centers, mass poverty, and the rise of the labor movement. Most of Austria, however, remained pastoral and agricultural (Sandgruber 1995: 233–313).

When the Habsburg Empire collapsed, the small new republic consisted of the Viennese metropolitan area and the alpine regions of old Austria, the latter based on agriculture with only a few industrial districts.

The First Republic was not able to overcome this economic cleavage. It was the war industry of Greater Germany that started a new wave of industrialization. As a consequence of the "Anschluss" in 1938 and of Nazi Germany's war machine,

TABLE 6.1   The Ten Wealthiest Countries: GNP per Capita in U.S. $, 1994

1. Luxembourg	39,850	6. USA	25,860
2. Switzerland	37,180	7. Germany	25,580
3. Japan	34,630	8. Austria	24,950
4. Denmark	28,110	9. Iceland	24,590
5. Norway	26,480	10. Sweden	23,630

SOURCE: Fischer Almanach 1996: 944.

TABLE 6.2   Unemployment Within the European Union, 1995

Luxembourg	2.9%	Greece	9.1%
Austria	4.3%	Belgium	9.3%
Denmark	7.0%	Italy	11.8%
Portugal	7.1%	France	11.9%
Netherlands	7.5%	Ireland	12.0%
Germany	8.2%	Finland	17.0%
United Kingdom	8.7%	Spain	22.7%
Sweden	8.9%		
European Union	10.7%		

SOURCE: *Taschenbuch* 1997: 37.

the German leadership used the still-underdeveloped regions of Austria for its war efforts. New industries, for example, in Linz, were established to serve this purpose (Sandgruber 1995: 403–438).

The Second Republic brought even greater modernization, but without the military focus that was typical of the short period of modernization under Nazi Germany. Austria started to become an industrialized Western society. After 1945, the Austrian economy changed rapidly. Between 1951 and 1991, the percentage of Austrians living in communities with fewer than 2,000 inhabitants—the communities typical of an agrarian society—declined from 34.7 to 21.5 percent (Sandgruber 1995: 497). The percentage of Austrians working in agriculture declined dramatically: In 1934, 32.1 percent of Austria's labor force was in the primary (agricultural) sector, but in 1991, the figure had fallen to 7.2 percent. This trend is still ongoing, and the sector that is profiting is not the secondary sector, industry, but the tertiary sector—the service sector in a broad sense. In 1991, 55 percent of the Austrian labor force was working in this sector (Sandgruber 1995: 500).

This economic modernization resulted in Westernization in a twofold sense:

- The Austrian economy and therefore the Austrian society became more and more like the economy and society of Western European nations.
- One decisive motor behind these changes was the political interest of the United States.

In 1947, Austria was invited to participate in the Marshall Plan. Unlike countries such as Czechoslovakia and Poland, which were not included in the American recovery program due to Soviet pressure, Austria decided in favor of the Marshall Plan despite Communist protests. The result was not only economic recovery and growth in Austria fueled by Western (American) investments but also the beginning of Austria's integration into the West. The Marshall Plan became the Organization for European Economic Cooperation (OEEC) and later the Organization for Economic Cooperation and Development (OECD)—the first of the many Western-oriented organizations in which Austria was able to participate despite its occupation by the Allies (including the USSR) and its neutrality status afterward.

The Marshall Plan created incentives that were significant for the period of economic growth starting in Austria in the early 1950s (Tweraser 1995). The combination of foreign investment and political stability, intensified by the State Treaty and the Declaration of Neutrality 1955, shaped Austria's new image as a prosperous country.

In the field of international politics, Austria abstained from full integration into the Western alliance as a consequence of its neutrality declaration of 1955. But economically, Austria became an industrialized Western nation. In contrast to other smaller industrialized nations such as the Netherlands, Sweden, and Switzerland, Austria is not home to traditional industrial conglomerates. Austria has no corporations comparable to Philipps, Volvo, or Nestlé. Austrian banks cannot command empires like Swiss banks can. Austria's rise to economic prosperity proves that such success is possible on the economic periphery. Austria succeeded despite its peripheral position.

Austria's position on the economic periphery of Western Europe is the consequence of economic delay. Prior to 1918, Austria's industrial development lagged far behind that of Western Europe, including Germany. German, British, and French capital played an important role within Austria. During the last period of Habsburg Austria, French banks used Austria's lagging development to establish their influence (Sandgruber 1995: 296–301). British capital was influential in developing a modern infrastructure for cities such as Vienna. The Austrian response was typical: Karl Lueger, mayor of Vienna from 1897 to 1910, and his Christian Social Party strengthened the influence of the Viennese municipal government over the local economy by taking over some of the service industries and founding special municipal institutions in the banking and insurance sectors (Sandgruber 1995: 304–306).

Lueger's reaction to the Austrian economy's dependence created a pattern that post-1945 Austria would try to repeat: Through the pragmatic application of socialist (or at least nonmarket, interventionist) methods, Austria reduced the impact of its dependence. The nationalization of main parts of the industrial and banking sectors in 1946 must be interpreted in this way. But this kind of government intervention was one more factor that delayed the development of specific capitalist attitudes in Austrian society. The Austrian tradition of dependence on government prevailed as the only alternative to dependence on foreign interests.

In the interwar period, especially after 1933, German capital became an instrument of the destabilization of Austrian independence. Nazi Germany specifically used the Styrian steel industry as a bridgehead to strengthen the Austrian NSDAP (Pauley 1972: esp. 160 f.).

Again, this experience confirmed the Austrian inclination to fight economic dependence by political means. In 1945, the Austrian economy could be defined as capitalism without capital and capitalists. Anxious to avoid a complete takeover by foreign interests, the Austrian parliament passed two nationalization acts, in 1946 and 1947. At that time, the main foreign power interested in and capable of completely dominating the Austrian economy was the Soviet Union.

The economic development after 1945 was responsible for another kind of Westernization: Geopolitics gave the western parts of Austria—the states of Vorarlberg, Tyrol, Salzburg, and Upper Austria—an economic advantage. The eastern and southern states were less successful in attracting the capital that was flowing into Austria and stimulating the economy. Until 1955, the presence of Soviet troops was an obstacle. And after the Allied forces had left Austria, the Cold War slowed the economic development of eastern and southern Austria, states that bordered on Communist countries and were considered economic dead ends.

The result was a shift of balance: Western Austria became more prosperous than the eastern and southern states. This can be seen in the European Union's allocation of development funds to Burgenland, the easternmost Austrian state and the only one to be designated an economically underdeveloped region. It can also be seen in the regional differences of unemployment figures (see Table 6.3). The Cold War continues to have an impact on the Austrian economy.

The dependence of the Austrian economy is also manifested in its international trade relations. Austria is strongly dependent on both its exports and its imports. This is a result of its small size. Smaller countries tend to be, all other factors being equal, more dependent on international trade. But the Austrian economy is especially dependent on imports and on one trading partner, Germany.

The first aspect of dependency can be seen by comparing Austria with the other highly developed, smaller EU countries: Belgium, Denmark, Finland, Luxembourg, the Netherlands, and Sweden (see Table 6.4). All of these smaller EU countries export more than they import. Even Ireland, one of the less-developed smaller EU countries, has a positive balance of trade. Of the smaller EU countries, only less-developed Greece and Portugal, plus two of the larger countries, Spain and the United Kingdom, are in the same boat as Austria: They export less than they import (*Taschenbuch* 1997: 35).

Tourism has traditionally compensated for this trade deficit, and Austria is a main focus of international tourism. The western part of the country—especially Vorarlberg, Tyrol, Salzburg, Carinthia—attracts international tourism in both winter and summer. In addition, Vienna and the city of Salzburg have become

TABLE 6.3   Unemployment in Austrian States, 1996

Western states	
Vorarlberg	5.3%
Tyrol	6.1%
Salzburg	4.6%
Upper Austria	5.5%
Other states	
Burgenland	8.6%
Lower Austria	6.9%
Vienna	7.8%
Styria	8.4%
Carinthia	9.4%

SOURCE: *Taschenbuch* 1997: 139.
NOTE: The statistical basis of these data is different from that used in Table 6.2.

TABLE 6.4   Exports and Imports of the EU Countries, 1995 (in millions of European Currency Units [ECUs])

	Exports	*Imports*
Austria	43.729	50.292
Belgium/Luxembourg	133.255	123.331
Denmark	37.760	33.739
Germany	389.265	338.647
Finland	30.955	22.530
France	230.245	221.245
Greece	8.246	18.952
Ireland	33.412	24.196
Italy	176.654	155.948
Netherlands	155.328	141.612
Portugal	14.190	24.931
Sweden	61.069	49.681
Spain	71.684	83.786
United Kingdom	181.000	207.703

SOURCE: EUROSTAT, in *Taschenbuch* 1997: 35.

important destinations for the kind of tourism that draws people from all over the world to cities with a unique cultural profile.

Tourism helps to stabilize the Austrian balance of payments. Foreign tourists spend more money in Austria than Austrians spend abroad, thereby helping to balance the trade deficit. However, income from international tourism is growing at a much slower rate than the expenditure of Austrian tourists abroad (see Table 6.5). In the 1990s, Austria's income from international tourism has even started to decline.

This trend is the result of Austria's economic success. In the 1990s, Austrians have enough money to spend more and more on international travel. Vacations in

TABLE 6.5 International Balance of Austrian Tourism (in millions of Austrian Schilling)

	Ingoing	*Outgoing*
1986	106,169	61,289
1990	152,441	87,775
1995	147,140	117,479

SOURCE: Taschenbuch 1997: 312.

the Caribbean, Greece, Spain, and East Africa have become popular—to the disadvantage of the Austrian balance of payments. On the home front, Austria has lost its reputation as a rather moderately priced tourist attraction: It has become expensive. The consequence is that tourism, while still extremely important for the Austrian economy, is losing its function as a remedy for the trade deficit.

Austria's economic dependency is exemplified not only by the trade deficit but also by the structural bias within Austrian trade relations: Austria's international trade is first and foremost trade with Germany. In 1995, more than 50 percent of Austria's imports came from Germany; and almost 50 percent of Austria's exports went to Germany (*Taschenbuch* 1997: 290).

This specific dependence on trade with Germany is compounded by the specific dependence on German capital. In the 1990s, the privatization of the nationalized industries and the nationalized banks opened Austria's economy to foreign investment, especially German capital. The Austrian media, both electronic and print, became more and more dependent on its German counterpart. In addition to this particular effect of denationalization, the process of economic concentration in Europe is increasing Austria's general economic dependence, especially its dependence on Germany (Aiginger 1996: 123 f.).

After 1945, Austria implemented a plan to countermine this dependency: nationalization. In 1946, parliament passed the first nationalization act, and the republic took over basic industries—steel, mining—and the major banks. The main reason for this step toward socialism was not a belief in socialist doctrines but a desire to avoid economic dependence and its political implications. The major industries and banks, the objects of this nationalization act, were "German property"—leftovers from the German war economy. And in 1946, the only alternative to nationalization seemed to be a takeover by the Soviet Union. The USSR claimed most of the "German property" as part of the restitution to which it felt entitled. In an effort to avoid such a development, the first nationalization act granted the Austrian government control of major industries and banks.

The second nationalization act, passed in 1947, made the republic and the nine states owners of the energy industry. Again, in the aftermath of World War II, there were few alternatives to making the country's energy supply the responsibility of the federal and state governments. But the underlying philosophy was to guarantee a maximum of independence—first by preventing a repetition of the

1930s, when German-owned industries became the instruments of Nazi interests in Austria, and second by preventing the instrumentalization of the Austrian economy by Soviet interests.

But when the nationalized industries entered a period of structural crisis in the 1980s, the Austrian government saw no alternatives to privatization. In compliance with its newly confirmed orientation toward the European Community, Austria started to denationalize its industries and its banking system.

Privatization included the Austrian oil company OMV; the steel industries in Upper Austria, Styria, and Lower Austria; the major Austrian banks; and the traditional Austrian federal monopolies, such as salt and tobacco. By 1997, the Austrian government no longer owned most of these groups and corporations.

The privatization of one of the two major banks, the Credit-Anstalt Bankverein (CA-BV), caused a political crisis in early 1997, when Bank Austria, the other major and previously privatized bank, bought the majority of the CA-BV's shares. The political background of this crisis was that the ÖVP had traditionally enjoyed influence over the CA-BV, while the SPÖ had wielded influence over Bank Austria. Despite privatization, the political aspects of the developments were the subject of heated debate. When the ÖVP protested and openly discussed the possibility of leaving the coalition with the SPÖ, it had to be appeased with other arrangements in the savings bank sector. The crisis surrounding the privatization of the CA-BV demonstrated that privatization was not an altogether clean break with the traditional Austrian pattern of political intervention in the economy.

The process of privatization had to follow the rules established by the European Union. One especially important provision was that non-Austrian EU corporations be allowed to buy into the Austrian market. Privatization has therefore had a significant impact on the Europeanization of the Austrian economy. Austria's economic structures are inevitably becoming more dependent on Europe, and for that reason, the pattern of political intervention will weaken despite the experience with the sale of the CA-BV.

The process of privatization marked the end of one feature that especially characterized the Second Republic: the "mixed" economy. Due to its high degree of nationalization, Austria was seen as the most "socialist" of the Western nations. The Austrian economy had been following two different logics: the logic of the market economy dominated in principle, but at the same time state control and state intervention created a different logic. In the early 1980s, the Austrian economy was seen as an example of how much socialism a market economy could incorporate. Now, at the end of the 1990s, the Austrian economy has become more or less an average market economy within the European Union.

These changes had to have an impact on the second economic quality that strongly influenced Austria after 1945: corporatism. The government's major economic role was instrumental in establishing the specific Austrian pattern of business-labor relations, called "social partnership." Many factors contributed to the decline of Austrian corporatism beginning in the late 1980s, but the crisis of Austria's nationalized industries and the resulting process of privatization is one of the most important.

Privatization was the final step in the Austrian blueprint for economic independence, and its consequence is increased dependence (Karazman-Morawetz and Pleschiutschnig 1997: 422–426). Although the Austrian economy of the 1990s can no longer be called "capitalism without capital and without capitalists," foreign capital is now taking over more and more of the Austrian economy, and foreign means first and foremost German.

In 1979, 62.2 percent of the employees of the 100 biggest corporations worked for nationalized industries or for enterprises owned by nationalized banks. By 1994, this figure had fallen to 30.8 percent. In the same period and within the same group, the percentage of Austrians employed by German corporations in Austria rose from 9.5 to 16.7 percent, and those employed by other foreign corporations increased from 9.9 to 17.4 percent(Karazman-Morawetz and Pleschiutschnig 1997: 423). The beneficiaries of denationalization are not Austrian but rather foreign and especially German corporations.

At the end of the 1990s, the Austrian economic dependence on Germany appears to be greater than ever. During the interwar period, the Austrian economy's involvement with the economies of the other successor states of Habsburg Austria balanced this dependency to a certain degree. Forty years of Communist domination in all these successor states destroyed many of the traditional relations that Austria was able to maintain until 1938. By the early 1950s, Germany was increasingly filling this gap, thereby becoming economically dominant in a broad sense. In the 1970s, the Austrian government and the Austrian National Bank—the equivalent of the Federal Reserve—tied the exchange rate of the Austrian schilling to that of the German mark. The main reason for this policy was the strong trade dependence of small Austria on its larger neighbor. But it was the impact of privatization, the end of nationalization as a systematic pattern, that significantly increased the role of the German economy in Austria.

From a political point of view, the most interesting aspect of this increased dependence is that economic dependence does not correlate with political dependence. Between 1918 and 1938, the dominant Austrian political attitude—including foreign policy—was pan-German: Austria was considered a second German state, bound to the larger country by both specific and mythical loyalties. Beginning in 1945, Austria—the Austrian government and the Austrian people—stopped defining itself as "German" in any political sense. Austria does not perceive its international role as one influenced by a specific German identity or specific loyalties toward Germany. Prior to 1938, a lesser degree of economic dependence did not prevent a strong pan-German political orientation. After 1945, an increase in economic dependence did not lead to a parallel political outlook. Pan-Germanism as a political program in Austria died during precisely the same period when Austria's economy became extremely dependent on Germany's economy.

But there is another probable connection between the stabilization of an Austrian identity and Austria's economic development. After the collapse of Habsburg Austria, conventional wisdom maintained that the small new republic was not economically viable. One justification of the pan-German Anschluss orientation after 1918 was the belief that Austria was too small and too underdeveloped to survive economically. And the First Republic seemed to confirm this prediction: Economic stagnation and mass unemployment were interpreted as Austria's economic inability to exist as an independent and sovereign state. The Anschluss movement had a strong economic rationale.

The Second Republic disproved the prediction that Austria would be too weak to survive economically. The experience of a period of unbroken economic growth and unparalleled prosperity provided the basis for a new belief in Austria's stability. The fact that this stability was based, among other things, on a strong dependence—on Western Europe in general, on Germany in particular—did not shake that belief.

One of the two main factors that characterized Austria's economy, delay, has been overcome. The other one, dependence, seems to be stronger than ever. But this is less and less dependence in a traditional sense—the dependence of a small country in the economic periphery of a major country in the economic center. It is increasingly a new kind of dependence: dependence on an economic logic that goes beyond national boundaries. The foreign corporations that play an important role in Austria may be based in Germany, but they are not part of a political conspiracy to undermine Austria's independence, as was the case prior to 1938. These corporations are not German (or French or American or Italian) in any traditional sense. Their sole interest lies in maximizing profit, not in fulfilling a political mission.

This is the logic of globalization. The global economy is not ruled by players with specific national interests. In the field of global economic competition, nationality has become obsolete. Austria's dependence is not so much on Germany and certain German interests. Instead, it has become the dependence of a rather prosperous but smaller country, a country that—for historic reasons—is not home to major corporations. But in principle, Austria's dependence is no longer different from the economic dependence all nations have learned to accept. Austria's economic dependence has ceased to be specifically Austrian.

Austria has accepted this kind of dependence by joining the European Union. In dropping the illusion of economic independence, Austria has become a minor factor in the attempt to counter some of the effects of globalization. By establishing themselves as one major player with a single market and a single currency, the prosperous countries of Europe are trying to redefine the global economic game (Matzner 1996). Austria's intention to participate in this game of globalization is now based on the Europeanization of its interests.

7

A FAREWELL TO
CORPORATISM?

Corporatism is a concept that must overcome some historical burdens, among them its continuing association with fascism. The Italian, but also the Spanish and the Portuguese, variety of corporatism claimed to replace class war with class cooperation dictated and guaranteed by an authoritarian state. The goal of fascism Mediterranean-style was to put an end to parliament and political parties and all the ruffians who used democracy as a pretext to make profits for themselves or for their employers, who were sometimes seen in the Kremlin and sometimes on Wall Street.

Social partnership is the friendly Austrian version of this skeleton in the closet. It is friendly because it is not the product of authoritarianism. Nobody is forced to participate in corporatist arrangements, and labor unions are not disbanded and reestablished under the immediate dictate of a nondemocratic government. There is no claim that social partnership is the antithesis to competitive democracy, the multiparty system, and parliament. Austro-corporatism is a very decent, very civilized way of doing the same thing: replacing class war with class cooperation (Bischof and Pelinka 1996).

There has been a less friendly Austrian version of corporatism. The authoritarian regime was a "Ständestaat"—the German term for "estato corporativo." And Mussolini was one of the protectors of the experiment that Dollfuss and Schuschnigg wanted to succeed. The "Ständestaat" was called "Austrofascism" for good reasons (Tálos and Neugebauer 1988).

The authoritarian regime had another protector, and that was the pope. Pius XI's encyclica "Quadragesimo anno" was seen as a basic document for the social order the "Ständestaat" wanted to construct. The leading philosophy was to reconcile the classes, which were incited by the two extremes that the Catholic social doctrine blamed for the "social question": liberalism and socialism. The former was identified with unrestricted capitalism, the latter with the message of atheism and social hatred. Mussolini, the former socialist, supported the antisocialist and antiparliamentarian tendencies of the Austrian government; Pius XI moderated fascism. The fact that the Ständestaat called itself "Christian" made a difference, not only to Nazism but to Italian fascism too.

The influence the Catholic Church had in defining the authoritarian regime's self-image was the consequence of the influence the pope, the bishops, and the their social doctrine had already had on the Christian Social Party before 1934 (Diamant 1960). Political Catholicism, the formula of the Christian Social Party in the First Republic, was still the formula of the authoritarian regime whose elite consisted of the very same people who had ruled Austria under democratic and republican auspices until 1934. Austro-corporatism between 1934 and 1938 was considered at least as "Christian" as it was "fascist."

What was defined as social partnership in Austria after 1945 had nothing to do with this nondemocratic experience. But it had something to do with the perspective of both the Dollfuss and the Schuschnigg governments. And it had something to do with the key players that the authoritarian and the democratic version of Austro-corporatism had in common: Almost all the People's Party representatives involved in constructing social partnership after 1945 had already had experience in pre-1938 corporatism.

Social partnership was and is intended to moderate the main conflict of modern society: the conflict between business and labor, between employers and employees. All three models the pope had in mind—liberalism, socialism, and corporatism—were based on that conflict. All three models agree that this conflict is the primary one and had to be adapted or transformed into a stable political system. The liberal approach tended to declare some basic rights and rules and then abstain from interference. The socialist approach was based on a zero-sum game hypothesis: Nothing but the ultimate victory of socialism would end the contradiction between the classes. The corporatist approach was and is compromise oriented and interventionist.

It was not this philosophy that distinguished post-1945 from pre-1938 corporatism. It was the inclusion of Social Democrats that made all the difference. Pre-1938 corporatism was built on the breakup of the republican constitution and on the defeat of the Social Democratic Party and social democratic labor unions. For the left, this kind of corporatism was nothing but dictatorship in disguise. Post-1945 corporatism had to be based on the Second Republic's consensus, on the historic compromise between the Christian-conservative and the socialist camps. For the left, social partnership had to begin from zero.

Not so for the right. The ÖVP had about the same political personnel as the authoritarian regime, and the social partners dominated by the ÖVP had to make use of that personnel. For the Chambers of Commerce and the Chambers of Agriculture, the new social partnership was not so different from the old. Elitist continuity was the rule on the right—a continuity broken by seven years of Nazi rule.

The case that best exemplifies this continuity is that of Julius Raab (Brusatti and Heindl n.d.). Raab, born in 1891 in St. Pölten, was a typical product of the Christian-conservative camp. He was politically socialized by the Catholic milieu into which he was born. During his studies to become an engineer, he joined one of the Catholic students' fraternities from the Cartellverband (CV), which was the most important recruiting base for the Christian Social Party and later the ÖVP. After World War I, in which Raab served as an officer, he entered politics. By 1927, he had become member of parliament. He represented both of the two competing wings within his Christian Social Party, the traditionalists with their roots back in the monarchy and the "young Turks" who were strongly influenced by the antiparliamentary tendencies from the more extreme right.

Raab became leader of the "Heimwehr" of Lower Austria in 1928. The Heimwehr was a right-wing militia with a radical antisocialist and somewhat antidemocratic agenda. Raab's intention was to maintain the linkage between the more and more openly anticonstitutional tendencies of the Heimwehr movement and his party. In that sense, he was a moderate among the militant leaders of the Heimwehr. But even the moderate Raab accepted the official program of the Heimwehr as expressed in the oath of Korneuburg in 1930 (Wiltschegg n.d.). The Korneuburg oath consisted of several paragraphs, some of them as antidemocratic as the following: "We reject western democratic parliamentarism and the party state." But there were also passages that could be read as the blueprint for a corporatist state. Instead of parliament and party-state, the oath declared: "We want to put in its place the self-administration of the corporations and a strong state leadership. . . . We are fighting against the disintegration of our people by the Marxist class struggle and the liberal capitalist economic order" (Edmondson 1978: 98 f.).

Here it was, the theoretical claim that corporatism was something antithetical both to socialism and to capitalism. The Korneuburg oath was the combination of the Catholic social doctrine and fascism as already established in neighboring Italy.

The moderate Raab and his Lower Austrian Heimwehr organization stayed within the Christian Social Party. Other regional organizations broke away, competing for seats in parliament independently from the Christian Socials in 1930. Raab was reelected on the Christian Social ticket. His power base was the "Deutschösterreichische Gewerbebund" (German-Austrian Business Organization), whose name indicated the still self-evident pan-German feeling that dominated the political thinking far beyond the borders of the pan-German camp (Dippelreiter n.d.). In 1933, Raab along with all the other leading Christian Socials joined the "Vaterländische Front" (Fatherland Front, VF), the umbrella organization Dollfuss wanted to build for his authoritarian regime. In 1934, the VF became the monopolistic political organization of the "Ständestaat."

Raab was influential in constructing the corporate elements of this regime. He represented the owners of small business. In 1934, he became chairman of the

"Österreichischer Gewerbebund" (Austrian Business Association), which was integrated into the VF. One year later, he also became chairman of the "Bund Österreichischer Gewerbetreibender" (Association of Austrian Businessmen), the parallel organization within the corporate structures of the authoritarian regime. As the employers' representative, he was a leading figure of the regime. In 1938, he was even in the top echelon of Austrian politics: for about three weeks (February 16 to March 11) he was minister of trade in Schuschnigg's last cabinet before the "Anschluss."

During the Nazi years, he worked as an engineer and was observed by the Gestapo but not imprisoned. He was one of the small group of people who founded the ÖVP in Vienna on April 17, 1945, and belonged to the innermost circle running the People's Party from its very beginning. He was a member of the Provisional Government the Social Democrat Karl Renner founded with the ÖVP and the Communists on April 27, 1945. He was the only member of the last Schuschnigg cabinet who also served in the first cabinet of the Second Republic—an example of continuity second only to Karl Renner, who as state chancellor and head of a provisional government was twice "founder" of the republic, in 1918 as well as in 1945.

In the Renner government, Raab was responsible for public construction, economic transition, and reconstruction. He represented the business interests and helped form the Austrian Business League (ÖWB), which became one of the three pillars on which the People's Party was built: the ÖAAB for employees, the ÖBB for farmers, and the ÖWB for employers. This structure reflected the corporatist thinking the People's Party wanted to carry over from the authoritarian regime into the new democratic era.

Raab was elected to the National Council on November 25, 1945. The elections put to an end the Provisional Government and the tripartite balance between SPÖ, ÖVP, and KPÖ. The KPÖ won only 5 percent of the votes, significantly less than expected, and was relegated to a minor role. The ÖVP received 50 percent of the votes and a majority in the National Council, but as agreed in advance, wanted to prolong the coalition with the SPÖ and even—until 1947—with the KPÖ.

The grand coalition was born as a consequence of elitist learning. The very same politicians—the most prominent among them Renner and Raab—who had not been able to find a way to stabilize Austrian democracy by means of compromise before 1938 were now responsible for the construction of the institutionalized networks of consociational democracy.

When Karl Renner became federal president, and Leopold Figl as federal chancellor and Adolf Schärf as vice-chancellor nominated the members of the new government, which was no longer called "provisional," Raab should have become minister of trade. Surprisingly, the Soviet authorities vetoed Raab's appointment to this cabinet position (Bergmann and Wögerbauer n.d.: 128). It was a surprise in many respects:

- The USSR had accepted Raab as a member of the Renner cabinet in April 1945, when the Soviet influence on Austrian politics was much stronger than in December of the same year. In April, more than half of Austria was still occupied by German troops. At that time, the Western Allies, who had not yet arrived on Austrian territory, had no say in accepting or rejecting the Provisional Government. More than half a year later, when the Western powers had fully established their presence and already had played a role in the planning of the first free general elections in Austria since 1930, the Soviet authorities vetoed a person who had already served as a cabinet member and managed to avoid any conflicts with the USSR or even specifically with the KPÖ.

- The USSR had shown no interest in insisting that the "antifascist" rhetoric and philosophy the Provisional Government had used to gain recognition should now be directed not only at the representatives of the Nazi regime but also at politicians of the Dollfuss-Schuschnigg era. The Soviets wanted Raab's position in the last Schusschnigg cabinet to be an obstacle for his further career in the Figl-Schärf cabinet because he was considered to be a "fascist" (Fischer 1973: 217). This inconsistency doesn't seem to have anything to do with Raab as a person. The only reasonable explanation for the new Soviet attitude was the Soviet irritation after the Communist electoral defeat. Raab had to be a kind of lightning rod.

It is especially ironic that Raab was not acceptable to the USSR because he was to become the Austrian politician the Soviet representatives could rely upon most. The future chancellor who came to be identified more than anyone else with the accord of 1955, the compromise with Moscow, was used as a scapegoat by disappointed officers of Soviet occupational forces. But Raab was elected to other positions at least as important as a cabinet position would have been. In 1945, he was elected chairman of the People's Party parliamentary group (faction or club) in the newly elected National Council, and in 1946, he became president of the Federal Chamber of Commerce, the newly founded umbrella organization of all the already existing chambers of commerce.

It was the latter position that Raab used to enhance his reputation as a man of social compromise, of social peace. As head of the most important employers' association, he was able to bridge the gap with the labor organizations, the Federation of Austrian Trade Unions (ÖGB), which like its counterpart the Federal Chamber was also an offspring of the Second Republic's network-building tendencies.

Raab's counterpart was Johann Böhm, representative of the construction workers' union and president of the ÖGB. Böhm, like Raab, was a political product of the Austrian Empire's twilight and the First Republic's centrifugal democracy (Böhm 1964). Böhm was prominent in the SPÖ leadership. Together, he and Raab were an ideal combination of the authority necessary to maximize the legitimacy of overcoming traditional limits and moving on to new frontiers. Raab and Böhm had the greatest possible formal power within the rather centralized new institutions the coalition had shaped for employers and employees. Furthermore, Raab and Böhm both belonged to the top elite of their respective parties. They were able to combine what was to become the corporate state with the already existing party state. Raab and Böhm became the personification of Austro-corporatism because they came out of the past and because they were able to speak not only for employers and employees but also, at the same time, for the ÖVP and the SPÖ.

Between 1947 and 1951, the major economic interest groups and the government agreed on a total of five accords on wages and prices. The background was the "stagflation" that had to be dealt with in the first years of the Second Republic: high unemployment and low economic growth accompanied by extremely high inflation. The institutional structure responsible for the accords was the Economic Commission founded by the Federal Chamber, the ÖGB, the Chambers of Labor, and the Chambers of Agriculture in 1947. This was the same "mix" that would be able to create the Joint Commission on Wages and Prices ten years later.

From the very beginning of the Austrian brand of corporatism, of social partnership, Raab expressed a clear creed: Employers must exercise self-restraint. If they did not wish to be controlled by the government and especially if they did not want to produce any pretext or reason for successful Communist propaganda, they had to abstain from exploiting any opportunity to raise prices. Voluntary price control—this was the golden rule Raab preached in the late 1940s (Klose n.d.: 168). And in the late 1940s, it was comparatively easy to convince employers that moderation would be in their own interests. In Austria's neighboring countries, Communist takeovers established "People's Democracies" as "anticapitalist" regimes: in Hungary in 1947 and in Czechoslovakia in 1948. To prevent a similar development in Austria, the formula of consociational democracy had to be respected, and the ÖVP and SPÖ, as well as employers and employees, had to compromise. Raab successfully convinced his side that it was better to negotiate with the labor unions than to confront them.

The fourth wage and price agreement from late summer of 1950 provoked a Communist attack on social partnership. The Communist policy of September and October 1950 had been the object of a double myth:

- The Communists insisted that their call for a general strike was purely for reasons of social protest, that it was highly legitimate and widely accepted—not only by Communists. The ÖGB leadership's strong condemnation of the strike was clear proof of how far the ÖGB and the SPÖ had already followed the path toward treason in class warfare.
- For the anti-Communists from both major camps, the KPÖ's strike slogans were just the beginning of a "putsch" designed to bring about in Austria the same fate Hungary and Czechoslovakia had to endure. Thanks to the heroic resistance of Austrians, this master plan did not succeed.

The truth is somewhere in between; or rather the truth lies elsewhere. The Communists' policy of using the fourth wage and price agreement as a pretext for a general strike was clearly politically motivated and had to do with the international situation. Just a few weeks earlier, the Korean War had started, and the United States began to have second thoughts about German disarmament. But a "putsch" in the real sense of the word, an extraconstitutional and violent takeover of the government, was not in the cards and was never really attempted. This would have been achievable only by engaging the Red Army, which still had its troops stationed in about one-third of the Austrian territory, and by confronting the Western Allies, which occupied the rest of the country. Any "putsch" would have only resulted in the division of Austria. This was clearly not the intention of Austrian Communists and especially not of Soviet leaders (Bader 1966: 155–183; Fischer 1973: 297–330; Gärtner 1979: 123–120; Ludwig, Mulley, and Streibel 1991).

The "great strike," as it was called by the Communists, or the "Communist putsch," as it was called by the anti-Communists, was an important watershed: It signified that the bond between Social Democrats and (former) Christian Socials was already strong enough to withstand attacks from the Communist left, even when the Communists used leftist paroles and appealed to leftist sentiments still existent among the majority of organized labor. But anticommunism had become an integral part of the consensus the two major camps had established on the elite level first. The strike that the Communists had organized was a kind of populist attempt against the compromise orientation of the elites. This attempt failed because both the "black" and "red" elites were able use anticommunism to mobilize the rank and file, especially within the social democratic masses.

The Communist attempt was directed against social partnership. The formula "compromise instead of confrontation" did not fit into the Marxist tradition that the SPÖ was still proud of. The class enemy was not to be trusted. A lasting compromise was contradictory to the nature of class warfare. For orthodox Marxists, the defense of social partnership was nothing less than capitulation.

The class enemy during these first years of the Second Republic was personified by Julius Raab. As an engineer who was never a top executive of any major corporation, he did not project the image of a bloodthirsty capitalist. He was a true representative of Austria's employers, most of whom were owners of small businesses. There was not much "big capital" in Austria after 1945, and the major industries and banks were nationalized in 1946 and 1947. Raab and his chamber represented not big but rather small capitalists.

Raab became chairman of the ÖVP in 1951 and chancellor in 1953. In both functions he was successor to his close friend Leopold Figl. From 1953 on, he was especially active in establishing confidence with the Soviet leadership. When a window of opportunity opened in 1955, Raab became the chancellor identified with the State Treaty, with the retreat of the occupational powers, and with Austria's declaration of neutrality.

But Raab was still the man who represented business interests. When it came to "historic compromises," he was in the unique position of being able to make use of his double function as head of government and as party leader. He had to resign as president of the Federal Chamber when he became chancellor. But he was still seen as the man business interests could identify with. In 1957, he and Johann Böhm made the crowning deal of their careers: They founded the Joint Commission on Wages and Prices. Raab asked the Council of Ministers to invite the presidents of the four economic associations, which had already established the Economic Commission in 1947, to join the government in a new institution, the Joint Commission (Klose n.d.: 172 f.).

This formal invitation was of course informally agreed on in advance by Raab and Böhm. Raab could speak for the government, for one of the coalition partners, and indirectly also for business. Böhm could speak for labor, for the second coalition partner, and indirectly for parliament—he was at that time second president of the National Council. Together, the two of them held all the strings that had to be pulled to get things moving.

There was also one aspect of this Raab-Böhm relationship that must be considered typical for Austro-corporatism: the lack of any constitutional function. Neither Raab nor Böhm were in the least interested in making the Joint Commission a legal institution with a specific place in the constitution. The Joint Commission was to be extraconstitutional. The reason behind this was the fear that some judges, perhaps even the Constitutional Court, might want to interfere by ruling on what the Joint Commission was allowed to do and not do. The social partners wanted to enjoy a maximum of flexibility. To this end, they were ready to relinquish any claim to a constitutional status. Another consequence of this flexibility was that the Joint Commission could not use formal sanctions. The social partnership had no power to enforce its policies. The only method of implementing its decisions was persuasion. And the task of persuading fell to the side involved: The Federal Chamber had to persuade the employers to refrain from overaggressive policies, especially concerning prices. The ÖGB had the same task: to moderate the unions' attitude, especially concerning their wage policies. The biggest success of Austro-corporatism is that it worked because it was based on voluntary agreements and not on laws (Pelinka 1981; Marin 1982).

The Joint Commission started with an emphasis on price control. In 1957, there was only one subcommittee—the one on prices. The idea was to have any price increase justified by voluntary control through this subcommittee. In 1962, a second subcommittee on wages was added. This subcommittee was to approve any wage agreement between any specific union and any employers' branch, thus providing for a balance in wage developments. In 1963, the third subcommittee was added, the Council of Social and Economic Advisers (Beirat für Wirtschafts- und Sozialfragen).

Raab was involved in all these developments. When he left the chancellorship in 1961, having stepped down as party chairman one year earlier, he again became president of the Federal Chamber. In this old-new capacity, he was still a key figure in Austro-corporatism and in Austrian politics in general. It was Raab and Johann Böhm's successors in the ÖGB presidency, Franz Olah (1962) and Anton

Benya (1963), who signed the documents creating the Joint Commission's second and third subcommittees.

In 1963, Raab was nominated as the ÖVP candidate for the federal presidency. He lost the election to the incumbent, Adolf Schärf. When Raab died in 1964, he was the honorary chairman of the ÖVP and still active president of the Federal Chamber of Commerce. Johann Böhm, who was five years older, had died five years earlier, in 1959.

The golden age of social partnership was the era after the establishment of the Council of Social and Economic Advisers. The subcommittees on wages and prices had given the Joint Commission the power to make decisions, and that power was in the hands of experts from the four major economic interest groups. The Joint Commission had always had the reputation of not needing its own bureaucracy. It made use of the apparatus that already existed in the three chamber organizations (labor, commerce, and agriculture) and in the ÖGB. The subcommittees on wages and prices had to meet behind closed doors and reach unanimous decisions about very somber problems, for example, whether to grant the Austrian paper industry a 5 percent price increase or whether to approve the wage agreement between the steel industry and the union of metal, mining, and energy workers. Those decisions are (or at least can be) important but certainly not exciting.

Exciting is, however, the perfect word to describe the impact the Council of Economic and Social Advisers had, first on social partnership and then on Austrian politics in general. The basis of the council was a techno-scientific understanding of economics and economic policies (Marin 1982: 255–399). The council brought together the young generation of academically trained experts coming from both sides: from the social democratic camp, through the ÖGB and chambers of labor, and from the Christian-conservative camp, through the chambers of commerce and of agriculture.

The Council of Economic and Social Advisers is not a decisionmaking body. It is there to recommend certain policies and to work in a prognostic way. Its task is to plan the future. Because it does not have to make decisions and come to a consensus, the council allows dissenting opinions. From its start in 1963, the council was the level that produced the "new technocratic intelligence" and that at the same time endowed this intelligence with a specific assurance (Marin 1982: 266).

One of the council's key figures in its first years, Alfred Klose, uses the term "Versachlichung" (making politics less political) to describe the council's effect (Klose 1970: 66). This term includes a variety of aspects:

- De-ideologization. The goal of the Council of Economic and Social Advisers was and is to play down "ideological" differences and to look for solutions based on "scientific" knowledge that go beyond interests. The gap between socialism and capitalism, between interventionism and the free market, was seen as secondary compared with the difference between "good" (consistent) and "bad" (inconsistent) solutions.

- Cleavage between an academic or "scientific" approach to politics and pure party politics. There was something of a generation gap in the attitude of the young, who were often experts with international experience in both labor and business, toward the old guard, who were less academic and less internationally oriented. The council was an assembly of "modernists" confronting "antimodernists."
- Philosophy of economic growth. In the 1960s and early 1970s, economic thinking had not yet been confronted with the basic opposition of environmentalists. Ecology was not a word many had heard. Therefore the council and its young experts emphasized the necessity of economic growth with almost no resistance. Growth was defined as the key to avoiding distribution conflicts. If everybody got more, then there would be no cost-intensive conflicts. Growth was the antithesis to class warfare.

From 1963 on, the council was used as a reservoir for a new breed of politicians. When Josef Klaus became chancellor in 1964, he appointed Wolfgang Schmitz as his minister of finance. Schmitz came from the Federal Chamber and had experience in the still very young council. When Bruno Kreisky nominated his cabinet members, he used the same reservoir. He recruited Ernst Eugen Veselsky, an expert employed by the Viennese Chamber of Labor and a leading member of the Council of Economic and Social Advisers, for the position of secretary of state in the Chancellery. These are just two examples of the generational takeover. The Council, the Joint Commission, and the social partnership all promoted a generation of political leaders who, despite being "black" or "red," had not been socialized by the conflicts and ideologies that ruled the First Republic.

In 1966, the cooperation between the social partners was seen as the prolongation of the grand coalition by different means. The SPÖ went into opposition, but the ÖGB and the chambers of labor still had the power of veto in all the fields ruled by Austro-corporatism. This was really the most important era of social partnership and of the Joint Commission especially: It functioned as a substitute for the grand coalition.

One of the factors responsible for the kind of mystique surrounding the term social partnership is that it is seen in combination with psychological and personal factors. There are two variations of this nonstructural interpretation:

- Social partnership is primarily the result of the personal chemistry between a small number of leaders, especially seen in a dualistic perspective. In the 1950s, it was Raab and Böhm. In the 1970s, the duo was Rudolf Sallinger, president of the Federal Chamber after Raab, and Anton Benya, who became ÖGB president after Franz Olah in 1963 (Gerlich 1992: 136).
- Social partnership is part of the Austrian national character. According to this interpretation, Austrians tend to be more pragmatic and more adaptive and more compromise oriented than other people. Social partnership is the way of life that distinguishes Austrians from the rest of the world.

TABLE 7.1   Economic and Political Reasons to Be Proud of Austria
Survey 1987, representative sample

Reasons to Be	Proud	Not Proud
Austria as tourist attraction	91%	6%
Domestic security, low crime rate	75%	18%
Social security	72%	23%
Vienna as a congress city	69%	23%
Social partnership	63%	28%
Austria's international role	56%	37%
Modern technological development	46%	44%
Position of Austria's economy	42%	49%
Dealing with environmental problems	23%	69%

SOURCE: Bruckmüller 1994: 29.

Another aspect of the myth of social partnership is that most Austrians are "proud" of it, like other countries are proud of Nobel Prize winners or of heroic aspects of national history (see Table 7.1).

The perspective on social partnership is linked to an overall orientation toward security. Social partnership provides Austrians with the feeling that they are protected and secure. This feeling is not at all irrational. One impact social partnership has, and probably its most important, is to minimize all sorts of social costs through low unemployment, a small number of strikes, and all sorts of welfare arrangements. Organized labor in Austria has been trading its power not for a socialist society, not for a transformation of capitalism into socialism, but for the establishment of the best possible welfare state within capitalism. Welfare state security—that is the formula social partnership is using, and that is the reason behind its extremely high rate of acceptance.

But power must be traded. There is nothing "natural" behind a system's transformation into a welfare state. It is a complex mixture of pressures and counterpressures. The employers who are conceding more social benefits in Austria are neither poor entrepreneurs nor "bleeding hearts" nor less intelligent than employers elsewhere. By compromising on all the social and economic policy aspects affected by social partnership, the employers are responding to a political situation, for instance to the relative strength of organized labor and to the relative weakness of organized business in Austria. The personal factor is the reaction to this situation, and that is where the elitist level comes in. The leading representatives of labor can overplay their hands—or not. The same is true in the case of business leaders. Moderation is not something that is a "natural" part of a "national character"; it is the result of learning in combination with objective factors. As soon as these objective factors begin to change significantly, the personal response either becomes obsolete or must also change.

When Austrian social partnership was at its peak, during the years between the grand coalitions, the acceptance of social partnership was also at its highest level.

But the tendency was to look for security at a time when the confrontation between the two major parties in parliament seemed to reduce consensus, which explains this preference for social partnership. A study in the Kreisky era showed that 21 percent of Austrians wanted to have a more influential social partnership but only 9 percent wanted a more influential parliament (Gerlich and Ucakar 1981: 185).

What both approaches—seeing social partnership as part of Austria's "national character" and seeing it as dependent on the good will of a small number of persons—have in common is that they avoid naming the political conditions of Austro-corporatism. They also forget that prior to 1938, the Austrian national character was not able to produce any kind of stability similar to the post-1945 social partnership. The political factors in their vertical (elite-followers) and their horizontal dimension (left-right), the pressures and incentives from the international system—all this can be ignored. The view of social partnership as something typical for Austria and the Austrians implies the tendency to see social partnership not as a dynamic but rather as a static phenomenon.

This static perspective is wrong from an analytical perspective. It is pure nonsense to think that "the Austrians" are less inclined to use violent methods in politics than Spaniards, Finns, Japanese, or Germans. A simple look into Austria's past, including the history of the First Republic, proves this interpretation wrong. But the static perspective is also wrong from a prognostic point of view. The perception of social partnership as something that belongs to Austria like landscape and climate precludes the sensitivity that is necessary for an early response to new challenges.

For analytical and for prognostic reasons, the conditions under which Austro-corporatism was developed after 1945 must be taken into account (Tálos and Kittel 1996; Kindley 1996). And because political conditions are never completely stable, the possibility of changes in those conditions must also be observed.

The conditions that made Austro-corporatism possible can be summed up as follows (Pelinka 1981: 15–61; Gerlich 1992: 135–138):

- Duopoly: The bargaining power must be reduced as much as possible. The optimal degree of reduction is to two: a labor organization that speaks with one voice as well as a business organization with the same ability. The foundation of the ÖGB in 1945 and of the Federal Chamber of Commerce in 1946 guaranteed this condition.
- Centralization: The leadership on both sides must command the maximum of internal authority. It is the ÖGB, and not the different unions, and the Federal Chamber, and not the different sections, that have to act. Decisions are made at the national level, and the state level has to follow. Social partnership is a system that works from the top down.
- Hierarchy: Internal discipline should be highly developed and respected. Internal democracy is of secondary importance. The hegemony that the leading factions (FSG in the ÖGB and in the Chambers of Labor, ÖWB in

the Chambers of Commerce, ÖBB in the Chambers of Agriculture) enjoy should be as dominant as possible.

- Informality: Decisionmaking within the Joint Commission and the other institutions of social partnership should be not formalized. Their extra-constitutional status is therefore desirable. The leaders of both sides should be allowed to confer behind closed doors. This increases the ability to compromise.
- Introversion: Each side has to exclude options that are simply unacceptable to the other side. "The participants tend to limit their attention only to those activities which fall into the framework of their common philosophy" (Gerlich 1992: 137).

The common philosophy is stability through economic growth. Social partnership by its very nature is not capable of agreeing on a redistribution of wealth that gives preferential treatment to one side over the other. That implies an orientation toward the status quo. And that makes social partnership vulnerable: It is not able to integrate new value orientations, new interests, or new movements that are not closely packed into the existing institutions. By virtue of its nature, social partnership is structurally conservative.

This is the first weakness of social partnership—its difficulty to adapt, to learn. The whole "techno-scientific" orientation, especially as expressed by the Council of Economic and Social Advisers, needs a stable framework. Any innovative changes that come not from within but from the outside must be seen as a disturbance.

The second weakness is that there are economic and international preconditions that cannot be influenced by Austrian institutions. The term "Austro-Keynesianism" (Seidel 1996) describes the ability to steer the Austrian economy by a mixture of state intervention and corporatist agreement. But what about the integration of Austrian economy into a European or even a global market?

In 1945 and after, the balance between labor and business was the balance between comparatively strong labor and comparatively weak business. There was not much big business in Austria. The industries and banks had to be nationalized because there was no private Austrian entrepreneurship willing and able to take over what was left of "German property." Private business was small business—as represented by Julius Raab. And the existence of nationalized industries and nationalized banks clearly helped the rise of social partnership: The fact that industry and banking were divided into "black" and "red" zones of influence and clientelism prevented some of the traditional profit orientations of the management. Due to this construction, management either was or had to be friendly toward organized labor (Mathis 1995). Even U.S. interests represented in the Marshall Plan cooperated in full harmony with the nationalized industry and with the corporatist arrangements the nationalization had strengthened (Tweraser 1995).

These two weaknesses existed only in theory until the 1980s. But in that decade, three factors disrupted the paradise of social stability and political harmony:

- New social movements challenged the philosophy of economic growth. Specifically, social partnership was unable to integrate the agenda of the ecological movement. The feminist movement also proved easier to integrate through political parties and parliament than through economic associations and social partnership (Natter 1987; Appelt 1993).
- The crisis of nationalized industry started the process of privatization, leading to the increase of foreign influence on the Austrian economy. The "flagships" of Austrian industry had to be broken up and some of them sold to foreign investors (Lauber 1992: 163–170).
- The new orientation of Austrian politics toward participation in the single European market further eroded a vital component of Austro-corporatism and Austro-Keynesianism, namely, the ability to steer the economy.

As a result of these developments, the importance of social partnership has been reduced. And this especially affects the Joint Commission on Wages and Prices because within a single European market the mechanism of voluntary price control by an Austrian institution can no longer work. The connection between the government and the Joint Commission, long symbolically expressed by the plenary meetings headed by the federal chancellor and attended by other cabinet members, ceased to exist in the 1990s: In 1995, a laconic report read: "In 1994, there was no plenary meeting of the Joint Commission on Prices and Wages" (Jahrbuch 1995: 38).

This has something to do with power. The decline of nationalized industry and the increasing importance of foreign capital reduced the relative weight of organized labor. The deterioration of the labor market added to this development. The power balance of the 1990s is not the same as it was in the 1950s, 1960s, and 1970s. Business has gained importance while labor has lost power as a result not of political and domestic developments but rather of economic and international developments.

Because Austro-corporatism is not the product of an Austrian national character, Austro-corporatism must be affected. And this effect has two aspects:

- Social partnership is becoming slim. Some areas of power will be eliminated because social partnership is no longer strong enough to conduct business as usual.
- Social partnership has embraced Europe. The main actors of Austro-corporatism have become prophets of the new Europe, especially of the European Union.

As early as in 1992, the presidents of the four major interest groups that make up the Joint Commission signed a paper that changed the responsibility of the Subcommittee on Prices—from price control to studying market tendencies (see Figure 7.1). And as a consequence of the European orientation, a new Subcommittee on International Relations was established (Karlhofer and Tálos 1996: 207–211).

FIGURE 7.1   The Structure of the Joint Commission

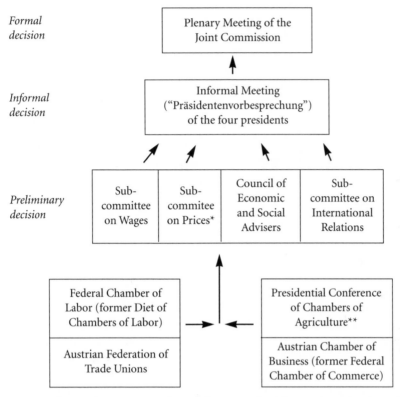

*According to the agreement of November 1992, the Subcommittee on prices will shift its price control authority to the general observation of market conditions.

**The Chambers of Agriculture are of minor importance for business-labor relations. They are members of the Joint Commission primarily to keep the balance between interest groups dominated by the SPÖ and ÖVP.

SOURCE: Karlhofer and Tálos 1996: 30.

The reform of the Joint Commission took place even before Austria entered the European Union. The end to any attempt at price control, started in 1957 (and based on the experiments since 1947), means that Austro-corporatism has surrendered its most prominent feature: voluntary price control without government regulation. Corporatism has capitulated. The market has thrown off the restrictions of corporate arrangements. Austria has taken a decisive step toward European normality—more market and less control.

The key players of Austro-corporatism were not passive observers of this development. They had actively participated in establishing the priority of a market economy over any "mixed" economy so typical for the golden era of Austro-Keynesianism and Austro-corporatism. The major economic associations played a very helpful role in legitimizing Austria's move toward full integration into the European market. In 1988, the federal government had asked the social partners for their opinion about possible Austrian European Community (EC) membership (from 1994 on, the EU). On March 1, 1989, this opinion was ready: All four associations of the Joint Commission openly emphasized the advantages EC membership would have for Austria. They stressed their readiness to actively cooperate in all further steps in that direction. Other joint declarations followed, all of them backing the government's orientation in favor of EC membership (Karlhofer and Tálos 1996: 203–206).

On the surface this might seem almost incredible: The economic associations applauded and actively supported the turn in Austrian politics that would no doubt significantly reduce their political weight. The main explanation for this astonishing behavior, which can easily be interpreted as a policy of self-mutilation, is the loss of creed. The social partners and especially the younger generation of experts with their "techno-scientific" approach—the generation that succeeded the council's founding generation of the 1960s—saw no alternative to this EC orientation. European integration and its new dynamics would affect Austria anyway. Therefore it would be better for Austria not just to wait for the effects but to participate in the process that would happen with or without Austria's consent (Karlhofer and Tálos 1996: 59–63).

This loss of creed is the loss of belief in Austria's ability to control its own future with the degree of independence implied by its nickname, "island of the blessed." There was no special Austrian way of circumventing the logic of a globalized economy. There was no policy or plan that Austria could rely upon to overcome negative tendencies in the labor market as a result of the global division in high-cost and low-cost production. Austria could mollify the social consequences, but only within certain limits. And even an Austrian policy of mollification would be easier to implement from within the European Union.

Economic dependence provided the background for the reduction of Austrian politics. It is not the dependence of small Austria on big Germany but rather the dependence of small, wealthy, and highly developed Austria on a market that is no longer divided into countries and nations. This kind of dependence is the product of processes that Austria cannot influence in any significant way. The conclusion is a kind of Machiavellian resignation: If you cannot prevent something, you should join and insist that it is of your own free will. If you can't lick 'em, join 'em.

Of course, corporatism is not dead. There is plenty for the economic interest groups to do, both in Austria and in the European Union. There are interesting signs of a new Euro-corporatism: the Social Dialogue, which started in 1992 and establishes permanent communication between social partners on the EU level; the Economic and Social Committee, which consists of social partners from the (now) fifteen member states, a committee designed to assist the EU Commission; the development of European umbrella organizations such as the European Federation of Trade Unions; and the development of codetermination that transcends national borders, one example being the Euro-Shop-Stewards (Karlhofer and Tálos 1996: 118–134).

Of course, corporatism will also continue to be in great demand in Austria. There are still enlightened entrepreneurs who believe that it is better to compromise with labor than to confront it. There is still the Second Republic's philosophy that Austrians are above taking to the streets to fight for social interests. There is still the need to bargain for wages, to find ways to finance social security, and to deal with the social and economic effects of immigration. These are just a few of the reasons why the best possible climate between social partners will be very much in demand.

The problem is only whether all the players can agree. And there are new players, who can no longer be ignored as they were in the past. The new players are corporations that are not based in Austria. Why should they accept the rules of the corporatist game? Why should they bother about social peace if rising unemployment in Austria virtually eliminates any threat of a strike? Why should any dynamic young Austrian industrialist accept cost-intensive agreements if he (or she) thinks that the market will reward the neglect of voluntary obligations? Why should an opposition party such as the FPÖ respect a political culture from which it justifiably feels excluded? Social partnership was never a love affair. It was always based on cost-benefit analysis.

There is not much likelihood of a total breakdown of Austro-corporatism in the near future. The most realistic scenarios are predicting not collapse but further decline. Corporatism will not disappear, it will simply fade away (Gerlich 1992: 143–145; Karlhofer and Tálos 1996: 171–180; Prisching 1996). There is a future for Austro-corporatism, but compared with its past, it will be a rather modest one. Economic interest groups, facing increasing internal criticism and their own diminishing capability to synchronize their policies with the (no longer so) major political parties, will represent a slim network of corporatist intermediation, which has already surrendered much of its power to the logic of the market.

Something called social partnership will continue to exist. But it will have little in common with what people like Julius Raab and Johann Böhm established as the Second Republic's proudest product of domestic politics.

Social partnership in the form of strong corporatism has outlived its usefulness. It is unlikely that a simple handshake between any future ÖGB president and his counterpart from the Chamber of Business will have the kind of decisive impact on Austrian politics that it had in the past. The interests are much less homogenous and are becoming even more fragmented. The more the Austrian economy follows the pattern of the market, the less control political organizations will have over it. The ideological spectrum within both labor and business will become too broad to be handled with old corporatist methods.

Social partnership has had its merits in the process of social, economic, and political stabilization. Now stabilized, Austrian society no longer needs such a strong cartel of interests. The true success of Austrian corporatism is that it is being eliminated as a result of its success.

8

■■■■■■

A FAREWELL TO
NEUTRALITY

Officially, Austria became a neutral country when the National Council passed the Neutrality Act ("Bundesverfassungsgesetz über die immerwährende Neutralität") on October 26, 1955. This unilateral declaration was accepted by the two coalition partners, the ÖVP and the SPÖ, and by the small opposition party, the Communists. The larger opposition party, the VDU, voted against it.

Officially, Austrian neutrality became part of International Law when the international community accepted this "perpetual" neutrality of Austria. This international acceptance happened either directly or indirectly, by tacit agreement. Every sovereign state in the world agreed in one way or the other. Austrian neutrality was and is part of the international order.

Officially, Austrian neutrality was from its beginning a set of specific rights and duties defining the relationship between Austria and the other international actors. At the core of the rights and duties was a military obligation: Austria did not want (and was not allowed) to join any military alliance; and Austria guaranteed that it would not permit foreign troops on its territory.

Officially, this neutrality has virtually never been jeopardized since 1955. Only a few brief conflicts arose out of misunderstandings. One of those minor incidents occurred in 1958, when U.S. aircraft crossed Austrian territory on the way to Lebanon during the deployment of U.S. troops. Austrian protests made it clear that the country wanted to have its rights respected.

Officially, this neutrality was (and is) armed neutrality. This was one of the preconditions the United States had insisted on, before the package deal including the State Treaty, the withdrawal of occupational forces, and the declaration of neutrality was possible. Austria has its armed forces—because it is neutral.

Officially, Austrian neutrality is perpetual. That means that Austria will stay out of all military conflicts, both present and future. Austria's perpetual neutrality—different from "ordinary neutrality," which binds the neutral party only in regard to a specific, already existing war—is an obligation for the future.

Officially, Austria's neutrality is based on the Swiss model. In the Moscow Memorandum of April 15, 1955, Austria expressed its intention to follow Switzerland's example. More than four decades later, Austria has joined not only the United Nations but also the European Union—and Switzerland has done neither.

Officially, this neutrality is based on a unilateral declaration. No other government has the right to force its interpretation of Austrian neutrality on Austria. Defining Austrian neutrality is the exclusive right of Austria.

Officially, Austrian neutrality has no obligation beyond the military aspects expressed in the Neutrality Act and in the rules of International Law. Neutrality has no special domestic or "ideological" impact.

These aspects of neutrality exist, and they have always been respected—by Austria and by other states, especially Austria's neighbors and the world powers, the permanent members of the United Nations Security Council. All the official parts of Austrian neutrality have been accepted, at both the national and the international political level. But the official version alone cannot describe what Austrian neutrality is really about. There is much more to this pattern than international or constitutional law can explain. There are politics behind neutrality, and neutrality has always be seen through the glasses of political interpretation and political interest, domestic as well as foreign.

Austrian neutrality can be explained by two logics that were behind the Austrian declaration in 1955. The first one was foreign policy oriented, and it was rather easy to understand. The second one was part of the domestic agenda, and it was much more difficult to grasp. But both logics were constructed and used by the elites who were running the Second Republic according to the rules of consociational democracy.

- The international logic can be explained by the window of opportunity that opened after Stalin's death; this was the first wave of détente the still rather young East-West conflict was able to produce. The USSR, trying to arrange terms with the West, was in untested waters. Since the beginning of 1953 the United States had been under the influence of Secretary of State John Foster Dulles's zealous anti-Communist rhetoric and was suspicious and hesitant about taking the new Soviet flexibility seriously (Bischof 1992). It was the professional skill of the Austrian government and its diplomats that found ways to deal with the USSR without feeding American fears (Stourzh 1988: esp. 42–51). The result was the compromise of Moscow: On April 15, 1955, the Soviet and Austrian governments agreed to trade the Austrian State Treaty for Austrian neutrality. The State Treaty would remove the occupation troops from Austria; neutrality

would guarantee that Austria would not use its newly increased freedom
to join NATO. To overcome American mistrust, the Moscow Memorandum included the term "neutrality according to the Swiss model."
Switzerland, as the Austrian government rightly thought, would sound
sweet in the ears of Americans who were afraid that a "neutralized" Austria would be under too much Soviet influence.

- The domestic logic can only be explained by history. After the end of the
Habsburg Empire, Austria was a small republic that lingered without
defining its international role independently. The First Republic staggered
from one dependence to the next: Orientation toward Weimar Germany
was followed by an orientation toward fascist Italy, only to be exchanged
for a dependence on Nazi Germany. But by 1955, the Federal Republic of
Germany had already been a member of NATO for one year. And the
German Democratic Republic cofounded the Warsaw Pact Organization
just one day before the Austrian State treaty was signed on May 15, 1955.
Declaring Austria neutral seemed to be an opportunity to define Austria's
role with a maximum degree of independence, especially independence
from any pan-German interpretation. This was the purpose of the Austrian National Holiday, October 26: The National Holiday was established
to recognize and celebrate Austrian neutrality; the declaration of neutrality was considered the act of defining a new Austrian self-understanding.
That fact that the parties of the pan-German camp, the VDU and the
FPÖ, voted against the Neutrality Act and later against the establishment
of the National Holiday strengthened this understanding. Neutrality was
to become part of the Austrian myth like so many other historical events
used for a similar purpose (Bruckmüller 1996: 123–125).

Both logics were designed, controlled, and promoted by the political and diplomatic elites of the ÖVP and the SPÖ. It was especially Chancellor Julius Raab who
overcame obstacles within both his own party and the SPÖ. In 1953, Raab dis-
missed Foreign Minister Karl Gruber, who was considered skeptical about Raab's
neutrality orientation. The new foreign minister was Leopold Figl, Raab's predecessor in the chancellery. Figl followed Raab's lead, thus effectively eliminating any resistance within Raab's party, the ÖVP. But Raab still had to overcome the pessimistic
attitude of Vice-Chancellor and SPÖ chairman Adolf Schärf about the new open-
ings from Moscow (Stourzh 1975: 93–96). On the eve of the breakthrough in 1955,
the SPÖ was more anti-Communist than the ÖVP, at least as far as foreign policy
was concerned. But in Moscow, in 1955, the coalition acted in full cooperation.
Consociational democracy's elitist methods worked (Kreisky 1986: 454–482).

At the beginning, the strategy of the pragmatic bargain—as agreed in Moscow,
as signed in Vienna in form of the State Treaty and as implemented by the Neutrality Declaration—was accepted more as a lesser evil than as a popular goal.
Neutrality was too abstract a concept to be identified with emotions. It was not

until ten years later, when the day of the Neutrality Act became the National Holiday, that neutrality started to fulfill some emotional functions.

The consequences of neutrality on the international level could be seen much more clearly. When the Treaty of Rome was signed in 1957, Austria's temptation to join the Common Market was understandably great because Austria's most important trade links were with Germany first and Italy second. The European Economic Community (EEC) was the economic center toward which Austria's trade and industry gravitated. Neutrality prevented Austria from applying for membership in the EEC, but not neutrality in its *legal* sense. The EEC was clearly not a military alliance, which Austria was not allowed to join by virtue of its Neutrality Act. It was neutrality in its *political* sense that prevented Austria from joining. In 1958, when the EEC was formed, its members were all members of NATO. The EEC was in effect the Western bloc's economic arm in Europe. To be a member of such an organization would have endangered the credibility of Austria's neutrality, especially toward the USSR. For that reason, the coalition cabinet decided Austria should not become a member of the number one economic club in Western Europe. Instead, it joined the softer version of European integration, the European Free Trade Association (EFTA), which was chartered in 1959 and came into existence in 1960. Compared with the EEC, the EFTA had the advantage of having Switzerland and Sweden, other neutral countries, as founding members. Ireland, another non-NATO country, also belonged to the EFTA, and Finland also later joined.

This preference for the EFTA was also justified in that the Free Trade Association had none of the supranational aspects that were so typical of the EEC concept from its beginning. The EEC was not only part of an overall system of the West but also a much more pretentious system of integration than the more traditional EFTA.

The way in which the Austrian government—still the first grand coalition—opted for the "softer" rather than the "harder" version of European integration expressed its dominant interpretation of the meaning of neutrality beyond the military level. Despite its neutrality, Austria wanted to participate in Western European integration, the reasons being both its economic interests and its political affinity. But because of its neutrality, Austria wanted no confrontation with the USSR. Austria interpreted its neutrality as an opportunity to be as Western as possible without alienating the Soviet Union.

The second aspect was motivated by geopolitical facts. After the Red Army's withdrawal from Austrian territory in 1955, Soviet troops were stationed at the Austrian-Hungarian border, about 60 kilometers east of Vienna. Geopolitics inspired Austria's neutrality policy, which should be distinguished from neutrality law. In its international dimension, neutrality was primarily the Austrian response to being caught in the middle, between Soviet troops stationed in Hungary (and after 1968 in Czechoslovakia as well) and NATO troops stationed in Germany and Italy. It was an instrument for dealing with geostrategical facts Austria could not alter.

The consequences of geopolitics became evident during the Soviet invasion of Hungary in 1956 and—together with other Warsaw Pact countries—of Czechoslovakia in 1968. These two military operations helped to define Austrian neutrality more clearly than any law could have done.

In both cases, Austria made it clear that it did not want to be involved and that it would consider any foreign military activity on Austrian territory a violation of its sovereignty and neutrality. Austria demonstrated that anti-Communist forces could not rely on any military help from Austria, despite official criticism of the interventions and overwhelmingly strong anti-Soviet public opinion (Schlesinger 1972: 34–55).

In both cases, Austria demonstrated its willingness to defend its neutrality by all means, including militarily. The Austrian army was stationed on the border with Hungary in 1956 and on the border with Czechoslovakia in 1986 to demonstrate this side of Austrian neutrality. But the main reason everybody, especially the USSR, respected Austria's neutrality during those years was not Austria's military might or its readiness to defend itself. The main reason was the overall European balance of which Austria's neutrality was an integral part. It did not make sense for Soviet politics to test U.S. willingness to defend the status quo in Europe. It did not make sense to invade Austria as long as the USSR was interested in maintaining the existing balance of power.

It was not the Austrian army that prevented any serious violation of Austrian neutrality. The Austrian armed forces are the weakest in Europe, judged on the basis of defense spending. During that critical year, when troops of the USSR and four other Warsaw Pact countries invaded Czechoslovakia, Austria spent significantly less on defense than any other comparable country in Europe, whether neutral, nonaligned, or a NATO-member (see Table 8.1).

Austrians could feel secure in their neutrality due to the power balance the United States and the Soviet Union had established in Europe. As long as NATO was strong enough to deter any possible Soviet expansion, Austrian security was protected too. Austria got a free ride on European security arrangements, independent of its own defense policy. It is remarkable that during the height of the Cold War Austria followed neither the example of the Swiss and Swedish, who felt they had to be better armed than the others because they were neutral, nor the example of small NATO countries, who had to be armed because they were facing a Communist threat. Austria lived in the best of all possible worlds, provided with a security umbrella without having to pay for it.

Not surprisingly, neutrality started to become popular, and people started to define it in their own way:

- For patriots, neutrality gave credence to their view that it was something special to be Austrian and to live in this Second Republic.
- For pacifists, neutrality was the guarantee that Austria could be a peaceful island in the midst of the most heavily armed military machines history had ever seen.
- For politicians, neutrality kept defense spending low, because Austrian security did not depend on Austrian expenditure.

TABLE 8.1   Defense Expenditures in 1968

Country	Per Capita Defense Expenditure (U.S. $)	Defense Expenditure As Percent of GNP
Austria	19	1.2
Denmark	60	2.3
Finland	27	1.8
Norway	84	3.8
Sweden	128	3.8
Switzerland	68	2.5
Yugoslavia	24	5.7

SOURCE: Schlesinger 1972: 124.

The only segment of the economy that was not satisfied with the situation was the military industrial complex. But because there was not much of it in Austria, it was not especially difficult to overcome its criticism and its interests. And when the Austrian armament industry became more important for the Austrian economy and the Austrian labor market, its dynamism was export oriented: tanks for Chile and Argentina, and cannons for Libya and Jordan, knowing fully well how they might be used. The tanks possibly helped military dictators put down popular uprisings, and the cannons were used to supply Iran and Iraq during the first Gulf War (Pilz 1982).

It was during the Kreisky era, between 1970 and 1983, when Austria's self-esteem reached its peak. The international media confirmed a new Austrian autostereotype. An analysis of the media at the end of those years showed how positively Austria and Kreisky were perceived internationally (Lendvai 1983). Kreisky and his government had made Austrians feel important again—not as participants in major power politics but as members of a nation whose government had established a policy of "active neutrality" almost everybody seemed to love (Höll 1994). And Kreisky was so confident in his image as a statesman that he even expressed open criticism of world leaders, including U.S. presidents (Rathkolb 1994).

Austria was back on the international map, not as an object of big power interests as it had been between 1945 and 1955 but as a much sought-after, neutral arbiter. The past seemed to be forgiven and forgotten. Hitler was a German, and the Austrian Empire was a peaceful power all the successor states mourned over. Neutrality was the recipe for reviving a feeling of positive uniqueness: Kurt Waldheim, an Austrian, was running the United Nations; and world leaders such as Presidents Nixon and Ford came to Austria to talk to Kreisky before meeting with the Soviet leadership. In 1979, Carter and Brezhnev signed SALT II in Vienna. Neutrality had paid off.

Austria was able to play an especially active role in the Helsinki process. The Conference for Security and Cooperation in Europe (CSCE), founded in 1975 in Helsinki, was based on the European status quo, on the balance between East and West. Nothing was possible against the will of either side. The neutral and nonaligned countries developed a special function as go-betweens: They established the "n plus n" group, which was a kind of third faction between the Western and the Eastern bloc. The Final Acts, signed in Helsinki, and the process that followed were seen as the perpetuation of the power balance.

Reaction to Kreisky's address at the summit in Helsinki was very positive: "Alone among the chiefs of state assembled to sign the Final Act, Austrian Chancellor Bruno Kreisky welcomed the 'clarification . . . that coexistence . . . cannot be understood as being valid for the ideological sphere'" (Mastny 1986: 9 f.). Neutral Austria was able to mediate conflicts but still preserve its credibility as a democratic country.

It was the era of the "small is beautiful" interpretation of the Austrian military defense. In order to remain militarily credible, Austria changed its defense doctrine from defending its borders to defending the essentials of its territory. With the exception of neutral Switzerland, tiny Liechtenstein and nonaligned Yugoslavia, all the countries that bordered Austria were fully integrated in the bloc systems. Any military aggression Austria might have to respond to was only thinkable as an aggression by one of those blocs. But this was only possible as part of a conflict that realistically would result in World War III. Therefore it did not matter whether or not Austria could effectively respond to such an aggression. Retreat into the mountainous regions and wait for help—that was the Austrian defense doctrine (Spannocchi 1976). According to the still dominant anti-Communist attitude in Austria and as a consequence of neutrality law, which permits any neutral country under attack to ally itself with its attacker's enemy, this was nothing more than a "waiting for NATO" doctrine.

During the years of SPÖ dominance, the "softer" version of Austria's participation in (Western) European integration had to be reinterpreted. In 1973, three EFTA members joined the European Community (EC), the joint organization made up of the EEC, Euratom, and the European Community for Coal and Steel. This was the beginning of the end of the EFTA. Without Great Britain, there was not much sense in seeing the EFTA as any real alternative to the EC. To prevent an isolation that would have threatened Austria's economic interests, Austria and the other remaining EFTA members signed a free trade agreement with the EC, which went into effect at the beginning of 1973.

This was still congruent with the interpretation of neutrality policy as Austria had defined it in the late 1950s: Austria should strive for any form of integration into the (Western) European common market short of full membership, thereby furthering its economic interests, but not become a member of the EEC, thereby maintaining its neutrality. In the 1970s, Austria's interpretation of neutrality was not different from the way the Swiss, the Swedish, or the Finns defined theirs. It was during the years of the free trade agreements with the EEC and the "n-plus-n" group in the CSCE that Austrian neutrality seemed to be in complete concordance with a European pattern of neutrality that Switzerland, Sweden, and Finland also followed.

Austria's neutrality was just a bit more active. Kreisky, especially his Middle East activities, stretched the understanding of neutrality more than the others, with the possible exception of Sweden's under Olof Palme. Kreisky helped the PLO gain international recognition. He helped bring Muammar Gadhafi into the international dialogue. And he risked alienating the mainstream of Israeli politics, including the Labor Party, which was linked with the SPÖ through their common membership in the Socialist International. Much has been written about the attitude of the Austrian with a Jewish background toward the Jewish state, from Jewish self-hatred and Jewish anti-Semitism on one side to Kreisky's great ability to throw over the restrictions of an outdated taboo on the other (Thalberg 1983: 293–322; Secher 1993: 152–165).

With the end of the Kreisky era, the best years of neutrality were over. In 1983, the FPÖ became the coalition partner of the SPÖ. Even after the FPÖ had started to accept the neutrality its predecessor had rejected in parliament in 1955, the party was rather cool toward this product of the old grand coalition. The FPÖ in its pre-Haider era still tried to gain a reputation as the only party that favored EC membership. Because the FPÖ wanted to demonstrate its predictability as a serious partner of the Social Democrats, it did not overplay its strong pro-EC stand or its less-than-enthusiastic position in favor of neutrality (Schneider 1990: 237–241). The changes, which started beneath the surface of Austrian politics, had different roots:

- International roots. In 1985, Mikhail Gorbachev became Secretary General of the most powerful Communist party; with him, the opening of the Soviet bloc began. Even before that, the events in Poland in 1980–1981 and less dramatic but similar developments in Hungary had made the Communist world less monolithic. Austria, with its geopolitical position and its justification from the Helsinki process, made cultural and humanitarian efforts possible—not so much on the level of official policy but behind the scenes, as provided for in the Helsinki accord. In this last phase of the Cold War, Austria functioned as a kind of bridgehead, promoting Western thinking in Eastern Europe. Because Austria was neutral, it was better prepared to exploit the developments in human rights, the "third basket" the Helsinki Final Acts had set in motion.
- Central European roots. Austria became instrumental in changing Europe—by demonstrating its Western nature. "Mitteleuropa" became the code word for nonofficial and semi-official policies. The code word underlined the things Austria had in common with the other Central European countries, despite the Communist rule the latter were still under. Dissidents from Communist Europe became partners in this new dynamism. The Middle East and other global problems had lost significance for Austria; its European neighbors had gained (Prisching 1996: 90–95). Before the Warsaw Pact was abandoned and the USSR collapsed, there

was a dynamic development that affected Austria in a specific way as a consequence of its geopolitical situation.

- Domestic roots. The SPÖ had lost its majority in 1983. Although the Social Democrats were still the biggest party and no government against them seemed possible, the influence of the other parties increased. The ÖVP was especially critical of Kreisky's involvement in global affairs. From the point of view of the People's Party, the SPÖ had neglected Austria's immediate neighbors. The ÖVP wanted to establish a special profile as the "Europe party." The ÖVP and its foreign policy specialists, first and foremost party chairman Alois Mock, wanted to distinguish between the Kreisky era, pictured as being full of illusions, and the more realistic and therefore more European orientation the ÖVP wanted Austria to follow. In 1995, ÖVP members of parliament demonstratively brought a motion before the National Council: Austria should intensify its relationship with the EC in close cooperation with other EFTA countries, but also bilaterally, if that was in Austria's own best interest. The motion was voted down by an SPÖ and FPÖ majority (Schaller 1994: 55 f.). The People's Party had not canceled the basic foreign policy consensus that both major parties had upheld even after the end of the grand coalition in 1966. The People's Party was just a little earlier and a little more outspoken than the Social Democrats in starting to redefine this consensus. Even before the ÖVP got back into the government and before Mock became foreign minister at the beginning of 1987, the accent had been shifted. The post-Kreisky SPÖ had also begun to subtly rearrange its foreign policy orientation. Peter Jankowitsch, the last social democratic foreign minister before the new grand coalition took over, was a prime example of this. In 1985, before Jankowitsch became foreign minister, he and Andreas Khol, an ÖVP member of parliament, no longer rejected an Austrian application for EC membership. The generation that now took over in both major parties was less influenced by the mystique of 1955 (Schaller 1994; Luif 1995: 188–199).
- Economic roots. In the mid-1980s, the faith in Austria's economic miracle was waning. Nationalized industry found itself in deep trouble due to a combination of management failures and international developments. It became obvious that Austria was economically more dependent than ever, despite the continued existence of the welfare system and rather favorable developments in employment and income. In 1986, the EC signed the Single European Act. The completion of the EC's internal market prompted the fears of more and more Austrian industrialists that the free trade agreement would no longer be enough to overcome significant disadvantages that Austrian exports faced in their by far most important market. The Association of Austrian Industrialists ("Vereinigung Österreichischer Industrieller," VÖI) mobilized to deal with the one decisive ob-

stacle, the traditional interpretation of neutrality. The VÖI entrusted two renowned professors of international law to give their expert opinions on the compatibility of permanent neutrality and EC membership. The opinion, published in 1987, was a breakthrough: For the first time, fully established legal scholars confirmed that Austrian neutrality was compatible with EC membership (Hummer and Schweitzer 1987). Big business, whose export interests explained their position, immediately began using this breakthrough to argue in favor of EU membership. Surprisingly, the other main social partners followed, including the Federation of Austrian Trade Unions (ÖGB) and the Chambers of Agriculture. Thus the new elitist consensus included not only the two major parties but also corporatist Austria (Schaller 1994: 98–11).

This was not the end of neutrality, but it was the beginning of the end. The political incentives to remain neutral were eliminated step by step as a result of the end of the East-West conflict. The economic disadvantages of nonmembership became more and more significant. And now even the law had spoken: Austria's primary justification for decades, that its neutrality did not allow it to enter the EC, was no longer valid. Economic interests and legal doctrines converged—how convenient for Austrian politics.

There was a generation gap within Austria's political and intellectual elite groups. The old leadership of the major parties and economic interest groups as well as most leading scholars had seen the neutrality declaration as their ultimate success in their efforts to stabilize the Second Republic. Now, a younger generation had taken over, and the younger representatives of the SPÖ, the ÖVP, and the social partners viewed neutrality in a much more sober light. Rudolf Kirchschläger is typical for the older generation: In 1955, he, as a legal expert with the Austrian Foreign Ministry, was a member of the team that tried to make optimal use of the window of opportunity that presented itself that year. The wording of the Neutrality Act expresses an intention to view neutrality as more than just a foreign policy instrument. Kirchschläger, an independent, became foreign minister in Kreisky's first cabinet and was elected federal president in 1974. As a non–party member, he was nominated by the SPÖ and had the staunch support of Bruno Kreisky. At the end of the Kreisky era, Kirchschläger, still federal president, published an evaluation of the 1972 free trade agreement between Austria and the EC. A decade after its signing, this agreement was, in Kirchschläger's opinion, still the best possible way to combine neutrality with Austria's export interests. His article concluded: "For ten years, this settlement has stood the test" (Kirchschläger 1983: 95).

As this was published, there was increasing doubt from other sides that the settlement was the best possible solution for Austria' problems. And the younger generation within the elite groups, hungry to challenge the diplomats and lawyers identified with 1955, had little respect for what people like Kirchschläger considered a kind of final settlement. In combination with the other factors, the generation gap started to make itself felt. In the case of neutrality, it was a generation gap within the ranks of the elites. The result was the decision to apply for EC membership.

At the end of the 1980s, Austrian neutrality had lost one of its most important aspects: Joining the EC was no longer seen as incompatible with neutrality Austrian-style. And joining the EC was exactly what the elites of both camps responsible for the interpretation of neutrality had in mind. In 1989, they sent the "letter to Brussels," in which they emphasized Austria's desire to join the EC as a neutral state (Schneider 1990: 91–97). At that moment, Austria's position did not conform to those of the other EFTA neutrals. Sweden's and Finland's applications followed later: Sweden's in 1991, and Finland's in 1992. In the same year, Switzerland also applied for EC membership, a move that failed when the Swiss population rejected membership in the EEA (European Economic Area), a kind of intermediate stage on the way to EC membership (Luif 1995: 200–233).

Austria had made history. It had destroyed a European pattern of neutrality and become the catalyst of a development that was arguably the logical result of the end of the Cold War. But while the other neutrals had waited, Austria had acted. Only then had the other neutrals followed Austria's example. But Austria received no special reward for its vanguard role in destroying decisive aspects of neutrality. Austria, Finland, and Sweden were accepted as one group and became members of the EC, which had just become the EU, on January 1, 1995.

The most significant aspect of the old interpretations of neutrality still had not been disturbed by Austria's EU membership. Austria was not allowed to join any military alliance. But the ramifications of EU membership would soon set in motion a development that had the potential to erode even this aspect of neutrality. In Maastricht 1991, the EC had decided that the future European Union should also include a Common Foreign and Security Policy (CFSP). Because this issue was a very delicate one and a step that might violate the sensitivities of member states, the definition of the CFSP was kept rather vague. But the Maastricht Treaty did imply that the CFSP should make use of the already existing West European Union (WEU), and its defense clauses included considerable restrictions of national defense policies in favor of a revived WEU within the EU framework (Luif 1995: 37–45).

The WEU was nothing new. It was founded in 1954 as a successor organization to the Brussels Treaty, which from 1948 on had been an organization consisting of the United Kingdom, France, the Netherlands, Belgium, and Luxembourg, and was originally designed to prevent a revival of German expansionism. In 1954, the Federal Republic of Germany and Italy also joined the WEU. But the WEU, like the Brussels Treaty, was almost completely overshadowed by NATO. The EC decisionmakers in Maastricht remembered the WEU as a virtually untested and therefore completely underdeveloped military arm that had only one advantage over NATO: The WEU did not include non-EC members, especially the United States, the country that dominated NATO. The WEU option was also a way to avoid U.S.

hegemony. Legally, the WEU is even more binding than NATO. WEU members are automatically obliged to provide military assistance.

In joining the EU, Austria had to pledge full acceptance of the Maastricht Treaty. In 1993, all the applicant states jointly declared "from the time of their accession, [to] be ready and able to participate fully and actively in the Common Foreign and Security Policy" (Luif 1995: 310). The logical consequence of these additional obligations, supplementary to those Austria had agreed to in 1989, was that the accession treaty signed in 1994 did not mention Austrian neutrality. Neutrality was already history. Austria had applied, as a neutral state, to become an EC member and would be allowed to maintain its permanent neutrality. However, it was accepted as an EU member only after it had agreed on the additional obligations of establishing a common foreign and security policy with other states, the majority of which belonged to NATO and WEU. Whatever Austria's relationship to NATO and WEU would be, it would never be the same as it was before joining the EU. Neutrality had lost its original meaning. Now the only neutrality left was that which applied to Austrian domestic policy.

Since joining the EU, Austria has officially been involved in developing the CFSP, including its military implications. Austria is fully engaged in activating a military alliance. By saying yes to the EU, Austria said yes to the CFSP. And it is impossible to distinguish between the nonmilitary and military aspects of the CFSP. Austria is well on its way to becoming a member of an alliance that includes military obligations.

This can be called neutral. Any theory of neutrality is possible as long as it is accepted by international politics. There are no limits to new theories of neutrality if this endeavor is backed by a certain domestic and international consensus. Ireland's long-standing neutrality differs significantly from the policy Switzerland, Sweden, Finland, and Austria followed in the 1970s. Since 1995, there is a Swiss neutrality, which is very different from the model Ireland has in common with Austria, Finland, and Sweden. It is not so difficult to imagine further developments, for instance neutrality that permits or even demands military assistance in all actions legitimized by the UN Security Council or by the decisionmaking bodies of regional organizations recognized by the United Nations. If military action is defined as international solidarity, why not define it as legally compatible with neutrality? Neutrality is just a word whose meaning can be changed significantly if there is the necessary consensus. But such a consensus must exist.

Joining the EU after Maastricht and accepting Maastricht's terms was the end of the beginning of the end of Austrian neutrality. Now the final stage has begun. What is still missing is the coup de grace. But there is not much to be finished by such a coup anymore. It is primarily the semantics that are still alive. Neutrality is just a word, but one that still causes a lot of headaches in the upper echelons of Austrian politics. There are still the domestic problems to be taken care of because there is no domestic consensus, neither to stretch the definition of neutrality even more to include WEU or NATO membership nor to officially abandon the neutrality status.

At the end of the 1990s, most Austrians still have not realized how dead neutrality already is. They still believe there is much to defend. The reason for this divergence between public opinion and foreign policy is twofold:

- The political elites did everything in their power to convince Austrian voters to accept EU membership. The campaign mounted by the coalition government in the spring of 1994 assured Austrians that there would be no incompatibility between Austrian neutrality and EU membership. Austria would join the EU as a neutral country. The government then averted negative backlash by avoiding any serious discussion about the difficulties and impossibilities Austrian neutrality would be facing within the CFSP. Because the main opponent of the pro-EU campaign was the FPÖ, which opposed EU membership but favored Austria's entry into NATO, the problem became further blurred. The most outspoken anti-EU party violated the traditional understanding of neutrality to a greater degree and much more openly than the government itself. Therefore the coalition partners obviously did not have to worry much about the neutrality aspect, because criticism came from people who were intellectually wrong and politically right. Among the 34 percent who voted against Austria's entry into the EU in June 1994, only 15 percent gave neutrality as one of their motives (Plasser and Ulram 1994: 113). Given that a vast majority of Austrians still had a very favorable opinion of neutrality at that time, this is an interesting omission of obvious associations. Only 15 percent of that 34 percent or about 5 percent of the electorate opposed EU membership on the grounds of their consistently positive views on neutrality.
- The popularity of neutrality has almost nothing to do with the real aspects of foreign policy. Most Austrians do not believe in neutrality according to the doctrines developed by legal experts or foreign policy. Neutrality was and still is part of the overall perspective of Austria's role in the world: a bit of island mentality, some leftovers of the old empire's glory, a pinch of pacifism, and a good dollop of xenophobic resentment. These ingredients can be mixed together in different recipes: For some Austrians, neutrality is first and foremost an antithesis to militarism; for others, neutrality's primary function is distinguishing Austria from other countries. In the past, these contradictory images of neutrality allowed Kreisky's Middle East activities to be interpreted as part of Austrian neutrality. Now these same contradictions allow Austria, a country that has pledged its full loyalty to the EU's intention to include defense in its future common policies, to continue to define itself permanently neutral. Only because neutrality was perceived in such different ways was the government able to disregard the most obvious of all contradictions, that neutrality in its traditional sense was not compatible with the acceptance of the CFSP.

The government knew that during the period between application in 1989 and the plebiscite in 1994, majority consent rested on the compatibility of EU membership and neutrality. The results of public opinion polls by various institutes were always clear: When asked if they would prefer EU membership without neutrality or neutrality without EU membership, more than 60 percent of Austrians always preferred neutrality (Neuhold and Luif 1992: 98–104). The coalition must have been tempted to understate the downgrading that neutrality would undergo as a consequence of the Maastricht Treaty. It was in the interest of the Austrian government to stick to the semantics of neutrality in an effort to ignore reality. To bring Austria into the EU, the government had to predict "neutrality as usual" despite the clear evidence that nothing was usual anymore.

By joining the EU, Austria became an observer in the WEU. This is the same status Ireland and Denmark have had since 1973 and the same status Sweden and Finland also acquired in 1995. The observer status is a kind of waiting room. Austria is waiting for the clarification of the CFSP's meaning. The official Austrian position is as clear as possible: Austria supports a "step-by-step transition to a communitarian approach in foreign policy questions," including a "cautious transition to majority voting" in the CFSP (Luif 1995: 371). That means that the Austrian government is fully prepared to take the next step within the reasoning behind its accession to the EU: to accept and even to promote EU majority decisions in foreign and security policy matters.

It was also within the scope of this reasoning for Austria to join the NATO Partnership for Peace program, another waiting room, in 1995. Everything is happening according to a script that is not written by conspirators but by the champions of that reasoning. As soon as Austria had said "yes" to Maastricht-Europe, neutrality was reduced to domestic embarrassment. The purpose of Austrian neutrality policy is no longer to implement the general rules of neutrality in a specific political situation but rather to tell the domestic audience that neutrality is already dead.

And this domestic audience reflects the ambiguities that have always been a part of Austria's neutrality. There is still a strong feeling that neutrality has not outlived its usefulness. But there is also a feeling that Austria should not abstain from future security arrangements. A majority of Austrians are in favor of neutrality—and of membership in a European security organization (see Table 8.2).

Opinions on keeping Austria neutral differ significantly between women and men. Men are more inclined to exchange Austria's neutrality for a membership in an international alliance. The difference along party lines is also significant: Green voters, followed by SPÖ voters, have the strongest preference for neutrality, ÖVP and LIF voters the weakest. Interestingly, the opinions of FPÖ voters are most representative of all Austrians (Fessel+GFK 1995). FPÖ sympathizers not being on the fringes of general opinion is a notable exception to a general rule.

Austrians distinguish not only between NATO and the WEU but also between a security organization that includes the security interests of Eastern European

TABLE 8.2   Public Opinion on Neutrality and Membership in Alliances, 1995

	Percentage of Austrians in Favor of Joining		
Staying Neutral Unconditionally	*a new all-European Security Organization*	*WEU*	*NATO*
67	50	40	33

SOURCE: Fessel+GFK 1995.

countries and the purely Western organizations, which already exist. But as soon as the WEU and/or NATO are defined and accepted as general European arrangements that integrate and respect Eastern European security interests as well, the Austrian public opinion is prepared to shift toward favoring membership in one or both of them. In 1995 NATO membership did not have majority backing; in fact, the majority of those polled were openly against it: 51 percent of Austrians opposed NATO membership, compared with 43 percent against WEU membership and 37 percent against membership in a possible all-European security organization. NATO still polarizes more than the other options (Fessel+GFK 1995).

Many Austrians wish to have their cake and eat it too: They want to keep their neutrality and join the new security structure the EU promised in Maastricht. This is a contradiction—if neutrality is seen solely as a foreign policy concept. But neutrality is more, and the majority of Austrians still want to preserve that feeling of security that had to do with aspects of Austrian politics extending far beyond foreign and military policies.

Public opinion cannot change the basic realities of Austria's geopolitical environment. With the end of the East-West Conflict, Austria's neutrality has lost its principal "conflict of reference" (Neuhold 1995). It would be wishful thinking to dissociate Austrian neutrality from its preconditions. And these preconditions do not exist anymore. Public opinion in Austria will eventually recognize the unavoidability of this development—it is only a question of time and of whether this timing can be controlled politically or if it will just happen.

In a report published in 1996, two Austrian legal experts—one a former foreign minister—have carefully described what is the "de facto end of Austrian neutrality" (Cede and Pahr 1996). It is still possible to identify special roles a neutral country can play within the security umbrella that WEU and/or NATO and especially the European Union's CFSP will soon provide. It is arguably in Austria's best interests to be included in any such security arrangement—with or without special roles. But there will be no role that can seriously be called neutral.

Neutrality served Austria's national interests for a certain period. The elites responsible for declaring neutrality successfully promoted their product in Austria, by enshrining it as a kind of national mystique. But the winds of change did not circumvent Austria. Austrian political leaders have concluded that Austria's interests are now better served within a (Western) European security system, and it will require all their political skills to convince public opinion in Austria. Their main task now is to present the fait accompli of discarded neutrality in such a way that most Austrians support or at least accept it. To succeed, they must undo the belief they worked so long and hard to instill in the Austrian people: the belief in neutrality.

9

AUSTRIA'S
DARKER SIDE

A computer search for the Austrian most frequently quoted worldwide would be easy to predict: It would be the Austrian Catholic Adolf Hitler (Heer 1968). Hitler more than anyone else was instrumental in shaping Austria, the country of his birth, Germany, his country by choice, and Europe, the continent he wanted to dominate. Hitler made history.

There is an old joke about the Second Republic's ability to make people forget Hitler's Austrian background: The biggest success story of post-1945 Austria was making the world believe that Beethoven was an Austrian but Hitler was a German. Of course, there is some truth in it: Beethoven's career took off in Austria, notably in Vienna, whereas Hitler had no career at all until he moved to Germany. But the importance of Hitler's roots has to be dealt with. How Austrian were his policies, and how strong an influence did his Austrian upbringing have on his ideological beliefs?

Adolf Hitler, the Austrian Catholic

Adolf Hitler was the product of Austria. His success was German based, but his ideological background was very Austrian. He was influenced by the Austrian environment he grew up in, an environment rife with ethnic conflicts and rivalries, which paralyzed the Austrian empire at the end of its existence. Hitler's personal response was typically Austrian: He declared himself not only to be a German but even more German than the Germans from the "Reich." His nationalistic attitude came directly from Georg Schönerer's ethnocentrist and racist nationalism (Whiteside 1975). "Blood" in the sense of heritage; "nation" in the sense of purity;

"people" in the sense of homogeneity: Austrian pan-Germanism of the late nineteenth century was the ideological testing ground for things to come. Austria was, as Karl Kraus was to later put it, the "rehearsal of global doomsday" (Zohn 1971: 68–85; Pfabigan 1976: 170–191).

Hitler openly declared that these roots were decisive for his creed, for his "Weltbild." In *Mein Kampf* he expressed his gratitude and admiration for the clarity of Schönerer's "Weltanschauung." Hitler wanted to mix Schönerer's ideological consistency with Lueger's pragmatic populism. Schönerer lacked the ability to instrumentalize the prejudices of the masses, and Lueger lacked the consistency of a true anti-Semite and pan-German. Hitler considered Lueger and his Christian Social mass movement much too pro-Habsburg. But Lueger's techniques for winning popular support were as important to him as Schönerer's ideological consistency (Hitler 1938: 107–111). Hitler, the strange maverick from Upper Austria who could not make a life for himself in Vienna never experienced success in his native land, but his attitude toward the world was shaped in and by Austria.

Hitler experienced Austria at the turn of the century as a battlefield between Germans and non-Germans. His identity was German, in full accordance with the dominant understanding of his time: He spoke German, and therefore he was German. As a German, he felt the same superiority as most Austro-Germans: The Austro-Czechs and other Austro-Slavs as well as the Austro-Italians were not to be considered equals in spite of the minority status Germans had in Austria. It is a fact that Hitler never learned or even tried to learn any of the other major languages spoken in Habsburg Austria. German was the language of the elite; anyone who wanted to have any impact on Austrian society had to speak German; there was no need to speak any other language.

One example of the dominance to which Austro-Germans thought they were entitled was the brief and ill-fated history of the Italian law school in Innsbruck. As the regional capital of Tyrol, Innsbruck was the political center for some hundreds of thousands Tyroleans with an Italian identity, Austrian citizens from the southern part of Tyrol more or less identical with the later Italian province of Trentino. Together with Austro-Italians from the Trieste region, about one million Austrian citizens who spoke Italian as their mother tongue lived in Austria. Those Austrian citizens were the target group of the "risorgimento" and "irridenta" propaganda from Italy, which was not satisfied with the borders it had been assigned after the 1866 war. It made a lot of sense to give the Austro-Italians the chance to feel at home in multinational Austria, to provide them with an identity that was Italian but at the same time also Austrian.

This policy of integrating Austro-Italians was implemented more or less on the political level: Austro-Italians represented their constituents in parliament in Vienna. The most prominent among the Italians in the Austrian parliament was Alcide de Gasperi, who after World War II became prime minister of the Republic of Italy. But on the cultural level, the integration did not succeed because of the attitude of pan-German Austrians. The Austrian government wanted to establish possibilities for the Austro-Italians to study in Austria, at an Austrian university, without being forced to struggle with German as the language of instruction. In 1904, the University of Innsbruck started its Italian law school, which as a complement to the already existing German law school was to teach the Austrian law curriculum in Italian.

This went against the dominant pan-German nationalistic feeling. Riots in Innsbruck organized by militant pan-Germans "forced" the authorities to close the Italian law school immediately after it opened. It was never to reopen again (Gatterer 1972: 87–91). The logic of any multinational balance had decisively lost against the logic of German hegemony. The Austro-Italian elite was tempted more than ever before to look for answers beyond the Austrian borders.

The Austrian Adolf Hitler despised the multinational potential of Habsburg Austria. The fact that Germans had to live with non-Germans and that the official philosophy of Habsburg Austria was multinational was reason enough for the young Austrian to see his country as "decadent" and its mere existence as a contradiction to the interests of the German nation. He became convinced "that this state was bound to be a disaster for German nationhood" (Hitler 1938: 134).

This was the basic accord of pan-German nationalism in Austria: Austria and national interests as defined by pan-German nationalists in Austria could not coexist. For Adolf Hitler, the consequence was obvious: He did not want to be drafted into the army of this "decadent" state. He emigrated to Germany, where he voluntarily answered the German call to arms in 1914, when he was still an Austrian citizen.

But it was not the incompatibility of nationalism and pre-1914 Austria that constituted the dark side of Austria. It was the racist, "völkische" idea, which nationalism in Austria created, that produced that darkness. The antirational effect so palpable at the turn of the century in Europe sprang from many backgrounds and manifested itself in many different ways. The antirational sentiment directed against the enlightenment played an important role in preparing Europe for the Third Reich (Angebert 1974; Goodrick-Clarke 1985). But its most sinister and most destructive variety came from Austria. The madhouse that the Austrian Catholic Adolf Hitler represented and its alliance with the German war machine produced World War II and the Holocaust. This consequence had already been articulated by the time Hitler defined his "Weltanschauung." He did not have to create it, he had only to pick it up and implement what already existed.

Anti-Semitism was seen not only as an aspect of religious faith that divided Christians and Jews but also as a general explanation of the world that defined Jews as a "race" and as such responsible for all of modern society's woes. This view was deeply ingrained even in the "Christian" version of (not only) Austrian anti-Semitism of the nineteenth century. Hitler assimilated what was the self-evident part of the Catholic culture in his Upper Austrian environment and even more in Vienna. It was especially the lower clergy who preached a violent anti-Jewish creed to the Catholic masses. In the tradition of Abraham a Sancta Clara, a popular and crude anti-Semitic preacher in Vienna around 1700, these priests two hundred years later made "the Jew" the personification of evil.

One of the most prominent clergymen to use the "anti-Semitism from below" was the Viennese Josef Deckert (Heer 1968: 70 f.). He was the parish priest in a middle-class suburban parish. Deckert assured his parishioners that overt racist justification for anti-Jewish sentiments was fully compatible with the Church doctrine. He did in theological terms what Lueger did politically: mixed anti-Semitism with anticapitalism in a message exhorting the lower-middle class to recognize "the Jew" as the only culprit. And this Jew was defined not by creed but by birth.

The more intellectual among the first who organized what would later become the Christian-conservative camp tried to differentiate among religious, racist, and cultural elements. Karl von Vogelsang, the leading theorist of the Christian Socials in the 1880s, was careful not to criticize Jews for being Jews in the religious sense or for being a "race." For him, capitalism was the result of a cultural trend mainly represented by Jews; he was culturally anti-Semitic (Heer 1968: 70; Pauley 1992: 40–42). But the average Catholics, who did not read Vogelsang's essays on social reforms and social policy but who every Sunday heard the parish priest preaching that "the Jews" were responsible for Christ's death and for all their economic hardships, could not make this distinction.

For the Austrian Jews, the two elements of the "new anti-Semitism" of the late nineteenth century as represented by Lueger and Schönerer, by the Christian Socials and the pan-Germans, were not distinguishable. They observed not only the general hostility they were traditionally used to. They watched the rise of modern political parties with new organizational skills and psychological techniques built primarily on anti-Semitism. Anti-Semitism was no longer just an attitude of most Christians; it had suddenly become a political program. "The multi-ethnic Habsburg Empire was the cradle of the most successful modern political movement based on anti-Semitism to emerge anywhere in nineteenth-century Europe" (Wistrich 1989: 205).

The traditional escape Christian anti-Semitism had offered Jews in the past was no longer seen as the answer to the "Jewish question." If race and not creed determined the essence of Jewishness, there was no sense in converting. Friedrich Funder, editor of the Christian Socials' daily newspaper, *Die Reichspost,* reported on the experience of baptized Jews who realized that baptism was not enough to free them of their Jewish identity (Funder 1952: 299). In spite of being members of the Church, they were still victims of anti-Semitic attacks, even from Catholics. It was a foreboding of the fate in store for the "non-Aryan" Catholics, who Theodor Innitzer tried in vain to save after the "Anschluss."

Even after his conversion to Catholicism, Gustav Mahler continued to be "the Jew" for his environment. He described his experience in the following sentence: "I am thrice homeless, as a native of Bohemia in Austria, as an Austrian among Germans, and as a Jew throughout the world" (Wistrich 1989: 628). In 1938, Gustav Mahler's music was not allowed to be played in Austria, now part of the

Greater German Empire. Mahler's conversion could not change his Jewishness. Not long before his death in 1911, Mahler realized that baptism no longer provided an escape route.

The official Christian Social platform, which was based on the thinking of people such as Vogelsang and Lueger, was free of racist anti-Semitism. The reality of "Christian" anti-Semitism was that it secularized its religious justification by redefining Jewishness as a biological phenomenon. The pan-German attitude, in contrast, was even officially racist. At the end of the nineteenth century, the Austrian pan-German milieu as represented by the dueling fraternities, the "Burschenschaften," was already a combination of all the elements that were to become the ideological mixture of Austrian Nazism some decades later: They showed "contempt for classical liberalism, democracy, the Habsburg dynasty, the Catholic church, and the conventional social hierarchy," but also "worship of popular sovereignty, the Junker Bismarck, the Hohenzollern rulers and the whole militaristic-autocratic-aristocratic idea of Prussianism. . . . [It] exhibited xenophobia, anti-Semitism and racism . . . and suspiciousness and preoccupation with conspiracy" (Whiteside 1975: 57).

At the end of the nineteenth century, most of the organizations within the pan-German camp, as well as some of the Christian Social organizations, restricted their membership to "Germans" only. At the vanguard of this policy of exclusion were the "Burschenschaften," the most important recruiting base for the pan-German political elite in Austria even after 1945 (Pauley 1992: 30–34; Perner and Zellhofer 1994). In reality, the exclusion was an "Aryan paragraph": German was considered the antithesis of Jewish. No Jew could become a German, not even if he had been born into a German-speaking family and baptized immediately after birth. The Austrian anti-Semitism closed the social escape route Jews had been able to use in the past. And all this happened years before Hitler arrived in Vienna.

Hitler did not have to invent anything. The ideology was waiting on the streets of Linz and Vienna, and he only had to absorb what was already there. The Vienna Hitler observed during his stay from 1907 to 1913 was a madhouse. He needed someone to blame for his lack of professional success, and the racist ideology of the Jewish conspiracy fit the bill perfectly. He perceived Vienna as being dominated by Jews. Jews had taken over everything: the media, the economy, even the political left. Everything was under Jewish hegemony. Hitler was not responsible for his own failure. Vienna was responsible—and in Vienna, the Jews. He left, not to return until twenty-five years later (Jones 1980; Hamann 1996).

Ideologically, not much separated pan-German racism from the thinkers on the very fringe of society. Austria at the turn of the century was full of crazy theories that tried to explain everything as the fault of one evil, one conspiracy, one culprit only. The atmosphere of Vienna was poisoned, full of sinister accusations. And at the center of most of them was "the Jew."

Fin-de-siècle Vienna included many aspects: It was the city that Lenin, Stalin, and Trotsky visited; the political arena that played such an important role in the careers of people such as Thomas G. Masaryk and Alcide de Gasperi; the society that gave birth to the three camps that Victor Adler, Karl Lueger, and Georg von Schönerer represented; the cultural and scientific center that shaped so many of the minds crucial to any understanding of the intellectual history of the twentieth century (Johnston 1972; Schorske 1980: esp. 116–180). But Vienna was also home to great numbers of intellectual freaks who might never have had a role in history if others had not put their crude ideas into political effect. And most important among the others was Adolf Hitler.

One of those intellectual freaks was Georg Lanz von Liebenfels, a dissident Catholic and former monk. Lanz was responsible for the creation of a fantastic concept of the perpetual global struggle between the forces of light and the forces of darkness. But in contrast to early Christian versions of this dichotomous thinking, the Lanz version had a racist pseudo-biological slant. Whether a person was good or evil was predetermined by birth: The blond nordic type was by definition part of the light; its counterpart, the non-Aryan, was among the forces of darkness. "[Lanz] combined anthropology and zoology with the Scriptures in his account of the heroic Aryan good-men, their near extinction due to the wiles of racial inferiors, and the possibility of their resurrection through a racist-chivalrous cult. . . . [Lanz] clearly expressed a widespread sense of German insecurity in late imperial Austria" (Goodrick-Clarke 1985: 202).

The young Hitler was among the readers of Lanz's "Ostara" journals, and after 1945 the aged author remembered Hitler visiting him in 1909 because he wanted to buy some of the journals he hadn't yet read (Daim 1958).

It was precisely this Lanz-style mixture of vulgar Darwinism and vulgar romanticism that was to feed the thinking of the Nazis and especially of their order, the SS. The image of a deadly global battle between the races was already in place, as was the belief in the existence of an "Aryan" race, which would face extinction if it did not succeed in exterminating its inferior foe. Hitler only had to embrace the ideas he found in Austria and especially in Vienna.

Another intellectual freak was the philosopher Otto Weininger. Weininger was much less an outsider than Lanz was. His book *Geschlecht und Charakter* (*Gender and Character*) was a remarkable literary success (Weininger 1916). Weininger considered race and gender to be the variables that explain the history of mankind. The male principle was as morally superior to the female as the "Aryan" principle was to the non-Aryan. Weininger combined biological misogyny with racist anti-Semitism. It fit perfectly into the Nazi "philosophy" because it was the justification of male and "Aryan" predominance. But Weininger's analysis was deficient in one important point: He himself was Jewish. His suicide was the tragic consequence of his understanding (Janik 1987).

The self-destructive neuroticism Weininger represented reflected the all-embracing anti-Semitic atmosphere of fin-de-siècle Austria (Pulzer 1988; Oxaal, Pollak, and Botz 1987; Pauley 1992; Sottopietra 1997). This anti-Semitism, which was so obviously a part of the hegemonic cultural climate, left the Jews living in Austria with two options.

The first option was to deny the criteria the anti-Semitic environment had invented and to insist that being Jewish was purely a matter of religious affiliation. The consequence was assimilation. Politically, the blatant anti-Semitism all political camps with the exception of Social Democrats cultivated forced most of the politically vocal Austrian Jews to move to the left. Most prominent among the first generation of Socialists was Victor Adler, who became a Marxist despite what Marxists would have called his own "class interest." Adler's counterpart two generations later was Bruno Kreisky. The two men shared a common tendency to play down anti-Semitism—including the anti-Semitism that existed informally even among the rank and file of the Social Democratic Party (Pauley 1992: 133–149).

The second option was to accept their Jewish identity by transforming their religious belief into a national identity. It is no coincidence that the founder of modern Zionism was Austrian. As a reporter for the Viennese *Neue Freie Presse* covering the Dreyfus trial in Paris, Theodor Herzl saw firsthand what anti-Semitism was capable of doing. Ready to accept the challenge, Herzl started to fight anti-Semitism by organizing the Jews as a nation, as a "Volk" (Schorske 1980: 146–180). It was the secularized form of anti-Semitism, which declared that Jewishness could not be overcome by baptism, that was responsible for the secularized form of Jewishness. And it all started in Austria.

But Hitler was also the product of his Catholic environment. The Austria he was born into was the Austria formed by the Counter Reformation and dominated by the alliance between the crown and the Church. There was not much traditional Catholicism in Hitler after he left his mother's home in Linz. But he was a religious person in that he frequently referred to his "Herrgott" (Lord and God) and to Providence, which were guiding him and his movement. Hitler did not respect the real Church and spoke with contempt about the clergy. But he retained his regard for the Church as a principle, as a hierarchy, and especially as an organized, permanent liturgy. His architectural daydreams (Speer 1969: 166–175) and his fascination with mass spectacles like the Party Congresses in Nuremberg reflected something profoundly religious in him.

Hitler represented the secularized baroque version of Catholicism as expressed nowhere more clearly than in Austria. Before his family moved to Linz, Hitler spent two years at a monastery school in Lambach, run by Benedictine monks (Heer 1968: 21 f.). He was influenced by his father's anticlerical attitude as well as by his mother's traditional piety. Nothing is known about the young Hitler's church attendance or other religious activities after he left his Upper Austrian home and moved to Vienna, but Hitler never openly broke with the church he was born into. The neo-pagan tendencies others in his party followed were not his own.

Hitler ran the Greater German Empire almost as if it were the permanent organization of an infantile image of paradise: good and evil were clearly divided, and the forces of good had a standing invitation to enjoy perfectly arranged festivities, which were theatrical in their joyful celebration of countless victories. But Hitler's Catholic background may lead to speculation about more than just his subconscious and secularized baroque Catholicism. His background enabled him to deal successfully with the Catholic clergy. No one was easier for him to fool than the Archbishop of Vienna, Cardinal Theodor Innitzer.

When Hitler returned to his native country in March 1938, he emphasized his strong interest in the welfare of the Church. Innitzer visited Hitler on the very same day of the Nazis' perfectly organized rally on the "Heldenplatz" in Vienna. Innitzer did not contradict an official communiqué, which underlined Innitzer's "joy over the unification of German-Austria with the Reich" and the "willingness of the Catholic population to cooperate effectively in German restructuring" (Botz 1978: 76). The effects of this restructuring were already visible: Political opponents were being imprisoned, and the Jews from Vienna were forced to clean the sidewalks under the insults and mockery of some of their neighbors. The number of suicides skyrocketed.

Many Catholics were active in bridging the gap between Hitler and the bishops. One was Franz von Papen, the German envoy in Vienna from 1934 to 1938 whom Hitler recruited especially because he was a Catholic. Another was Bishop Alois Hudal, the Austrian who ran the German "Nationalstiftung" in Rome, the "Anima," established to represent German Catholic interests at the Holy See. In 1936, Hudal published his book *Die Grundlagen des Nationalsozialismus* (*The Foundations of National Socialism*) (Hudal 1936). In this book, which because its author was a bishop could only be published with the Vatican's approval, Hudal emphasized the parallels between the Nazi doctrine and Church doctrine and insisted that cooperation between the Nazis and the Church was possible. The main obstacle to a friendly agreement was, as far as Hudal could see, the Nazis' neo-pagan tendencies as represented by Alfred Rosenberg and not the principal anti-Semitic orientation the Nazi regime had already expressed in the Nuremberg Laws of 1935. In later years, Hudal played a rather important role in sheltering Nazi criminals and helping them to escape to South America (Hudal 1976; Aarons and Loftus 1991: esp. 26–42).

Another would-be "pontifex" (bridge builder) was the Austrian economist Othmar Spann, professor of economics at Vienna University. He tried to reconcile the corporatist thinking rooted in the Catholic tradition with modern fascism. His "universalism" represented a combination of all the nonsocialist, antimarket, and antidemocratic theories that could provide the missing link between Nazism and Catholicism (Siegfried 1974).

Spann did not get the reward he must have hoped for. In 1938, he and other representatives of his "school" lost their academic positions when they were removed to make room for the true believers. Hitler no longer needed go-betweens. Some of Spann's followers were even persecuted and jailed. A similar fate awaited Georg Lanz von Liebenfels: Not only was he not recognized as "the man who gave Hitler his ideas," he was also forbidden to publish (Daim 1958: 170). Hitler did not want anyone digging in his past and uncovering proof that there was nothing new in his ideas.

Hudal was also never rewarded for his efforts. The outcome of World War II made this bishop, known as a Nazi sympathizer, a burden and a public nuisance for the Vatican. Contrary to his expectations, he never became a cardinal—a failure he lamented at length in his memoirs, blaming the Vatican's post-1945 opportunism. The person he held especially accountable for his fall from grace was Archbishop Giovanni Montini, later Pope Paul VI (Hudal 1976: 264–312). Neither Hitler nor the Church was anxious to have the parallels between them fully recognized: not Hitler in 1938, when he had everything he wanted from Austria; and certainly not the Catholic Church in 1945, when evidence that its appeasement attempts had gone as far as Hudal's would have been damning.

On March 15, 1938, Hitler had promised Innitzer a "religious spring" for Austria (Botz 1978: 120). The Austrian bishops responded with an official recommendation to vote "yes" at the referendum the Nazis had organized for April 10, 1938. The referendum's purpose was to legitimize the already executed annexation ("Anschluss"). Despite the many differences between Hitler and the Austrian bishops, they still had one thing in common: the belief that Jews did not belong with the (German) people, to the Aryan race. The bishops' laissez-faire attitude toward the regime's racist anti-Semitism, already prevalent years before the "Anschluss," corresponded to the unwavering anti-Semitism of the Austrian Catholic Adolf Hitler.

Another card the Austrian Adolf Hitler was able to play successfully during the days of his triumphant return was socialism. During the last decades of the empire, the First Republic, and the four years of authoritarian rule, "capitalism" was a dirty word in Austria. Rhetorically, all three camps had an anticapitalistic orientation. This was easy to understand in the case of the Austro-Marxists. But what about the anticapitalism of the Christian-Socials or the pan-Germans?

Schönerer had already succeeded in his electoral campaigns by using strong anticapitalistic rhetoric. In 1879, he fought against the "Jewish domination of finance and communication" (Whiteside 1975: 84).

In its manifesto of 1920 ("Salzburger Programm"), the Pan-German People's Party, the party of the bourgeois element of the pan-German camp, declared that the Jews were a "foreign body" ("Fremdkörper") hostile to the "ethnic organism" ("Volksorganismus") (Berchtold 1967: 478). This biological view, the same as can be found in Hitler's *Mein Kampf,* was added to a lot of other extremely hostile and racist clichés in the manifesto. The Pan-German People's Party distanced itself from "internationalism," represented by the Jewish leadership of social democracy, as well as from the "materialistic" ideology ("Weltanschauung") of market-oriented "liberalism," also dominated by Jews (Berchtold 1967: 444). The consequence was a concept that was neither capitalist nor socialist—a kind of organic corporatism, which differed from the Catholic version in its critique of the "Roman-Christian" creed. The enemy was Jewish if he was not Roman. The (Austro-)German answer was first and foremost exclusion: exclusion of Jewish capitalists, of Jewish socialists, and of "Roman Christians." Xenophobia, not capitalism, dominated the thinking of the First Republic's most bourgeois party. And this xenophobia had already acquired a distinctly racist tone four years before

Adolf Hitler dictated his book in the Bavarian fortress where he had to live quite comfortably for some months after his putsch in November 1923.

For the Austrian bourgeoisie, anti-Semitism was more important than a clear position in favor of a market economy. Anti-Semitism put capitalism and socialism into one basket, labeled "Jewish." This was not so different from the Christian Socials' point of view. Anti-Semitism was less prominent in the official manifestos of the Christian Social Party than it was in those of the Pan-German People's Party, but the "Christian" version of anti-Semitism played a similar role, had a similar function. In their 1919 platform, the Viennese Christian Social Party declared the Jews a separate "nation" to distinguish them especially from the "Germans" (Berchtold 1967: 364). And in its all-Austrian platform of 1926, the Christian Social Party called for a fight against the "hegemony" ("Übermacht") of the "decomposing Jewish spirit on the intellectual as well as economic level" (Berchtold 1967: 376).

In 1938, it was easy for the Austrian Nazis to profit from the anticapitalistic rhetoric that had been so dominant in Austria for such a long time. Immediately after the occupation by German troops, the new regime demonstrated its socialism by implementing the following policies (Botz 1978: 134–139):

- Reinstating (former) social democratic workers in their former jobs, especially with the city of Vienna, as long as they were not Jewish and not too prominent as Socialists.
- Redistributing Jewish property among non-Jewish Austrians, not only active members of the NSDAP, thus creating a climate of political dependence but also of social mobility.
- Creating new jobs—some of them not really new, but "aryanized"—by expanding the Nazi bureaucracy on the eve of World War II as a continuation of the quasi-Keynesian economic policy the Nazis had begun in Germany.

These policies were responsible for many Social Democrats' somewhat ambiguous attitude toward the Nazi rule. Karl Renner was not the only appeaser from the left. His voluntary declaration in favor of the "Anschluss" was similar to that of the Austrian bishops (Botz 1978: 139–145). But many blue-collar workers recognized elements of socialism in the Nazis' "Realpolitik." The anti-Jewish measures nobody could ignore did not seem to play any visible counterproductive role. Not even an intellectual with plenty of international contacts and experience such as Karl Renner was immune to this ambiguity. In Renner's case, this lasted until at least November 1, 1938, when he wrote his praise of the Munich agreement (Pelinka 1989: 61–71).

Hitler was able to exploit his Austrian background. He played the role of the statesman interested in ushering in a new religious spring, and Cardinal Innitzer believed the seriousness of his intentions. Hitler promised to give workers jobs and housing—and many of them took the bait. He was an Austrian among Austrians and could play all the cards: pan-German, Socialist, and even Catholic. He succeeded because his message was not so different from that of so many other Austrians. The other Austrians had more or less accepted the theory that the Jews (and the gypsies) did not belong to the same race, to the same "Volk." So their fate was no obstacle to this spring of joy, this spring of 1938.

More than anyone else, the Austrian Adolf Hitler was able to overcome the deep fragmentation running through Austrian society. For the Catholics and their bishops, he was more acceptable than the Austro-Marxists; for the ordinary Austrian blue-collar worker, his social policy was more promising than that of the authoritarian regime. Hitler's pan-German background did not make him less attractive to the mainstream of the two other camps. His expansive nationalism and his anti-Semitic racism, whose murderous intentions were so obvious, were both acceptable even if they were not part of his attractiveness. The Austrians recognized Hitler as one of their own.

Of course, Hitler's Austrianness was only one factor that helped his rise to power. He had to succeed in a major European country before he could become the conqueror of Europe. Hitler as an Austrian dictator would not have made it. Austria was too small a country to serve as a power base for a totalitarian dictator who longed for global dominance. Hitler had to be a German dictator first.

The size of Hitler's following in Austria was not so different from that in Germany. To a certain extent, Hitler's henchmen were Austrian. The percentage can be disputed, but there is no doubt that among certain groups of Nazi leaders, Austrians were at least proportionally represented. And this is not only the case on the leadership level, whether party, SS, or Wehrmacht. This is also the case for the ordinary Austrian. In Daniel Goldhagen's work on the Holocaust, no doubt is left that the analysis of the Germans must also include Austrians (Goldhagen 1996). Willingness to accept the Holocaust, to actively participate in it, and to exploit the expulsion and murder of Jews in order to enrich themselves ("aryanization")—anything that can be said about "ordinary Germans" and their attitude must also be said about "ordinary Austrians."

Of course, this can be supplemented by naming: the Austrians Artur Seyss-Inquart and Ernst Kaltenbrunner, who were sentenced to death in Nuremberg; the Austrians Odilo Globocnik and Franz Stangl, who played such a deadly role in occupied Poland; the Austrian Alexander Löhr and the other officers who joined the Greater German Wehrmacht to fulfill prominent functions in the military aggression Hitler's plans included from the very beginning. The Austrian Adolf Hitler was not a deviant case in Austria—at least not as far as his beliefs were concerned.

The Roots Are Fertile Still

It would have been unrealistic to expect the Austrian roots of Nazism to vanish with the Nazi regime. The language of the Moscow Declaration of 1943, defining Austria as the first victim of Nazi aggression, and the antifascist rhetoric the Provisional Austrian Government used in 1945 did not and could not change the relationship between the past and the future. The truth about Austria's responsibility was too complex to fit into a neat formula of guilt or innocence. Just how complex the truth was can be seen in different cases:

- Austrian anti-Semitism was not restricted to Austrian Nazis. Many Austrians, who for good reasons considered themselves non-Nazis or even anti-Nazis, held the same attitude toward Jews as the Nazi leadership. Not all the registered members of the NSDAP in Austria were necessarily ardent Nazis, and many of the Austrians not registered were not immune to Nazi ideology.
- Austrian antidemocratic traditions were also to be found outside the NSDAP. The democratic tradition of the two other camps had to be reconstructed, too: The ÖVP had to make people forget its leaders' responsibility for the authoritarian regime, and the SPÖ had to rethink democracy as a concept that was more than just a step toward socialism.
- Austrian prejudices impeded the process by which Austrians came to fully accept the Nazi regime's persecution policies. Sentiments that justified the Nazis' treatment of the gypsies existed for a long time and condemnation of homosexuals even longer. Even the specific role of Jews as victims contradicted the predominant Austrian view of victims as "patriots" persecuted for political reasons.
- Austrian patriotism as an antithesis to traditional pan-Germanism was a fragile product of rather recent developments. The construction of a patriotic Austrian tradition against or even apart from German nationalism was politically motivated.
- Austrian social development was significantly influenced by the strong impact the Nazi years had on Austrian society. Nazism accelerated modernization, especially through economic input and educational reform.

The Austrian society of 1945 was significantly different from the society of 1938. There was continuity on the elite level of politics; there was continuity in political structures; but there was no continuity in society. The tendency of political elites—especially of the ÖVP—to see the year 1945 as a return to normality had nothing to do with the realities Austrian society was facing. There was no normality to which society could return.

One sign of this was both obvious and fully consistent with Nazi ideology: the nearly perfect "solution to the Jewish problem," as the regime had called it. By 1945, the Jewish community in Austria had practically ceased to exist: At the end of that year, it had only 1,730 surviving members (Embacher 1995: 101). Of some 200,000 Jews living in Austria before the "Anschluss," more than half had been able to escape before the transports started to the eastern ghettos. The official number of Austrian Jews murdered in the Holocaust is 65,459 (Embacher 1995: 28).

The Nazis had very nearly achieved their goal of a society without Jews. In the terms of Nazi racism, modern Austria was never more "ethnically pure" than in 1945. But anti-Semitism did not die with its victims. As in other countries, anti-Semites do not need Jews to justify their prejudice. If necessary, they invent them. And anti-Semitism continued to play a role in post-1945 Austria as an anti-Semitism virtually without Jews.

Some of the impacts the Nazi years had on Austria were contrary to the official goals the NSDAP was pledged to follow. They can be summarized by the term "modernization" (Mulley 1988):

- Industrialization. In a blatant contradiction of its romantic, retrograde economic ideology, the Nazi regime promoted not the agrarian but the industrial sector of the Austrian economy (Mooslechner and Stadler 1988: 85–87).
- Feminization of the labor force. Despite its anti-emancipationist ideology, the Nazi regime actually promoted a strong influx of women to the labor market (Mulley 1988: 40 f.; Berger 1988).
- Internationalization. Notwithstanding its exclusive ethno-nationalistic attitude, Nazism brought more Austrians than ever before into contact with foreigners—by invading foreign countries, by policing foreign regions, by using foreign labor at home.

Of course, all these consequences were the direct result of the war and the war economy. The need for an arms industry led to the political priority of industrialization. Because most of the men had been drafted into the Wehrmacht, the shortage of workers to staff this industry resulted in feminization and internationalization. In many cases, the demand for workers was filled with forced labor: An increasing percentage of the female labor force during World War II consisted of women brought to the Third Reich against their will. Internationalization had the same quality: It was not by choice that foreigners found themselves facing Austrian officers and soldiers in German uniforms, or Austrian employers, foremen, and farmers. It was an internationalization without balance, but it was an internationalization nevertheless. How many Austrians would have seen the Caucasus, northern Norway, or the Libyan desert if the war had not sent them there? How many Ukrainians, Poles, and later, Americans or Russians would have come to Austria? How many contacts were direct results of the war?

Years later, the mystique of a city such as Stalingrad would provoke a kind of negative nostalgia in Austria. Veterans would talk about it—in most of the cases ignoring the atrocities committed by the Greater German Wehrmacht. But for many Austrians of this generation, World War II was the great adventure of their lives. The war was also responsible for a huge wave of migration: Hundreds of thousands of non-Austrians came to Austria, and many stayed, including "Volksdeutsche" (ethnic Germans) from Central and Eastern Europe and non-German

Eastern Europeans, among the latter some thousand Jews. Many Austrians learned their English through contacts with the occupation forces, and many used those contacts to emigrate, especially to America.

The effects of the Nazi era and World War II on Austria were the most destructive in its history. But there was also an integrative effect of the war's outcome. As a result of World War II, Austria became an object of Cold War power conflicts. The Marshall Plan and its immediate impact integrated Austria into the Western economy (Tweraser 1995).

Modernization started with the German war economy. Production was stepped up by all available means. From 1937 to 1944, the production of electricity was increased by exactly 100 percent (Kernbauer and Weber 1988: 61). This had an important side effect on the labor market: Unemployment disappeared. Of course, neither the means of change nor the end must be forgotten—concentration camps plus forced labor; military aggression and the Holocaust.

The German war industry was responsible for the industrialization of Austria's post-1945 economy. The steel production established in Linz as the Hermann Göring factories became the "flagship" of Austria's nationalized industry after 1945, the VÖEST (United Austrian Iron and Steel Industries). And the German war machine's demand for more electricity was met by the construction of the Kaprun Dam, built during the war using forced labor and finished after the war under the auspices of the Austrian government. Some of the Austrian industries that the Second Republic used to bring about the "economic miracle" of the 1950s were built by forced labor during World War II (Freund and Perz 1988).

The Nazi era also had a modernizing effect on the Austrian society through education. As a consequence of its extreme exclusion and inclusion ideologies, the Nazi regime was radical in its repression and exclusion of all those who did not belong to the "German people." But for those who qualified as Germans, the regime's policies were of a comparable egalitarian approach. This was especially true in educational matters (Dachs 1988; Lichtenberger-Fenz 1988). The Nazi goal and ultimate impact was to secularize private, especially Catholic institutions, and to promote and encourage the underprivileged, especially the working class. Despite the bishops' appeasement, Catholic schools and other educational organizations fell victim to NSDAP policy soon after the "Anschluss." The NS state and the NS party, de facto one entity, had a perfect monopoly on education.

This had an egalitarian impact, which was to be of significant consequence for the Second Republic. "Aryan" working-class youths were systematically recruited for higher education by enlarging the number of state institutions, including strongly politicized schools like the NAPOLAs (National Political Educational Institutions). In Austria, there were seven such institutes, some of them in buildings confiscated from former Catholic schools (Dachs 1988: 225 f.).

The impact of seven years of NS education became obvious in the 1970s, when this generation reached top political positions. Many of those who had taken advantage of the opportunity of higher education during the Nazi years were from proletarian backgrounds, from families deeply rooted in the social democratic tradition. The most talented and ambitious of the young proletarians had been invited and encouraged to benefit from this "socialist" aspect of the educational system. Not all, but a significant number, of those who received this kind of NS education had joined the Nazi Party. Because they were young, not prominent, and not involved in any specific crime, it was no problem for them to be "denazified" after 1945. Most of them simply returned to the social background from which they had come—the milieu of the socialist camp. And because they were ambitious and better educated, they went into careers in areas now under the control of the SPÖ such as the nationalized industries or politics.

These facts explain the surprisingly large number of former NSDAP members in Kreisky's cabinet. Five of the ministers of this SPÖ-cabinet—all of that generation—were "uncovered" as former Nazis. Among the members of the first cabinet, there were "only" four. But when it became known that the minister of agriculture was not only a former party member but also an "illegal" SS officer, he had to resign for "reasons of health." His successor had also belonged to the Nazi Party, but only as a rank-and-file member (Secher 1993: 178).

That Austrians who had joined the Nazi party in their youth could ensue a successful career within the SPÖ and even achieve cabinet rank was the result of two combined factors:

- The modernizing effect of NS education was less important for the two camps traditionally seen as "bourgeois." It was far more important for the camp that was home to the working class. Education signified the osmosis between the Nazi regime and Austrian social democracy—a relationship that existed despite the theoretically unbridgeable gap between those two sides.
- The Second Republic had no qualms about former "ordinary" Nazi Party members. To have been just a "small Nazi" was not a career disadvantage. Only those who had held higher positions in the Nazi hierarchy were considered unacceptable for higher positions in the Second Republic. This was the case with Kreisky's first agricultural minister, Hans Öllinger, and with Friedrich Peter, FPÖ chairman from 1958 to 1978, both of whom were former SS officers. Öllinger could not become minister in 1970, and Peter could not become third president of the National Council in 1983.

Although Kreisky was not aware of Öllinger's SS background when he recruited him for a cabinet position, he was very much aware of Peter's because the two men had established a common bond approaching friendship (Kreisky 1986: 206 f.). Kreisky staunchly defended Peter against Simon Wiesenthal's allegations that Peter's SS unit had been involved in mass killings of civilians in the Soviet Union (Secher 1993: 182–185). Kreisky's emotional rebuttal provoked anti-Semitic attacks on Wiesenthal. The attackers felt justified because "another Jew," Bruno Kreisky, had also criticized Wiesenthal (Wodak et al. 1990: 282–322).

But when the FPÖ nominated Peter to be the third president of the National Council in 1983, during the founding of the SPÖ-FPÖ coalition, even Kreisky's protection could not change the SPÖ's refusal to accept him. Peter had to withdraw his nomination to make the coalition, which was both his and Kreisky's main goal, possible (Pelinka 1993: 30 f.).

By 1983, things had already started to change. The new generation of Austrians was becoming more sensitive to their country's Nazi past, to anti-Semitism, and to the dark side of Austria. The Waldheim affair was soon to come.

The careers of Kreisky's five cabinet ministers within the SPÖ between 1945 and 1970 were not careers based on their former NS affiliation. They were not appointed because they were former Nazis, but their past affiliation was not a career obstacle for them either. A simple lack of sensitivity made it possible for the SPÖ to follow policies that contradicted the Second Republic's official philosophy as well as their own programmatic tradition. The SPÖ was also very much in need of better-educated personnel when the rules of consociational democracy made it necessary for them to put people in leading positions. The Jews, traditionally so important for the intellectual ranks within Austrian social democracy, were not available in any significant numbers. So some of the former members of the same party that was responsible for the Holocaust benefited from the opportunities that opened on the political left after 1945.

And the SPÖ was not alone in its extremely pragmatic method of dealing with Austria's claim to be the first victim of Nazi aggression. The ÖVP had its parallel cases. Reinhard Kamitz, minister of finance in the 1950s, had also been an "ordinary" member of the NSDAP. And the case of Taras Borodajkewycz signified the same lack of sensitivity in the ÖVP as the case of Hans Öllinger in the SPÖ.

Taras Borodajkewycz was an Austrian Catholic with a traditional background in the elite of political Catholicism: He was a member of the Cartel-Verband (CV), the Catholic, nondueling students' fraternities. Born in 1902, he studied history and earned a doctoral degree. He was one of the organizers of the German "Katholikentag" (Catholic Day) in Vienna in September 1933. In 1934, he joined the NSDAP, at that time an illegal organization in Austria. He belonged to the group of Catholics who wanted to mediate between Nazism and Catholicism. After the "Anschluss," he got his reward from the new regime. When the Nazis occupied Prague and took over full control of University of Prague, Borodajkewycz became a professor. He published some historical articles that were pure Nazi propaganda (Fischer 1966: esp. 7–29).

After 1945, Borodajkewycz had a Soviet scholarship to do research in the Austrian Archives ("Österreichisches Staatsarchiv"). In 1949, he returned to his old role as a go-between, helping to recruit some prominent Nazis for the ÖVP. It was the time when most of the former NSDAP members reentered the political process after getting back their voting rights. The VDU was trying to become the successor of the Pan-German People's Party and the Landbund, which had been the two smaller parties of the pan-German camp before it was almost completely absorbed by the NSDAP. The SPÖ was extremely interested in bringing the VDU into existence in an effort to prevent most of the former Nazis from voting for the ÖVP (Riedlsperger 1978). Borodajkewycz was useful in the ÖVP's counterstrategy. On May 28, 1949, a significant meeting took place in the Upper Austrian village of Oberweis. Prominent ÖVP leaders met with prominent (former) NS representatives, among them some SS officers—and Taras Borodajkewycz (Fischer 1966: 27–32).

Borodajkewycz was once more rewarded with a professorship. With the active support of the ÖVP, which controlled higher education at that time, he became a professor of history at the University of Economics in Vienna. In this position, he was the subject of one of the affairs that characterized Austria's rather inconsistent methods of dealing with the Nazi past. Borodajkewycz was not pragmatic, not flexible enough. Too much of his old political creed influenced his teaching. He was not a turncoat: He still was teaching his own understanding of history, the same he had taught in Prague. Some of the aspects of this teaching were later described by an Austrian court: Borodajkewycz used anti-Semitic clichés, openly advocated a pan-German understanding of history, and justified some aspects of Hitler and his regime (Fischer 1966: 153–164).

This was the leading historian at one Austrian university during the 1950s and the first half of the 1960s. But in 1965, Borodajkewycz's position became undefendable. He had already sued for libel in response to an article condemning his Nazi past. In a second trial, the defendants, Social Democrats, were able to prove the validity of their allegations against Borodajkewycz. During the trial, witnesses testified as to the essence of Borodajkewycz's teaching at the University of Economics. Borodajkewycz was suspended and later forced into an earlier retirement.

The "Borodajkewycz affair" had a second consequence. Opponents of Borodajkewycz organized two demonstrations in Vienna. When right-wing students, among them members of dueling fraternities, organized counterdemonstrations, the police lost control and street fighting erupted. It appeared to be the return to the First Republic's confrontational style. On March 31, 1965, during the second of those demonstrations, a right-wing student killed a leftist demonstrator, Ernst Kirchweger (Scharsach 1995: 25–30). The death of Kirchweger, a survivor of Nazi persecution, had a "cathartic effect" (Kasemir 1995: 497). Almost all the members of the cabinet—with the exception of some ÖVP members including Federal Chancellor Josef Klaus—attended Kirchweger's funeral. Thus, in its last year, the (first) grand coalition presented a unified front against Nazism. But the lack of principles in confronting Austria's past, which had allowed Borodajkewycz to teach at an Austrian university, could not be changed in retrospect. What was called pragmatism was in reality pure opportunism.

But this opportunism had something to do with democracy in that the political elites responded to the demands and support of the electorate. The opportunism of the ÖVP and SPÖ reflected public opinion. Had the ÖVP and SPÖ done a serious cost-benefit analysis in the 1960s and 1970s, it would have shown one clear result: Confronting and offending the socially ingrained elements of Nazism, anti-Semitism, pan-German nationalism, and xenophobic racism would have a negative net effect. It would cost more votes than it would win.

This accounts for both the ÖVP's hesitant methods of dealing with its own protegé Borodajkewycz as well as the careers that put former NS members into cabinet positions under Kreisky. It was well-calculated opportunism that explained the somewhat unprincipled approach both major parties used in that period.

In the 1960s and 1970s, the social sciences began to have an impact on Austrian politics. Political leaders started to look at public opinion data before they made decisions. This was a much more sophisticated way to respond to electoral interests than the SPÖ's strategy of supporting the foundation of the VDU, or the ÖVP's strategy of promoting prominent (former) Nazis as demonstrated in the Borodajkewycz affair. But it was the same logic, the logic of sheer numbers: Many more voters would be repelled by a principled anti-Nazi policy consistent with the Second Republic's official philosophy than would be lost by an "opportunistic" policy of double-talk.

The social sciences made it clear that there was still anti-Semitism in Austria decades after the end of the Third Reich. Some of the characteristics of "postfascist anti-Semitism" in Austria were different from those of pre-1945 anti-Semitism (Bunzl and Marin 1982: esp. 197–224; Weiss 1984).

First, it was an anti-Semitism without Jews. Part of the anti-Semitic stereotype was that the number of Jews living in Austria was grossly overestimated. Jews had to be invented in order to construct some kind of justification for anti-Semitic clichés. Before 1938, the number of Austrians with Jewish identity was about 200,000. After 1945, it was about 10,000, the majority immigrants from Eastern Europe. In a 1976 study, only 16 percent of the Viennese questioned correctly estimated the percentage of the Austrian population consisting of Jews: less than 1 percent. The vast majority thought the percentage of Jews was much higher; 28.6 percent thought it was over 10 percent (Weiss 1984: 146). The anti-Semitic prejudice was not ready to accept and admit the consequences of the Holocaust.

Second, it was an anti-Semitism with shame. Before 1938, a great number of Austrians had no problem openly admitting that their attitude toward Jews was hostile. After 1945, most Austrians were anxious to explain that they had "nothing against Jews." The anti-Semitic prejudice had gone underground, in most of the cases beneath the level of consciousness. Austrian anti-Semites no longer consider themselves anti-Semitic. It was an "anti-Semitism without anti-Semites" (Bunzl and Marin 1982: 177). One consequence of the Holocaust was that being against Jews was no longer openly accepted in Austria.

Finally, it was an anti-Semitism of the uneducated. Before 1938, anti-Semitism was fully accepted in academic circles including universities (Pauley 1992: 89–101). After 1945, higher education became negatively correlated with anti-

Semitic attitudes. Once a prejudice overproportionally voiced by the socially and culturally privileged, anti-Semitism had now become more a sentiment of the underprivileged (Bunzl and Marin 1982: 180–182; Weiss 1984: 135). There was some hope that education would make a difference. Higher education had ceased to work in favor of anti-Jewish hatred.

But it was still an anti-Semitism that was correlated with party preference. In 1976, anti-Semitism was most prevalent among FPÖ voters and least prevalent among SPÖ voters, with ÖVP voters somewhere in between (Weiss 1984: 145). This correlates with other results (Pauley 1992: 307). The left was not immune to anti-Semitism, but it was less inclined toward it.

It is not so easy to evaluate the influence of religion on Austrian post-1945 anti-Semitism. There is some indication that the Catholic intellectuals changed most significantly in their attitude toward Jews. The young generation of better-educated Austrian Catholics showed a significant concern for the Holocaust, including its religious roots. Erika Weinzierl, an Austrian historian whose academic career spanned the 1960s, 1970s, and 1980s, represents this self-critical tendency among Austrian Catholics (Weinzierl 1969). The impact active Catholicism had on post-1945 anti-Semitism must be distinguished along the lines of education and generation: The younger and better educated they were, the less inclined Austrian Catholics were (and are) to nourish anti-Jewish sentiments.

The significance of the generation factor is more unequivocal: The above-mentioned study from 1976 shows a definite if not dramatic correlation between age and anti-Semitism. Younger Austrians were significantly less anti-Semitic than older (Weiss 1984: 135).

With these statistics, it is possible to construct an "Index of Anti-Semitic Predisposition" in Austria for the 1960s and 1970s. This index is analogous to the famous "Index of Political Predisposition" that Paul F. Lazarsfeld, Bernard Berelson, and Hazel Gaudet created for their classical study on electoral behavior, *The People's Choice* (Lazarsfeld, Berelson, and Gaudet 1944). For the 1960s and 1970s—the years of the end of the (first) grand coalition, the SPÖ's rise to dominance in the party system, and the Kreisky era, which can also be called the pre-Waldheim period—the inclination toward anti-Semitism can be distinguished as follows:

- Factors favoring anti-Semitic tendencies: lack of higher education, older generation, political sympathies right of the center.
- Factors opposing anti-Semitic tendencies: higher education, younger generation, political sympathies left of the center.

This index, like that in *The People's Choice*, only indicates probabilities; and it includes many crosscutting tendencies. The phenomenon that in this period the majority of less-educated Austrians tended toward the SPÖ whereas the majority of higher-educated Austrians leaned toward the ÖVP must especially be seen as factors responsible for cross pressures. So the profile of a person with the highest probability of being immune to anti-Semitism at that time would be left-leaning intellectual, socialized after 1945, either with strong Catholic motives or with no religious motivation at all.

The changes that started in the 1980s and became politically explosive in the 1990s lessened some of the cross pressures included in the "Index of Anti-Semitic Predisposition" of the 1970s and early 1980s. The blue-collar vote started to dissolve its traditional ties with the SPÖ. Younger workers gravitated more and more to the FPÖ, the party that traditionally showed the least restraint concerning anti-Semitism. The impact of the new mix of factors favoring anti-Semitic prejudice is difficult to predict. But it is probable that timid anti-Semitism is becoming less timid and is taking on, not necessarily a new importance, but a new candor. The restraint of cross pressures has decreased in the 1990s. The contrasts are clearer now than they were in the Kreisky era, and the confrontation is less complicated by ambiguities and contradictions of political ideology and social status.

Those changes did not come about as a result of the "affair" that put Austria in the international spotlight, the Waldheim affair. It would be misleading to overlook the deeply rooted social and political changes already taking place in Austria. Kurt Waldheim's election was not the reason that Austria's dark side was revealed. But the Waldheim affair was a catalyst in that it sharpened both the international and the domestic perspective of Austria. The affair unleashed sentiments that had been inconsistently restrained and removed obstacles that had obscured the view of Austria's past and present.

The affair had several aspects. One was the pure historical side of Waldheim's career. Had Kurt Waldheim, the former Secretary General of the United Nations, actively participated in Nazi atrocities? This question has caused heated debates. The intensive research into the subject of the controversy, which began in 1986, yielded rather clear results: Waldheim's role in the Greater German Wehrmacht, especially in the Balkans, was more important than he had previously admitted in his memoirs. But there was and still is no proof of any criminal wrongdoing on his part (Cohen and Rosenzweig 1986; Born 1987; Palumbo 1988; Herzstein 1988).

Waldheim himself tried to avoid a polarized debate. He made certain deliberately vague statements ("I was only doing my duty") purposely void of any anti-Semitic references. However, at the same time, he did not, at least not during the electoral campaign, clearly oppose the anti-Semitic overtones of some of his supporters (Wodak et al. 1990: 59–120; Mitten 1992: 198–245).

More important than all the details about Waldheim's intelligence activity in Greece and Yugoslavia was the function the debate took on. On a second metalevel, it was also a debate about Austrian anti-Semitism, about Austria's Nazi past. One principal aspect was the role that the World Jewish Congress played in the whole business, or rather, the role attributed to it by some of Waldheim's supporters and defenders. Waldheim was turned into a "victim" of the Jews, and many of the arguments involved used various transparent euphemisms: references, for example, to "certain circles" on the East Coast of the United States who control the American media.

One example of this aspect of the controversy was the public letter the ÖVP deputy mayor of Linz, Carl Hödl, wrote to Edgar Bronfman, President of the World Jewish Congress. The new dimension was the newfound respectability of an anti-Semitism that was no longer timid, as the post-1945 anti-Semitism had been. Hödl wrote: "Your co-religionists two thousand years ago had Jesus Christ condemned to death in a show trial because he did not fit in with the ideas of the rulers of Jerusalem. . . . An eye for an eye, a tooth for a tooth is not our European way. The promulgation of this fundamental talmudic tenet throughout the world was left to you and your kind" (Pelinka 1990: 85 f.).

This letter revealed the essence of traditional Christian anti-Semitism. It came as no surprise that it was still possible to think along those lines in Austria more than four decades after the liberation of Auschwitz. It was however surprising that a fairly influential leader of the People's Party dared to declare his anti-Semitic attitude in an open letter. Hödl may have speculated that the time had come to be more frank about "the Jews." His personal anti-Semitism had become less timid. But he had miscalculated: Following the publication of his letter he had to resign.

Another aspect of anti-Semitic clichés came into the open during the Waldheim debate: Anti-Semitism is negative, but the Jews are responsible for it. Ilse Leitenberger, a leading conservative Austrian journalist, wrote an editorial for *Die Presse*, a highly respected conservative paper, about Waldheim's opponents, especially the World Jewish Congress. In it, she said: "They are the ones who bear a considerable amount of blame for the fact that a new anti-Semitism can no longer be denied, the escalation of which we can hardly imagine". (Pflichterfüllung 1986: 35). How lamentable, this Austrian anti-Semitism. But who is to blame? Jews!

Perhaps the most important outcome of the Waldheim affair was the internationalization of Austrian anti-Semitism. Ongoing controversy over Kurt Waldheim opened a general discussion of the specifically Austrian roots of anti-Semitism, and particularly the continuing existence of that anti-Semitism. Never before during the Second Republic had Austria been the subject of so much international scrutiny. But there had to be also a domestic reaction, and this reaction was a polarized one.

One indicator of this polarization is that few Austrians still avoid taking a clear stance on anti-Semitism. In a representative survey done in 1991, 39 percent of Austrians agreed with the anti-Semitic cliché: "Throughout history the Jews have caused a lot of trouble," but 55 percent rejected the statement. Only 6 percent had no opinion (*Journal für Sozialforschung* 1991: 450).

It is the decline of the "don't know" answers that is important, compared with studies of Austrian anti-Semitism in the 1970s. And it is again the readiness to have and express strong opinions that distinguishes the Austrian attitude of the 1990s from attitudes in former Communist countries at the same time (*Journal für Sozialforschung* 1991: 450–452). The debate was now an open one. The elites had lost control. Politicians like Hödl no longer hesitated to openly confess opinions they had kept to themselves during all the years of the Second Republic. Journalists like Leitenberger continued to openly express their contempt for anti-Semitism, but contended that the people responsible for it were Jews and Jewish organizations.

But there was also another side to the ambiguous reaction. For the first time, official representatives of Austria recognized Austria's co-responsibility for the Holocaust. Federal Chancellor Franz Vranitzky used that language at formal occasions many times: in 1988, when the Austrian federal government remembered the fiftieth anniversary of the "Anschluss," in 1991 in parliament, and again in 1993, when he visited Israel. Federal President Thomas Klestil did the same at his state visit to Israel in 1994, using the same rhetoric, which has now become a kind of official version of contemporary Austrian history: "All too often we have spoken only of Austria as the first state to have lost its freedom and independence to National Socialism—and far too seldom of the fact that many of the worst henchmen in the Nazi dictatorship were Austrians" (Antisemitism 1995: 90).

What a difference from the official attitude of ÖVP and SPÖ representatives immediately after 1945, when they insisted that Austria had had nothing to do with Nazism and therefore bore no responsibility whatsoever, especially for the financial consequences (Rot-Weiss-Rot-Buch 1946; Knight 1988). But the responses of the 1990s went far beyond the level of rhetoric when police and criminal courts started to crack down on right-wing extremism (Heindl 1994; Gallhuber 1994). One direct consequence was that Gottfried Küssel, the self-proclaimed "Führer" of the VAPO ("Volkstreue Außerparlamentarische Opposition"), perhaps the most notorious of the violent neo-Nazi groups in Austria with international links to Germany, the United States, and elsewhere, was found guilty of Nazi activity by an Austrian jury and sentenced to years in prison (Purtscheller 1993: 400–417).

Neo-Nazism and/or Right Populism?

Both the international and domestic attention has shifted from the Waldheim generation to the post-1945 type Austrians. Jörg Haider has replaced Waldheim as the person who provokes domestic polarization. In the 1990s, it is the FPÖ chairman who seems to elicit few "don't know" responses, and he attracts most of the criticism from those who observe tendencies to use xenophobic and racist clichés (Antisemitism 1995: 80 f.). In the 1990s, Haider plays the polarizing role that was Waldheim's in the 1980s. It does not matter that the two are very different with regard to generation, background, ideological roots, and political style. Waldheim is a product of the Christian-conservative camp, a professional diplomat, and a typical representative of post-1945 consociationalism, who happened to have had selective amnesia about his years in the Wehrmacht. Haider is deeply rooted in the

Nazi past of his family; his politics were shaped by the post-1945 isolation of Austrian pan-Germanism, and his style is confrontational (Bailer and Neugebauer 1994: 368 f.). Waldheim was always oriented toward elitist compromise (Waldheim 1996); Haider behaves like a typical populistic challenger (Scharsach 1992; Haider 1993; Scharsach 1995).

The FPÖ was a party standing at the crossroads when Haider took over the chairmanship in 1986. In the tradition of Friedrich Peter, the FPÖ leadership had tried to win respectability by behaving in the consociationalist way. Norbert Steger, chairman from 1980 to 1986, had what German chancellor Helmut Kohl called the "grace of late birth" to avoid the obstacles Friedrich Peter's generation of Austrian pan-Germans had to face. Steger established the coalition with the SPÖ, hoping to make the FPÖ the kind of pivotal centrist party the FDP has been in Germany since 1949 (Pelinka 1993). But he had underestimated the strong resentment of the pan-German rank and file within his party. Haider used this internal opposition to overthrow the Steger leadership in 1996.

Haider's leadership was both successful and unsuccessful at the same time. The FPÖ more than quadrupled its share of the electorate—from just 5 percent in 1983 to more than 22 percent in 1994. But the FPÖ became isolated to a degree unknown even to the VDU when the ÖVP's invitation to join the grand coalition in 1953 had to be withdrawn because Federal President Theodor Körner threatened to veto it (Riedlsperger 1978: 124–128). The Haider FPÖ was able to win more public support than any other leader of the pan-German camp after 1945 could have ever dared to hope for. But the Haider FPÖ paid dearly for this electoral success on the elitist level, when his habit of breaking taboos by mobilizing xenophobic resentments and flirting with elements of the Nazi past made him unacceptable in any power configuration.

The FPÖ is a rather unique party. Since its break with the Liberal International in 1993, the party has not belonged to any of the European party families. The other established Austrian parties, in contrast, are all members of a party family, with a corresponding party group in the European parliament: the Social Democrats, the Christian Democrats and Conservatives, the Liberals, and the Greens.

Is the FPÖ a neo-Nazi party? Yes and no. No, because many elements in this party, especially since Haider took over leadership, would not be possible in a hard-core fascist party. Yes, because the Haider FPÖ virtually absorbed all the smaller right-wing parties that existed in the pre-Haider days. In 1980, for instance, when the FPÖ under the leadership of Norbert Steger had nominated the moderate Wilfried Gredler for the office of the federal presidency, the small neo-Nazi NDP (National Democratic Party) nominated its chairman, Norbert Burger. Burger got 3.2 percent of the vote, a remarkably good showing for an extremist (Müller, Plasser, and Ulram 1995: 547).

There is a legal reason behind the vanishing of parties like the NDP: Austrian authorities have narrowed their interpretation of the liberty to which parties with clear links to Nazism are entitled. The parties simply no longer have much legal leeway in Austria. But the electoral success of the FPÖ gives rise, at least hypothetically, to a second explanation: The Haider FPÖ satisfies a fundamental need of some right-wing elements, a need not satisfied by the policies of Haider's predecessors Peter and Steger. The history of the Second Republic's right-wing extremism until Haider took over the FPÖ was the history of activists from the pan-German camp who became disillusioned with the moderation of politicians like Peter or Steger. Burger, the founder and leader of the NDP, was himself a former FPÖ activist and the best example of this background of right-wing extremism (Dokumentationsarchiv 1994: 98 f., 131 f., 168–174).

But there are some important factors that distinguish the Haider FPÖ from hard-core neo-Nazism. One is the kind of respectability Haider wants to establish. Whereas Steger's goal of respectability meant winning the acceptance of ÖVP and SPÖ leaders, Haider's goal is acceptance of the FPÖ as a broad protest movement consisting not only of fringe elements of the Austrian political spectrum.

The party is using some of its more intellectual activities to prove that it represents not only the most extreme facets of political thinking. The FPÖ academy (Freiheitliches Bildungswerk), like the academies of the other established parties financed by federal funds, regularly invites authors with other points of view to contribute articles for its annual publication. The 1995 yearbook, for example, contains the writings of internationally respected philosophers, political scientists, and journalists (including Hermann Lübbe and Marion Gräfin Dönhoff), less-respected authors with revisionist tendencies (such as Werner Pfeifenberger), authors from the FPÖ's own extreme right wing (such as Otto Scrinzi), authors with single-issue attraction (such as Karl Socher and his critique of Austria's entry into the EU), and authors who deal with traditional pan-German topics (such as Walter Marinovic's attack on multicultural concepts) (Höbelt, Mölzer, and Sob 1994).

The function of this yearbook and other publications with an academic approach is to provide arguments against reproach that the FPÖ is simply the party of Austrian neo-Nazism. Nazism? There is "even" a Jew among the authors. Extremism? There are prominent liberals among the authors. The NSDAP as well as the NDP would not have bothered to invite Jewish and liberal authors to publish their thoughts in a semi-official party yearbook.

Another factor, which perhaps distinguishes the Haider FPÖ more from the fringe parties of post-1945 neo-Nazism than from the historical NSDAP, is the party's electorate and its motivation. The FPÖ's electorate has changed dramatically since 1986, and although the motives responsible for that change may be called nationalistic, they have almost nothing to do with the traditional values the pan-German camp has always esteemed most.

The electoral structure has changed dramatically with regard to gender and profession (see Table 9.1). The FPÖ's rise has been due to the significant increase in its popularity among the blue-collar and the male segment of Austrian society. Age is less significant: the FPÖ is most attractive to members of not only the

TABLE 9.1 Changes in the FPÖ Electorate, 1986–1994

The FPÖ's share of ballots cast	1986	1990	Difference
General electorate: All voters	10%	23%	+ 13%
Men	12	28	+ 16
Women	7	17	+ 10
18–29 year-olds	12	25	+ 13
30–44	11	22	+ 11
45–59	6	22	+ 16
60–69	8	15	+ 7
70 and older	9	29	+ 20
With no school degree	6	21	+ 15
With compulsory school degree	11	26	+ 15
With high school degree	10	19	+ 9
With university degree	15	15	0
Skilled workers	11	33	+ 22
Unskilled workers	8	24	+ 16
Public sector (white-collar) employees	9	14	+ 5
Private sector (white-collar) employees	13	22	+ 9
Self-employed, freelance professions	15	30	+ 15
Farmers	5	15	+ 10
Retired	7	24	+ 17

SOURCE: Plasser and Ulram 1995: 485.

youngest but also the oldest segment of the population. The general trend can be characterized as the proletarianization and the masculinization of the FPÖ.

This fits into the pattern of parties to the far right of the center in other democracies (Lipset 1960). But it fits only to a certain degree into the pattern of the NSDAP's rise. The NSDAP was much more the party of the cultural elite, a fact expressed by its overproportional popularity with university students and graduates. The FPÖ's rather new attraction for blue-collar voters is reminiscent of the NSDAP's ability to attract the workers' vote in Germany at the end of the Weimar Republic. But in relative terms, this was much less significant than the blue-collar proportion of the FPÖ vote in the 1990s in Austria. And the FPÖ has almost no comparative attraction for better-educated voters. The FPÖ has a clear deficit with the cultural elite—a deficit the NSDAP clearly did not have (Childers 1983; Falter 1991).

A look at the factors that motivate people to vote FPÖ reveals some of what has been "new" in the FPÖ since Haider became chairman. Various opinion polls showed that people associated three areas of concern with the FPÖ in the 1990s and saw the FPÖ as being most competent to deal with all three (Plasser and Ulram 1995: 477):

- solving the "foreigner problem,"
- fighting corruption and mismanagement ("Privilegienwirtschaft"), and
- eliminating waste in public spending.

The second and third areas of concern encompass issues usually attributed to parties in opposition. But the first concern has something to do with xenophobia. The FPÖ is synonymous with the topic "foreigners," which was the issue of its popular initiative in 1993 (Bailer and Neugebauer 1994: 450–456). But it is precisely this combination of at least potentially xenophobic motives and traditional protest motives that helps to explain the FPÖ's popularity. There are many reasons to criticize and to oppose government. In Austria, there are specific reasons for political protest. Consociational democracy Austrian-style and aspects of intensive party influence provoke enough discomfort among those who feel excluded. Voting for the strongest opposition party is within the logic of liberal democracy because the administration seems to ignore legitimate demands.

It is the mixture that makes the difference because it is the mixture that is obliterating the difference. Anyone with racist views has reason to find the FPÖ attractive: The antiforeigner slogans it directs against migrants from Eastern and Southeastern Europe as well as from countries outside Europe are an invitation to those with right-wing sympathies to vote for the FPÖ. But even those who are unmoved by slogans against migration and migrants but who are motivated to protest against the political insensitivity of the ruling elites may be inclined to vote for the opposition party that commands the loudest voices of protest. The FPÖ is both the standard-bearer of Austria's traditional dark side and the legitimate opposition party voicing the protests of those who do not feel recognized enough by the government.

It takes an integrative leader to combine two aspects that theoretically have nothing in common. This integrative role is being played by Jörg Haider. He sends signals in both directions, feeding the protest motives and the xenophobic motives as well. His rhetoric is full of attacks on the "old parties," which he says are unwilling to respect the freedom of the citizens. The Second Republic is pictured as a semi-Communist system that manipulates Austrian society in a pre-democratic way (Haider 1993; Tributsch 1994). But at the same time he stirs up aggressive resentments by claiming that foreigners are responsible for unemployment as well as for political violence and the crime rate (Bailer 1995: 140–148).

The most significant signals Haider is sending are those concerning the Nazi regime. As early as 1977, he argued that the Treaty of Versailles was responsible for the totalitarian Nazi dictatorship. In 1986, he praised Austrian Nazi leaders such as the Carinthian Ferdinand Kernmayr as models of democratic straightforwardness. In 1988, the fiftieth anniversary of the "Anschluss," he called political education "rape of the past" and "summary justice" ("Femegericht") of "reeducators." In 1992, he warned that there must be an end to the "criminalization of (our) own history." In 1995, following the murder of four Roma in the worst case of political violence in Austria since 1945, he spoke of Auschwitz as a "penal camp" ("Straflager") (Bailer 1995: 88–93).

Haider's constant efforts to play down the special character of the Nazi rule and to relativize the Holocaust has occasionally backfired. In 1991, two years after being elected governor of Carinthia on the strength of votes from the ÖVP and his own party, he spoke during an official session of the Carinthian diet on the subject of employment policies, comparing the Second Republic with the Nazi regime: "In the Third Reich, they had a proper employment policy, which cannot be said of the government in Vienna" (Bailer 1995: 94; Riedlsperger 1996: 359).

His use of the term "proper employment policy" ("ordentliche Beschäftigungspolitik") for the NS concept of forced labor and militarization of production was too much. The ÖVP canceled the alliance, and the SPÖ and ÖVP voted Haider out of the governor's office. This was a drastic setback for his further ambitions. Haider's first attempt to overcome his isolation was a failure, but this did not diminish his electoral attractiveness in any significant way.

In the aftermath of this failure and the disappointing echo of his popular initiative of 1993, Haider's strategy was to play down traditional pan-Germanism. Even the name of the initiative, "Austria first," was a slogan pan-Germans like Schönerer would have abhorred. More and more he began to speak of his party as the "Austria" party, as the party of Austrian patriotism. He even criticized what he called "Deutschtümelei" (pan-German exaggerations) and argued in favor of a "strong Austrian identity" (Bailer 1995: 54).

The background of this official farewell to pan-German traditions was a strategic assessment. The FPÖ had nothing to gain by emphasizing its pan-German roots. There was no competition from the right to contend with. The FPÖ's new constituency, especially the blue-collar segment, could not have cared less about constant reflection on Austria's German character. The question of an Austrian national identity separate from the German one had been already answered— against the intentions of traditional pan-Germanism. To bind his new electorate, it was necessary for Haider to integrate Austrian patriotism with whatever was left of (Austrian) pan-Germanism.

The fight against immigration is the ideal issue for that strategic effort: Pan-German ideology can be mobilized easily against non-German speaking foreigners; and the working-class element, which was never much inclined to follow Schönerer's ideological leadership, would respond to the offer of protection against cheap labor from abroad.

The farewell to "Deutschtümelei" did not mean a real farewell to those organizations that constituted the pan-German camp. Haider never distanced himself from his "Burschenschaft," the dueling fraternity to which he belongs, and the type of organization that is one of the main sources of "Deutschtümelei" (Perner and Zellhofer 1994). The Styrian umbrella organization of all the academic pan-German fraternities publishes a monthly magazine called *Die Aula,* which reflects the current strategic position of the FPÖ and the pan-German camp (Gärtner

1996). Haider is one of the authors for the *Aula,* as are many other FPÖ leaders. The *Aula* had backed Haider during his rise to the FPÖ chairmanship and after.

The *Aula* is an instrument to bridge the gap between the respectable, moderate image the FPÖ at least occasionally wants to project and the extreme, violent, neo-Nazi image the right wing of the pan-German camp represents. One indication of the moderate image is that the *Aula* publishes articles by many authors who are neither in any respect extreme nor in any way affiliated with the FPÖ. The *Aula* uses these authors for their own purpose, reprinting articles already published elsewhere without even asking for the author's permission (Gärtner 1996: 287–312). The other, neo-Nazi aspect was verified in 1995, when an Austrian criminal court jury found *Aula* editor Herwig Nachtmann guilty of publishing Nazi propaganda: An article that appeared in the *Aula* denied the reality of the Holocaust (Gärtner 1996: 75). A judicial court of appeals upheld the verdict.

There is a difference between the FPÖ as the third biggest party in the Austrian parliament and hard-core, right-wing extremism, but there is no clear and evident line of division. Every analysis of the milieu that is violence oriented, openly racist, and unapologetic about Nazi crimes, including Holocaust denial, demonstrates a certain fluidity between FPÖ organizations and this right-wing extremism as represented by Gottfried Küssel. Austrian neo-Nazis are not only very sympathetic toward the FPÖ but also very understanding about the party's strategic need to sometimes distance itself from Nazism (Purtscheller 1993; Bailer and Neugebauer 1994; Scharsach 1995).

Beginning in December 1993, a wave of terrorist bombings shook Austria. Its victims all had one thing in common: They were the "natural" enemies of the right-wing milieu: leftist politicians and private individuals who actively opposed discrimination against foreigners (Antisemitism 1995: 87). Letter bombs addressed to individuals injured several people seriously. In February 1995, a bomb killed four Austrian Roma in Burgenland. The Roma, gypsies who were victims of the Holocaust, are "natural" enemies of Nazi terrorism, like Jews and the persons who received the letter bombs. An anonymous letter that claimed responsibility for the fatal bombing was full of Nazi rhetoric (Scharsach 1995: 15 f.).

How "Austrian" is this right-wing extremism? Can it be explained by specific Austrian roots? There are other cases of murderous political extremism stemming from racist prejudices in other European countries and outside Europe as well. And there are many parallels, especially in attitudes toward immigrants and the fear of social decline. "Foreigners," even if they are Austrian born like members of the Roma minority in Austria, are all too often targets of violence. This is the case in Austria and elsewhere. But in Austria and in Germany, specific national history and responsibility for the Holocaust have to be taken into account.

There is little quantitative difference between the murderous violence emanating from the right-wing milieu in Austria and violence elsewhere. The difference is the fluid borderline between a very small group whose acts of violence are based on Nazi beliefs and a party that is one of the most successful right-of-center parties in Europe. This is an Austrian peculiarity. Or is it an Austrian peculiarity?

A comparative analysis of David Duke, a member of the Louisiana state legislature and second in a runoff gubernatorial election, and Jörg Haider reveals several striking similarities. One is the profile of their voters (in both cases overproportionally lower-class males); another is the ambiguity between legitimate protest and rhetorical duplicity based on beliefs not considered "politically correct": white supremacy in Duke's case; Nazism in Haider's case. The most striking difference is the degree of acceptability: Duke is a political maverick who articulates broad resentments but lacks the permanent legitimate power base Haider has had as chairman of the third strongest party in the Austrian parliament (Howell and Pelinka 1994).

But the comparison can go even further. Evidence of anti-immigrant rhetoric and policy can be found within well-established parties such as the U.S. Republican Party, for instance as expressed by California Governor Pete Wilson, usually seen as a moderate. It can be argued that the Haider FPÖ represents a "new Right that is closer to the 'Libertarians,' 'Moralists' and 'Enterprisers' of the United States Right ... than it is to the traditional, Christian-conservative Right or the Nationalist Socialist extreme Right of the Austrian past" (Riedlsperger 1996: 352; see also Warren 1996).

There is no doubt that the FPÖ's protest attitude against the remnants of post-1945 consociationalism, especially clientelism by parties and interest groups, must be seen in that light, which makes the FPÖ's style since 1986 appear "populistic" in that it mobilizes protest against a political establishment (Plasser and Ulram 1995). Ideologically and socially, this protest has nothing to do with Nazism. But the FPÖ's flirtatious approach to Nazism cannot be ignored.

This is the ambiguity of the most successful party representing strong right-wing elements within the European Union. The FPÖ combines pan-German traditions with Austrian patriotism, mixes opposition rhetoric with an appeal to xenophobic resentments, and plays with Nazi revisionism and Holocaust denial. The FPÖ is populistic and has a "New Right" agenda, and both aspects are legitimate in liberal democracies. But at the same time, the ideological parallels to Nazism have not ceased to exist (Scharsach 1995: 244–265). This is the version of Austria's dark side more than fifty years after the founding of the Second Republic.

To achieve such an amalgamative effect, some political preconditions must exist. It is the timing that explains Haider's electoral success. The FPÖ's policy is based on the strategy of combining and fulfilling different functions: mounting legitimate protest against government mismanagement and mobilizing racist aggression in the form of undisguised xenophobia. Why was that kind of policy unsuccessful in the late 1940s and early 1950s, when the economic situation of most Austrians was much worse and the number of citizens who identified with many aspects of the Nazi regime much higher? The answer is that the xenophobic, racist, anti-Semitic potential existed, but it was under control. The benign power cartel of consociational democracy satisfied some of the extremists' needs by accepting and defending ordinary and not so ordinary former Nazis (some of whom were not always just former) in the "affairs."

This contradictory behavior of the old power cartel has now lost its grip on society and its problems, so different from the post-1945 era. The protective umbrella that the post-1945 political system was able to hold over most Austrians is leaking:

- Economic development continues to expose social differences, and the socially weaker segments of the population feel increasingly lost. The impact of ever-greater global mobility exacerbates the decline of subjective and objective security.
- Political development has eroded the traditional camps and their ability to maintain loyalty from generation to generation. The stabilization of democracy after 1945 freed the citizens from their need of guidance from above.

Both Vranitzky and Klestil represent the post-Waldheim style of official Austrian politics, in that they acknowledge Austria's co-responsibility. But this style fails to fulfill certain aspects of populistic need. The politics of double-talk, at which Austrian consociationalism after 1945 excelled, no longer worked—or was at least less effective than it used to be. The new frankness about Austria's darker side opened a strategic opportunity that the Haider FPÖ fully exploited. The fears and prejudices and aggressive moods so typical for the "authoritarian character" (Adorno et al. 1950) got out of control. The polarization that had begun to be politically effective in the 1980s made the elitist control of populist resentments impossible.

The rise of the FPÖ from a small traditional party to a medium-sized party with some new elements is the result of political modernization. The highly ideological, quasi-religious functions of the camps and the traditional parties are now gone. The "new" FPÖ is benefiting from the same effect of political modernization that has served the Greens and the Liberals so well. Children no longer follow their parents' political footsteps. Instead, the young generation makes its choices on a case-by-case basis, from election to election. This modernization involves certain risks, but from the viewpoint of liberal democracy, it cannot be seen as purely negative.

Perhaps the most significant difference between the NSDAP, the most successful catchall party of the Austrian past, and the FPÖ, the successful catchall party of the 1990s, is the latter's lack of quasi-religious functions. Despite all its similarities with the NSDAP, the FPÖ is also a product of the secularization that works in its favor. The masses voting for the FPÖ now are not believers. They are bound to their leader neither by an ideology nor a certain creed. The FPÖ's style is somewhat American, and Haider's TV appearances have great entertainment value (Plasser and Ulram 1995: 480 f.). He is not a messiah the crowd wants to follow but a clever politician who knows how to exploit existing prejudices and sentiments from case to case by using the media. His sound bite messages are effective even with an audience that is not a pious community eager to accept everything its leader says.

There is no danger of a revival of National Socialism in its Hitler-era form. The substance of these populistic resentments never truly died, so it makes no sense to speak of a rebirth. And the substance is more complex than just Nazism, although that is certainly one component of the mixture. But Nazism as a creed, a quasi-religious faith, was also only one part of the mixture that brought Hitler to power.

The present situation is more complex and thus less predictable than the past. This does not necessarily make Austria's darker side less dark, but it indicates that there is no danger of history simply repeating itself.

But there are other differences, especially on the international level. In the 1930s, Austria was surrounded by dictatorships and strongly influenced by fascist Italy, by Nazi Germany, even by semi-fascist Hungary. In this context, the Austrian madhouse factor responsible for the political socialization of the Austrian Catholic Adolf Hitler was multiplied by the international impact factor.

This is a fundamental difference between the 1930s and the 1990s. The new blend of Austrian nationalism is full of aggressive xenophobia. But the political environment has changed in every facet of its structure: The international framework is now more important than ever due to Austria's EU membership, and the domestic framework is now influenced by a democratic continuity unknown in Austria in the past.

More than half a century after the collapse of the regime built on the mad dreams of the Austrian Catholic Adolf Hitler, the madhouse potential still exists, but everything else has changed. More than fifty years of stable Austrian democracy and Austria's integration into a democratic Europe have made all the difference.

10

AUSTRIA'S FUTURE

At the end of the twentieth century, Austria's qualities are less distinctive than they used to be. Social democracy is still strong in Austria—but its ability to force its socialist perspective on Austria is, to put it mildly, less than impressive. There is still an overwhelming Catholic majority in Austria, but the essence of being Catholic in that country has become extremely diffuse. Corporatism is not over, but its overall dominance has been reduced. Neutrality has not been declared dead, but those who are willing to see the realities of Europe since the collapse of the Soviet Union have already agreed the death certificate is ready to be signed.

There is still a tradition of crude right-wing attitudes in Austria, but even that seems to be changing. The most violent neo-Nazis are imprisoned, and the representatives of official Austria are confessing Austria's co-responsibility for the Nazi crimes. The culturally elitist version of Nazism has been largely replaced by the proto-Nazism of an uneducated underclass.

All that makes Austria less Austrian. All the characteristics used to describe and analyze post-1945 Austria have become much less visible: its stability through corporatist arrangements; its ability to be Western and neutral at the same time; its strong social democratic outlook, personified in the Kreisky phenomenon; its Catholic character, combining the heritage of the Counter Reformation with the sophisticated system of Church-state relationship; its stubborn insistence on having been a victim of Nazi aggression, and at the same time holding a more tolerant attitude toward former Nazis than Germany. At the end of the 1990s, Austria is much less the Austria it was during the 1950s, 1960s, or 1970s.

The Westernization of a Central European Democracy

All these changes have effects, which can be summarized in one impact: They are setting free a Western democracy. Layer after layer is being stripped away—layers of political structures whose main function was to protect specific Austrian qualities. The various subsystems that were so closely connected by an omnipotent consociational democracy are now gaining more and more autonomy. It is a general process of emancipation:

- The constitution is gaining autonomy from the party state as well as from the corporate state.
- Parliament is becoming more autonomous from the administration.
- States are becoming more autonomous from the federal level, municipalities more autonomous from the state level.
- Political parties and economic interest groups are beginning to dissociate, thereby winning autonomy from each other.
- The print media has already achieved full autonomy from the political system; the electronic media will soon follow.
- The economy has reached a degree of autonomy from political interference previously unknown in the Second Republic.
- Religious behavior, to whatever degree it exists, has never been less under the clerical hierarchies' control.

The quintessence of all these processes is the individualization of society. The typical Austrian at the end of the twentieth century is becoming much less dependent on hierarchical structures than previous generations of Austrians. But less dependence also includes a reduction of care and services the different subsystems were responsible for in the past. The Second Republic integrated the camps into one nation. One consequence of nation building was that the government took over many of the responsibilities the subsystems had before, especially those within the socialist and the Christian-conservative camp. But later, beginning with the 1980s, government proved less willing or at least less able to deliver what people had come to expect from it: welfare.

The emancipation process is an ambiguous one. Some of the qualities that are being lost or at least diminished are very popular among Austrians, who perceive the effects of losing them as negative. This is especially true of the decline of the welfare state. There is less politically organized solidarity (Zulehner et al. 1996). The gap between the haves and have-nots is widening. Since the 1980s, the distribution of income has become increasingly unequal. Austria is approaching the status of a two-thirds society: a significant minority is more and more excluded from the economic success the majority still enjoys. The "golden era" of the welfare state ended somewhere around 1980 (Tálos 1995).

But this process has also brought about some very positive changes, especially from the democratic point of view. It reduces the Josephinic guardianship of an enlightened and well-intentioned government. It increases the opportunities of individual citizens to participate in the political process without having to use the instruments of the party state or the corporate state. New social movements, citizens' initiatives, and political parties of a new type started to have an impact in the 1980s (Gottweis 1997). The political arena became much more open to new-comers and the political system much more responsive to nontraditional demands and supports.

All these changes resulted in the awakening of the constitution and its agencies from their dormancy. The constitution had not disappeared after 1945—it had always been observed and respected, but it had little impact on the political process. The positivism and simplicity of the amendment procedure allowed the two major parties the freedom to shape the constitution according to their interests on a case-by-case basis. This flexibility in dealing with constitutional matters also gave the parties centralized control over the different constitutional organs: the parliament, cabinet, administration, and even the Constitutional Court all had to follow a script written by the consociationalist elites. Their most effective instrument was the control of access to the most important positions in politics and society.

This recruiting power started to erode in the 1980s, and it started with parliament. The National Council elections of 1986 marked the beginning of a dramatic breakdown of the party system's concentration (see Table 10.1). For decades, the two major parties had been able to control the constitution's main institutions and the entire political system because they had the democratic legitimacy to do so. Their approval ratings were among the highest in the world: Together, the SPÖ and ÖVP had a combined voting share of around 90 percent in elections with voter turnout of more than 90 percent. As the popularity of the SPÖ and ÖVP declined, it reduced their control capability by increasing the other parties' ability to gain access to parliament and thus also control the access to other institutions.

In Table 10.1 the second column is even more significant than the first because it shows the decline in voter turnout. In 1994, the two major parties responsible for the establishment of the Second Republic were only able to mobilize one out of two Austrians to vote for one of them. This is not dramatic at all if compared with data from other Western democracies: In the United States or Switzerland, for example, voter turnout in national elections has only averaged about 50 percent for decades (Powell 1980). But it is dramatic compared with the data of the Second Republic's first thirty years, when more than 90 percent always turned out to vote in general elections, and of these, about 90 percent voted either SPÖ or ÖVP.

Of course, it is not possible to evaluate the turn of the concentration's decline in 1995. In the general elections of that year, the two traditional major parties—especially the SPÖ—got back some of their ability to mobilize the electorate. Voter turnout that year was 86.0 percent, up from a low of 81.9 percent in 1994 (Plasser, Ulram, and Ogris 1996: 344). Although the results of the 1995 elections might appear to indicate the beginning of a reversal or a decisive recovery in the downhill trend of the traditional party system, this is not very probable. A more realistic interpretation, which can be projected from the elections of Austrian representatives to the European parliament in October 1996, is that the 1995 rebound was an exception to the rule brought about by the generation gap and the

TABLE 10.1   Development of the Party System's Concentration

General Elections to National Council	Percentage of SPÖ/ÖVP Votes Combined	
	Valid Votes	*All Registered Voters*
1975	93.4	85.8
1979	92.9	84.7
1983	90.9	83.0
1986	84.4	75.0
1990	74.9	62.6
1994	62.9	50.2
1995	66.4	55.7

SOURCE: Official data.

decline of party affiliation. The steady decrease in the percentage of hard-line voters ("Stammwähler"), who consider themselves loyal to their party as a matter of principle, affects SPÖ and ÖVP in about the same degree (see Table 10.2).

There is no indication of a return to "normality" in the sense of post-1945 concentration, loyalties, and discipline. The 1995 election results only indicate that the SPÖ and ÖVP might be able to halt the decline and to maintain their ability to mobilize voters at its 1995 level. But the old party state is unquestionably dead.

This is the most visible aspect of the Westernization of Austrian politics. The functions political parties fulfill in Western democracies are less concentrated and therefore less effective. The institutions that benefit from this development are parliament and other constitutional agencies such as the federal presidency and the Constitutional Court.

The sharp increase of pluralism in parliament was like the prince's kiss for Sleeping Beauty. Five parties have been sharing power in the National Council since 1993, and this has given rise to new configurations of ad-hoc coalitions. Discipline within the party groups started to decline in general because the Greens and the LIF had a different, more individualistic understanding of parliamentary behavior. Were it not for the Haider FPÖ's unacceptability as a partner even for ad-hoc coalitions in parliament, this trend would be even more pronounced.

The most dramatic break in traditional discipline occurred in 1987, after the Greens, as a fourth party, had broadened the parliamentary spectrum and the FPÖ had started its new "populistic" style of opposition. People's Party members of the National Council from Styria called for a vote of no confidence concerning the Minister of Defense Robert Lichal, also a member of the ÖVP. The minister, in agreement with the cabinet, had decided to base the newly purchased interceptor fighters of the Austrian Air Force almost exclusively in Styria. The Styrian ÖVP responded vehemently by canceling its confidence in the minister, who came from the Lower Austrian People's Party. Lichal's position was saved by the discipline of

TABLE 10.2   Decline of Party Loyalists (by self-definition)

Loyalists	1969	1972	1976	1980	1986	1990	1994	1995
Percentage of electorate	65	61	56	47	39	34	31	28

SOURCE: Fessel+GFK 1995; Müller, Plasser, and Ulram 1995: 346.

the ÖVP representatives of the other states and all the SPÖ members of parliament (Nick and Pelinka 1996: 48). There is a distinct possibility that it could happen again, with certain groups within one party siding with other parties against their own party's leadership.

The probability of different ad-hoc coalitions is just one of the factors that are animating parliament. Another is the individualization of parliament indicated by the new independence individual representatives have enjoyed since the 1992 decision giving them the freedom to choose their own offices and personnel without party interference (Schwimmer 1993). The average member of the National Council is no longer merely an interchangeable party puppet with the party's central leadership holding the strings. The average Austrian member of parliament now appears to be at least slightly more like the independent individual Edmund Burke or the authors of the Federalist Papers had in mind. This does not mean that the individual representative enjoys complete independence from the pressures of the party or any interest groups. Things do, however, appear to be moving in that direction.

One strong indicator of this tendency is that there is less corporatist involvement in parliament. For several years now, the number of members of parliament who not only represent their voters and their parties but also indirectly represent major economic associations has been declining (see Table 10.3). Consociationalism enabled the major economic interest groups, the main pillars of the social partnership, to get their leaders into parliament by getting them elected on party tickets. One particularly important aspect of Austrian-style consociationalism was to have more political roles than political personnel. Casting a small number of people in a larger number of roles on different stages had an integrative effect.

There are two possible explanations for this trend: The rise of the FPÖ, Greens, and LIF was the rise of parties much less interrelated with corporatism than the SPÖ and ÖVP, which were in decline. But even within the SPÖ and ÖVP, the number of representatives with parallel functions in the major interest groups had already begun to decline in the 1980s. The overall trend is therefore indisputable: Parliament is freeing itself from corporatist dominance, and corporatism is dissolving most of its ties to parliament. Both sides are gaining independence.

By dissociating itself from immediate corporatist entanglement, parliament is winning autonomy from corporatism—and corporatism is also gaining in autonomy from constitutional agencies and from political parties. The roles and func-

TABLE 10.3 Full-Time and Part-Time Representatives of Main Economic Associations in the National Council

	SPÖ		ÖVP		FPÖ		Greens		LIF		Plenary	
	n	%	n	%	n	%	n	%	n	%	n	%
Employees' Association (ÖGB, Chambers of Labor)												
1973	45	48	11	14	0	0	—	—	—	—	56	31
1978	42	45	13	16	1	10	—	—	—	—	56	31
1987	33	41	13	16	0	0	0	0	—	—	46	25
1991	30	38	7	12	1	3	0	0	0	0	38	21
1995	17	26	1	2	2	5	1	8	0	0	21	11
Employers' Associations (Chambers of Commerce, VÖI)												
1973	1	1	14	18	2	20	—	—	—	—	17	9
1978	2	2	19	24	2	20	—	—	—	—	23	13
1987	1	1	15	20	2	11	0	0	—	—	18	10
1991	2	3	9	15	2	6	0	0	1	9	13	7
1995	1	2	5	10	2	5	0	0	—	—	9	5
Agrarian Associations (Chambers of Agriculture)												
1973	3	3	18	23	0	0	—	—	—	—	21	12
1978	2	2	21	26	0	0	—	—	—	—	23	13
1987	1	1	14	18	1	6	0	0	—	—	16	9
1991	0	0	10	17	1	3	0	0	0	0	11	6
1995	0	0	4	8	0	0	0	0	0	0	4	2

All corporatist associations together

1973	49	53	43	54	2	20	—	—	—	—	94	51
1978	46	50	53	66	3	30	—	—	—	—	102	56
1987	35	44	42	55	3	17	0	0	—	—	80	44
1991	32	40	26	43	4	12	0	0	—	—	62	34
1995	18	28	11	21	4	10	1	8	1	9	35	19

SOURCE: Karlhofer and Tálos 1996: 45.

tions of each are becoming more distinct and discernible. Parliament and parties and corporatism and administration are no longer just different versions of the same thing.

One aspect of the constitution is having a particular impact on the new dynamism of the Austrian parliament: proportional representation. The effects of proportional representation accelerate the decline of the party system's concentration (Lijphart 1994). That makes it impossible for one party to have a majority in parliament, which in turn makes coalition cabinets necessary. Coalition building is becoming more and more complex, in direct proportion to the complexity of the decomposing party system.

This effect diminishes the power of the position that is the main beneficiary of clear one party-majorities in parliament—the head of government. The more dependent the federal chancellor is on complex configurations in parliament and on the goodwill of other parties, the less power he has to make decisions on policy. In the long run, proportional representation plus decomposition of the party system will make the role of the Austrian chancellor less like that of the British prime minister and more similar to that of the Italian, Danish, Belgian, and Dutch prime ministers, who are dependent on the confidence of a number of small political parties.

The complex nature of the chancellor's dependence in his role as the chief executive of Austrian politics is interrelated with the potential of the two possible constitutional arbiters: the federal president and the Constitutional Court. Both are arbiters with a much underused potential:

- If the decomposition of the party system either continues or at least stabilizes at the 1995 level and if the FPÖ becomes less unattractive and less isolated, there will be manifold possibilities to form majority coalitions. Then the federal president will be called into active duty as an arbiter. He will be able to use his direct democratic legitimation and his constitutional prerogative to appoint the chancellor and his cabinet. He will make use of those constitutional functions by freeing himself from a purely ceremonial, "dignified" role. He will become "efficient."
- If changing majorities destroy the established pattern of joint SPÖ-ÖVP control over access to the Constitutional Court and if interpretations of constitutional rules become more conflicting, the decisions of the court will become more important. The Constitutional Court will take on a significance more similar to that of the U.S. Supreme Court than to the old post-1945 Austrian court, whose main characteristic was constitutional restraint. The Constitutional Court will become more political because it will be less dependent on party control.

But the main beneficiary of this effect will be the constitution as such. Its "normative" aspect will become more important, and there will be more correspondence of the "reality of the power process with the norms of the constitution." Its "semantic" aspect will decline as a result of "the formalization of the existing location of political power for the exclusive benefit of the actual power holders in control of the enforcement machinery of the state" (Loewenstein 1965: 148 f.).

All this is a work in progress that began in the 1980s. The Austrian constitution is already taking over more of the functions a constitution should fulfill, according to Karl Loewenstein, especially the "differentiation of the various state functions and their assignment to different state organs of power holders, (in order) to avoid concentration of power" (Loewenstein 1965: 127). It is the deconcentration effect, starting with the changing voting patterns, that is bringing about an increase in constitutional function.

Crises and Integration

The decline of the distinctive political culture that post-1945 Austria established and was dominated by must be perceived as the rise of competitive democracy. Consociational democracy, the elitist restraint of competition, and a generally legitimized cartel of major parties and interest groups had to give way to competition, to more open conflict. The cartel's loss of control over society because of stable democratic conditions must also have an impact on the political system.

This did not happen gradually. It took place in the form of major pushes, made possible by major crises. The crisis of the 1960s resulted in the quasi-Westminster style of the Kreisky era. The crisis of the 1980s resulted in the unpredictability of the 1990s.

Both crises had an integrative impact. The first strengthened domestic integration; the second international (that is, European) integration. The 1960s crisis strengthened and streamlined the political system by making it a more chancellor-oriented democracy like the Westminster system, but it also overloaded the political system with expectations beyond its capabilities. The 1980s crisis resulted in the political system's escape from exaggerated expectations into the European arena. It was an escape that included a partial abdication from the powers the Second Republic had concentrated in the hands of a small number of persons.

In his comprehensive history of Austria from 1890 to 1990, Ernst Hanisch distinguishes between the two crises that led to the important changes in the Second Republic's development: the new emphasis on seeking more democracy in the 1960s and the decline of stability in the 1980s (Hanisch 1994: 456–483). In addition, another creative crisis must be added: the impact of the new international and European agenda on Austria in the 1990s. All these crises together changed Austrian society; and when the society and economy changed, the political system had to change too.

The crisis of the 1960s indicated that the old guard, the older generation responsible for consociational democracy in the post-1945 era, was beginning to lose control. Julius Raab died in 1964, Adolf Schärf in 1965. Both major parties were rethinking the politics of keeping the grand coalition alive at all costs—the ÖVP more openly, the SPÖ more internally. When the Borodajkewycz affair broke, some of the ghosts from the Nazi past came back to haunt the Austrians. The international student rebellion of 1968 had an impact even in Austria. The unrest in Paris and elsewhere challenged the belief that liberal democracy had already reached its zenith, and the events in Prague destroyed whatever credibility the Soviet system still had.

In Austria, the grand coalition was ended at the first opportunity, demonstrating that there was nothing really permanent about the "permanent" coalition between the ÖVP and SPÖ. In 1966, the People's Party and the Social Democrats separated after the ÖVP had achieved an overall majority in the National Council. This must be considered a first and important step toward normality. For the first time in the Second Republic, there was a Westminster kind of system, with one of the two major parties in opposition.

There were skeptics who did not see this development as a logical step within a system of Western democracy but as the repetition of the First Republic's tragic mistakes. The most prominent among these skeptics was Bruno Kreisky. Kreisky, who was soon to become the politician who would most benefit from the new flexibility in Austrian politics, warned that that very same flexibility could mean permanent opposition for his party, a situation well known from the years 1920 to 1934. When in 1966 the SPÖ voted not to accept the ÖVP's conditions for continuing the coalition, Kreisky disagreed with his party's decision (Kreisky 1981: vol. 1, 686–692). He lost the battle—but won the war. By opposing the decision, he became the spearhead of an internal opposition, which successfully backed him at the SPÖ's convention in January 1967. He was now party chairman and leader of the opposition.

Kreisky's attitude toward consociational democracy was ambiguous, to say the least. He had been one of the group that took over the party leadership after Schärf's election to the presidency in 1957: Bruno Pittermann became party chairman, Franz Olah president of the ÖGB, Felix Slavik chairman of the Viennese party and later mayor of Vienna, Christian Broda minister of justice, and Kreisky was appointed foreign minister in 1959. The members of this new leadership group were united by their commitment to rethinking the party's strategies and opting for more openness. The new party platform of 1958 was the result of their search for a new image (Sully 1982: 150–173). The most visible consequence was the modus vivendi between the Catholic Church and the SPÖ, expressed in the solution to the concordat question in 1960 and the school laws of 1962 (Steger 1982: 75–86).

Although none of the new Social Democratic leaders was old enough to have held a prominent position in the First Republic, they were especially intent on rethinking the strategy of permanent coalition. The SPÖ started to revive an old strategy that had been shaped by former minister of the interior Oskar Helmer: To prevent any "bourgeois bloc" as was the case in the First Republic, the SPÖ itself had to cultivate a special relationship with the pan-German camp (Svoboda 1993: esp. 98–107). In using this logic to help to bring the VDU into existence, Helmer and his generation had liberated the pan-German camp from its post-1945 paralysis. The next generation of socialist leaders began to liberate that camp from its isolation. The SPÖ established certain contacts. Olah helped finance the FPÖ out of union funds (Svoboda 1990: 49), and Kreisky used his position as foreign minister to explore the possibilities of future cooperation with people such as Friedrich Peter, chairman of the FPÖ, and Gustav Zeillinger, the FPÖ's foreign affairs spokesman (Pelinka 1993).

Those contacts were both very informal and very delicate. In 1957, the ÖVP and FPÖ together had nominated a candidate for the federal presidency, Wolfgang Denk. Denk lost to Schärf, but the general perception was that the ÖVP had played its cards well in using the FPÖ as a means of getting a better deal with the other major party, still considered an unavoidable coalition partner. But in 1963, things started to get serious: The SPÖ leadership used the Habsburg crisis as an opportunity to talk to the FPÖ leadership about the possibility of a coalition. Although it was twenty years before that coalition was finally built, the first blueprints had been made (Olah 1995: 232–242).

It was too early. The SPÖ leadership lost its nerve when open debate started in the SPÖ and it became obvious that a large portion of the party was not willing to follow its leadership into an alliance with the party of the former Nazis. The Olah crisis in 1964 and 1965 was the consequence: Franz Olah, who had pursued the idea of an SPÖ-FPÖ coalition much more intensively than the others, started a mudslinging campaign against his successor in the ÖGB presidency, Anton Benya. This was the beginning of the end of Olah's career as a Social Democrat. The party considered his behavior inappropriate and expelled him. Olah attempted a political comeback as the head of a newly founded party, the Democratic Progressive Party, but failed. The *Kronen-Zeitung,* already on its way to becoming Austria's most widely read daily newspaper, was generous in backing the campaign of the man who had once appropriated union funds to finance the publication (Konrad and Lechner 1992: esp. 138–156)

The SPÖ's new flexibility seemed to end with Olah's fall. In the 1966 electoral campaign, the party tried to profile itself as the main defender of the grand coalition, and after losing the election, Kreisky still wanted to join the coalition despite the ÖVP's overall majority. Kreisky's attitude was extremely pragmatic and full of contradictions: He was the SPÖ leader who had been most friendly with Olah, but he still defended the grand coalition—for the moment. After having unsuccessfully argued that if the SPÖ went into opposition it would simply be history repeating itself (Kreisky 1981: vol. 1, esp. 690 f.), he became the most successful opposition leader in Austrian history. Four years after a devastating electoral defeat, he led his party to its most surprising triumph.

The Kreisky era had begun. Despite his hesitant approach to the new competitiveness, a result of the ÖVP's one-party cabinet, Kreisky was its greatest beneficiary. Despite his defense of the grand coalition in 1966, he became the most out-spoken opponent of repeating it and therefore opted—like his (former) friend Franz Olah had done in 1963—for the partnership with the FPÖ, a lesser evil than the coalition with the ÖVP.

Kreisky's success had much to do with the crisis of the 1960s: A new generation of voters was no longer worried about a civil war just around the corner. More than two decades of grand coalition and social partnership had not only stabi-lized the Second Republic but also established a belief in democratic normality. The fear of the "other" side had been diminished. There was a basic consensus not only among the elite but also more and more among the population.

Stabilization was interrelated with modernization. The percentage of Austrians living in prosperity was higher than ever (Sandgruber 1995: 529–535). The num-ber of students at Austrian universities had started to climb significantly and showed no signs of stopping. Austrians were more aware of what happened out-side their small country: in Paris and in Prague, in Vietnam and in U.S. cities.

The political consequence of that awareness was neither the end of consocia-tional democracy nor the collapse of the traditional party system. It was a new quality of flexibility within the Second Republic's political culture. There was a restless new mood, a desire to move toward new frontiers. And the party that would be able to direct this mood would become the country's dominant force—within the two-and-a-half-party system and under the condition of accepting the established system of corporatism and the church-state relationship. There was a new dynamism within consociationalism.

The crisis of the 1960s produced a new elitist attitude responsible for the 1970s' belief in progress and political management. Progress appeared possible by virtue of political decisionmaking. The two major parties and their camps successfully recruited and integrated those who had been strongly influenced by the crisis of the 1960s, especially by what had been called the "spirit of 1968." To recruit them, the parties had to change their attitude. Democracy beyond the political system was the key term used to express the innovative drive the generation of progres-sives demonstrated: democracy used to define not only politics but also other parts of society. In the 1970s, both the SPÖ and the ÖVP spoke about the need to democratize the society. The generation that joined the parties in the 1970s was united in its belief that politics could do almost anything (Welzig 1985). Later, the disillusion of this generation would play a significant role in establishing the Greens—first as a social protest movement, then as a new political party.

But generally, the Austrian political system was quite successful in managing to integrate the offspring of the 1960s' crisis. The old channels had been able to at-tract the most active elements of a generation that was the first to be called post-war in every respect. The system had been upheld, and nothing of political signif-icance was beyond its limits.

The next crisis, the crisis of the 1980s, was to go beyond those limits. There was no established instrument left to successfully channel the dynamism of the 1980s within the system. The SPÖ had to pay the price every dominant party has to pay after so many years of hegemony. The ÖVP had to pay for being the opposition on the parliamentary level and the coalition partner on the corporatist level. The dynamic mood had to look for new instruments outside consociationalism.

The Greens offered themselves to allay the disappointment of the left, which no longer had any hope of fulfilling its dream through social democracy. The Greens successfully combined the disappointed left with the new energy of social movements that the old parties could no longer integrate. And the FPÖ seized the opportunity to shed its old-system image, that of the pre-Haider FPÖ striving for intra-elite respectability, and became the vanguard of a new populism from the right.

The crisis of the 1980s resulted in an anti-elitist protest with a new type of radicalism that challenged the establishment from the outside and from below (Warren 1996). The representatives of the Greens and of the "new" FPÖ were not interested in being invited to join the old arrangement. Consociationalism had lost its attractiveness for outsiders and therefore its integrative power. The speakers for the outsiders were representing interests that existed below the traditional level of awareness of the two major camps. How were they to deal with the ecological issues the Greens articulated? How could they reach a compromise with those protesting against a new dam on the river Danube? There was no way to build just half the dam; and there was no possibility of trading the dam for something else. The old mechanism of exchange relationships so crucial for consociational democracy simply could not grasp the logic of the new social movements. The same happened with regard to the FPÖ. How could they begin to deal with a party that did not respect the cost-benefit formula of equating electoral strength with elitist respectability and that did not bother to hide that it wanted to overthrow the old system and its "old parties" ("Altparteien")?

The left-right contradiction still existed, but it no longer corresponded with the bipolar conflict between the SPÖ and the ÖVP. The old clusters of voters, the old patterns of political behavior could not explain what was happening, so new clusters had to be developed, new patterns had to be explored (Plasser 1987). The rise of the FPÖ, the establishment of the Greens in the second half of the 1980s, and the foundation of the LIF in the first half of the 1990s made party competition extremely complex.

The first crisis, the crisis of the 1960s, resulted in a nearly perfect Westminster system. At least on the surface, the Austrian party system resembled the British— one party in government, the other one in opposition. Third parties did not count. The corporatist networks working beneath that surface to keep consociationalism alive made a big difference. But this was not so visible during the years of chancellors Klaus und Kreisky.

The second crisis, the crisis of the 1980s, resulted in the breakup of the two-and-a-half-party system. The illusion of a Westminster-type system was over. Austria moved away from the British model and toward the deconcentrated party systems of smaller European democracies with proportional representation, such as the Netherlands and Switzerland and Denmark. Among the major European democracies, Austria did not move toward Britain, as many assumed in the 1960s and 1970s; nor toward Germany, an obvious choice due to its two-and-a-half-party system; nor even toward France, despite its constitutional similarities of presidential components in a parliamentary system. The most striking parallels are with Italy, whose party system was just starting to collapse around 1990. The Italian development seemed of special relevance to Austria (Ulram 1990: 299–306). Italy was a possible model for Austrian democracy in the near future.

In Austria in the 1980s, the scenario was the same as it had been in the 1960s: increased competitiveness as the result of the system's move toward more differentiation and less integration. But in the 1980s, the consociational elites were not able to integrate the generation influenced by the crisis of the 1980s into the traditional system. This time, the current level of SPÖ-ÖVP conflict could not satisfy the general trend toward more competitiveness as it had in the 1960s and 1970s. This lack of ability to integrate alienated parts of the electorate was parallel to the Italian development. The Italian elites had lost their integrative potential a little earlier and in a more dramatic fashion, but the increasing distance between the elites and the masses was the same phenomenon.

The Italian pattern teaches an important lesson for the future of Austria: society's emancipation from government, from the state. The specific control the Italian parties—first and foremost the Demcrazia Cristiana—were able to establish over society, especially over important segments of the economy, in many ways paralleled the Austrian situation. Joseph La Palombara's description of Italy's "classe politica" includes many similarities with the Austrian consociational elites (La Palombara 1987: 144–165). His description of the "Rashomon syndrome" (La Palombara 1987: 127–129) also explains a lot about the dynamic process Austrian democracy had to go through beginning with the elections of 1986.

With the dramatic decline of party concentration in Austria, it became impossible to declare indisputable winners and losers. In the years when Austria's democracy had been similar to Westminster's, to name winners and losers was an easy task: Klaus and the ÖVP won in 1966, Kreisky and the SPÖ won in 1970, 1971, 1975, and 1979. Even the result of 1983 was comparatively easy to evaluate: Compared to its significant victories in the 1970s, the SPÖ was considered the loser, even though it successfully defended its position as the strongest party.

The Rashomon syndrome describes the absence of a result in politics, as explained by the Italian elections of the 1980s (La Palombara 1987: 129–131). As in Akira Kurosawa's outstanding films or Luigi Pirandello's plays, there is no reality; there are only different perspectives of reality. Reality is substituted by different viewpoints, which are the results of different interests, experiences, and cultures. Political systems like the Italian of the 1980s and the Austrian, beginning with the elections of 1986, have no method to clearly define winners and losers. This is a total contradiction of the Anglo-American understanding of democracy, of the two-party system in which there is always a clear distribution of roles: winner and loser, government and opposition. The Rashomon syndrome is based on the experience that all competing parties have reasons to argue to have lost or won, depending on the criteria used. The ultimate consequence of the Rashomon syndrome is that it suspends the zero-sum nature of competitive democracy.

The best example of the Austrian version of the Rashomon syndrome is the FPÖ's fate beginning in 1986. Before the elections, the party was in power because it was a coalition partner in command of three ministries. At election time, the FPÖ won almost twice as many votes as in the previous elections, thereby significantly increasing its number of seats in parliament. But at the same time, it lost its seats in government and had to move from the cabinet benches to the opposition. There was a causal connection between those two consequences: The FPÖ won votes because its new "populistic," antiestablishment, anti-elitist style paid off with the electorate, but strategically it lost because its confrontational methods had alienated all the other parties. The FPÖ became isolated and unable to ally itself with any other party.

The question is whether the SPÖ was also a loser because the share of votes it lost roughly equaled the share the FPÖ gained. But can a party be called a loser if it defended its leading position in parliament and in government? Conversely, can the same party be called a winner if it lost some hundred thousand votes in a short period? And what about the ÖVP? The People's Party's decline to an electoral percentage of less than 30 percent signaled the end of its role as a major party. But in 1994 as well as in 1995, the ÖVP was still holding all the cards of the power game: Given the unbridgeable gap between the SPÖ and the Haider FPÖ, there was no way to build a majority without the ÖVP. Is this monopoly as a power broker the quality of a losing party?

There will be even more of this syndrome in Austria's future, and it will affect some or even all of the parties. Austria's political system approaches the new millennium with a diffused understanding of the roles of winners and losers. The current unpredictability is creating an unintelligible situation on the political market. What the market has gained in importance, it has lost in clarity.

The impact of the crisis of the 1980s on Austrian politics can also be called the "Andersen syndrome." Politicians, like the figure in the Hans Christian Andersen fairy tale "The Emperor's New Clothes," can no longer fool their audience. Their nakedness became obvious when the government and social partnership stopped being able to deliver the benefits the public had come to expect of them: steady economic growth, universal welfare, full employment, and a generally optimistic outlook.

Until the 1980s, most Austrians believed that by working in close cooperation, the government and the social partnership could guarantee all the advantages associated with the "Austrian way." In the 1980s, however, this belief was badly shaken. It was not so much the rising unemployment—the government could still argue that Austrians were comparably much better off than most other Europeans. It was more the sinking of Austria's economic flagship, the VÖEST, and the end of nationalized industry's success story (Sandgruber 1995: 491 f.).

The attitude of an entire generation was determined by the belief that anything can be achieved through politics. The crisis of the 1960s confirmed that belief, but the crisis of the 1980s destroyed it. The traditional side of this belief was characterized by predemocratic attitudes: The good emperor would take care of everything. The progressive side of this belief had an overall perspective of what democracy could achieve: Once freed from restraints, the people's government would be able to satisfy all its citizens' needs.

In the 1980s, people suddenly discovered that the emperor was naked. The Andersen syndrome made the Austrians realize how very limited political power was. Government was neither a good nor a bad Leviathan. It was not a powerful monster at all. The belief in government was shaken. Society had begun to realize that it already had a greater degree of autonomy from the government than it had imagined before. Government by consociationalism was no longer seen as either good or bad, but simply as exposed in its nakedness.

The discovery of this nakedness was soon followed by an increasing realization of Austria's smallness and dependence. The Austrian media was dependent on German TV productions, and German print media was taking over Austrian papers. The privatization of Austria's nationalized industry was largely dependent on foreign investment because not enough capital could be raised within the country. Later, its position of dependence in security matters became evident when the post-Yugoslav wars started being fought practically on Austria's borders.

The consequence was integration—intentional or not. Austria became economically integrated into the huge market Western Europe had established, or rather Austria had to face the fact that this economic integration had already taken place and no amount of wishful thinking would be able to change it. Austria also became socially integrated. Although unemployment figures in Austria were strongly dependent on the global trade cycle, it had managed to maintain a higher rate of employment than most of the other industrialized nations. But when the OECD countries began to suffer a decline in employment, Austria had no way to fully protect its own labor market.

The realization that economic and social integration had already taken place was the basis for the decision to allow political integration to follow. The crises of the 1960s and 1980s had proved that the Second Republic's independence was only relative. And when international developments began to set Austria free from the neutrality necessitated by the Cold War, the next step was inevitable. EU membership finalized Austria's political integration.

It may be paradoxical that the two social crises of the Second Republic resulted in Austria's full participation in European integration. The process of emancipation had a disintegrative effect on Austrian society and politics. It significantly increased the autonomy of the different subsystems but decreased the control of the political system and the Second Republic's political culture over Austria. The response to this decline in domestic integration was to increase European integration. The political elites were losing their power to control Austria, so they went European—and ultimately lost even more power. The elitist interest in maximizing control cannot explain that development. Development is the substitution of domestic by European integration.

In their newly detected nakedness, the traditional elites did not want to risk putting up resistance in their retreat from the power positions they once held. Instead, they wanted to position themselves at the head of the new trend. They did not remain as the rear guards of the Second Republic's old philosophy of maximizing Austria's independence; they became the vanguards of Austria's integration into Europe.

Old Cleavages, New Cleavages

The camps that reflected the existence of cleavages in Austrian society are no longer subjects of studies in social sciences but in history. However, that does not mean that Austria has become a fully harmonized society. On the contrary, new contradictions have surfaced and new conflicts are becoming explosive. Cleavages that were frozen for a long time are starting to heat up. Three cleavages seem to be of increasing importance for the future of Austrian politics: gender, ethnicity, and region.

The age-old gender cleavage has awakened from its dormant state. For decades, political parties have expressed their willingness to recognize the equality of women under the law. For decades, nothing happened to change the discrepancies between equality as guaranteed by the constitution and inequality that existed in the political, economic, and cultural spheres. Austria's political system proved perfectly capable of covering up that contradiction, and traditional elites were able to placate any signs of female unrest (Rosenberger 1992). The SPÖ was especially responsible for creating that dissonance by preaching equality but exercising male prerogatives. Officially, the Social Democrats pointed proudly to their party's programmatic tradition of insisting on equality between men and women but did nothing to change the inequality within their own ranks.

One example of this inequality was the de facto freeze on the proportion of women in parliament. The percentage of female representatives in the National Council had always remained below 10 percent. Neither the SPÖ nor the other parties traditionally less committed to egalitarian doctrines did anything specific to promote women in parliament. But after decades of remaining constant, the numbers began to fluctuate much like the needle on a seismograph predicting an earthquake. Sometime around 1980, the frozen gender gap began to thaw (see Table 10.4).

The percentage of women in parliament increased dramatically. Following the 1995 elections, there were four times as many female parliamentarians than there had been at the beginning of the 1970s. This was the consequence of a new

TABLE 10.4 Percentage of Women in the National Council

	SPÖ		ÖVP		FPÖ		Greens		LIF		Plenary	
	numbers	%	numbers	%	numbers	%	numbers	%	numbers	%	numbers	%
1971–75	8	8.6	3	3.8	0	0	—	—	—	—	11	6.0
1975–79	9	9.7	5	6.3	0	0	—	—	—	—	14	7.7
1979–83	11	11.6	7	9.1	0	0	—	—	—	—	18	9.8
1983–86	11	12.2	8	9.9	1	8.3	—	—	—	—	20	10.9
1986–90	13	16.3	10	13.0	4	22.2	3	37.5	—	—	30	16.4
1990–94	23	29.1	8	13.5	7	21.2	6	60.0	(2	40.0)	46	25.1
1994–95	16	24.2	8	15.7	9	21.4	6	46.2	4	36.4	43	23.5
1995	22	31.0	11	20.7	9	22.5	5	55.6	3	30.0	50	27.3

NOTE: Due to increasing fluctuation during legislative periods, from 1983 on the figures show the maximum number of women. The actual number of women could have been slightly lower at various times. The figures for the LIF for 1990–94 are in parentheses because the five founding members of the LIF had been elected on an FPÖ ticket prior to their break with that party.

SOURCE: Sickinger 1996: 48.

awareness of the gender gap. Political parties do not make dramatic changes in their recruitment patterns unless the electorate forces them to do so. The female electorate had become a mobile force, and the party system and the parliament responded.

This did not come about because of a new legal situation; it was the consequence of the openness of democracy. Women have risen more rapidly in politics, especially parliament, than in any other branch of society. Even the federal bureaucracy, which is officially dependent on political changes, has lagged behind parliament in opening positions to women. The bureaucratic elite is proving much more resistant to the women's movement than the parliamentary elite (see Table 10.5).

There is upward mobility of women outside the political system, but it is much slower. It follows a traditional pattern: the higher the position, the worse the chances for women. But even this is changing to meet women's higher demands. Women are no longer willing to settle for less.

The reason behind this development is education. In the 1990s, the percentage of female students at Austrian universities reached 50 percent. Women are entering the labor market in ever-greater numbers, but they are no longer satisfied with traditional female roles. The female autostereotypes are converging with the male. Women are insisting on the same right to a career as men.

But men, afraid of coming out losers in that contest, are defending their traditional prerogatives. Because it is a zero-sum game, the new situation is creating conflicts. The gender gap is deepening, and gender is now a cause of political cleavage.

Political parties are swift to react because they are immediately dependent on changing role expectations. Society is more hesitant in its reaction because men in leading nonpolitical positions are not as directly dependent on female demands and supports as elected politicians are. Within the political system, the process of feminization is forcing men out of parliament and out of the cabinet. Compared with the past, men's political career opportunities have worsened but women's have improved. But compared with the idea of proportional representation of men and women, women still have every reason to feel underprivileged.

Feminization will go on, and so will the conflicts that are the result of this process. The gender cleavage in Austrian politics will continue to be a decisive factor in mobilizing the social interests that divide men and women.

The second cleavage that is coming out of the freezer is the ethnic conflict. For decades, the Second Republic's stability and its Austrian national identity beyond the pan-German had hidden a socially dynamic factor that post-1945 Austria did not want to acknowledge: the consequences of immigration. Austria has long had a tradition of attracting immigrants. But the politics of the Second Republic refused to accept this reality. The most visible result is the absence of any viable immigration policy despite the fact that hundreds of thousands came to Austria after 1945 and stayed permanently (Fassmann and Münz 1995).

TABLE 10.5 Women in Leading Functions in the Federal Bureaucracy

Highest Level ("Sektionen")				Second Highest ("Gruppen")				Third Highest ("Abteilungen")			
1995		1993		1995		1993		1995		1993	
nums.	%	nums.	%	nums.	%	nums.	%	nums.	%	nums.	%
3	3.7	2	2.5	12	10.6	9	9.2	130	17.4	110	14.9

SOURCE: Schermann-Richter 1996: 55.

Beginning with 1945, immigrants came to Austria in many different waves consisting of different peoples. Distinctions should be made among the reasons for migration:

- Migration as a result of World War II. Many people from Eastern Europe fleeing the Soviet Army came to Austria in 1945 and stayed in the Western occupation zones. Most of them were "Volksdeutsche," or ethnic Germans.
- Migration as a consequence of the Holocaust. Tens of thousands of Jewish survivors came to Austria. The majority of them used Austria as a transit country, but some stayed and became part of the Jewish community in Austria (Albrich 1987).
- Migration as a result of ethnic cleansing immediately after the end of World War II. The majority of the victims were "Volksdeutsche" who went directly to Germany. But most of those who came to Austria stayed there.
- Migration as a result of political persecution. Most political refugees fled Communist regimes in Austria's neighboring countries. Hundreds of thousands came from Hungary in 1956, from the CSSR in 1968, and from Poland in 1981. The majority used Austria either as a country of transit or as a country of asylum before returning to their own countries, but many stayed in Austria.
- Migration as a result of economic development. Beginning with the 1960s, the Austrian economy had a shortage of workers in certain sectors. Hundreds of thousands were invited to stay for a certain period as "Gastarbeiter" (guest workers), most of them from the former Yugoslavia and from Turkey. Many of them stayed.
- Migration as a result of political and economic factors, especially after the collapse of the Communist regimes. Many of these migrants used Austria as a transit country, but many stayed, some of them without proper visas or working permits.

Migration was and is the consequence of political and economic factors, and its impact on Austria has never ceased. It was never a one-way street: After 1945, hundreds of thousands of Austrians emigrated to other countries (Fassmann and Münz 1995: 46 f.).

Migration has also created a legal problem. Because Austria never accepted its de facto status as a country of immigration, it never established special laws on granting citizenship to foreigners who wanted to stay. The assumption has always been that refugees and "guest workers" will stay only for a given period, so there is no need for full legal integration. As a result, in 1995, there were more than 700,000 "foreigners" living in Austria legally as noncitizens. This figure increases if the smaller number of "illegal" foreigners is added (Fassmann and Münz 1995: 47). By any calculation, the number of "foreigners" is an artificial one. A consistent immigration policy would have long since made many of those foreigners Austrians by granting them Austrian citizenship more easily.

The main reason for the lack of any consistent immigration policy is xenophobic resentment, which became especially strong after the fall of the "Iron Curtain," when more Eastern Europeans came to Austria legally or illegally. As the Communist dictatorship ended they fled; there was no longer political sympathy for them, and they were increasingly accused of being cheap labor competing with Austrians for cheap housing.

The demographic structure of immigrants in Austria is important because foreigners in Austria are significantly younger than Austrians. "Guest workers" not only pay taxes but also help finance the social welfare system. In fact, there are proportionally more foreigners than Austrians working and funding the system (see Table 10.6). This should be seen as an advantage for Austria.

The implication of the figures in Table 10.6 is obvious: The older generation is overproportionally represented in the Austrian population. It is the immigrant population that provides a certain demographic balance, especially immigrants from the former Yugoslavia and Turkey. Among the "other" foreigners are many West Europeans whose status, income, and demographic structure are similar to those of Austrians.

On the surface, there is no reason why migration should be responsible for the ethnic cleavage's new explosiveness. But the rebirth of ethnicity as a political factor has no such rational background. It is the result of fear, with which the socially weaker segments of Austrian society have always responded to the new and the unpredictable.

This is reflected by a new voter typology, which cuts across the old cleavages. An analysis of the voting behavior in 1994 identified the following clusters (Grausgruber 1995: 410–424):

- Social democratic labor: more or less the traditional SPÖ clientele and still overwhelmingly—over 80 percent—SPÖ oriented.
- Rural-Catholic milieu: traditionally a part of the Christian-conservative camp; almost two-thirds of this cluster still votes ÖVP.

TABLE 10.6   Austrians and Foreigners Living in Austria in 1993, by Home Country and
Age (percentage)

Age	Austrians	All Foreigners	From ex-Yugoslavia	From Turkey	From Other Countries
Under 15	18.4	25.7	25.1	38.9	17.6
15–30	22.8	28.5	26.9	29.4	29.5
30–45	21.1	29.0	31.8	22.4	30.5
45–60	17.7	11.6	13.0	8.3	12.4
60+	20.0	5.2	3.2	1.0	10.1

SOURCE: Fassmann and Münz 1995: 62.

- Traditional urban middle class: the bourgeois part of the Christian-conservative camp; like the second cluster, more than 60 percent still vote for the People's Party.
- Welfare state–oriented new middle class: the "leftist" segment of better-educated, white-collar employees with a plurality (not a majority) of SPÖ voters and with the Greens running a strong second.
- Market-oriented new middle class: the "rightist" version of the cluster above; the SPÖ is number one, the FPÖ a strong second.
- Destabilized blue-collar labor with less education: especially characterized by the term "losers of modernization," with a small plurality of the SPÖ ahead of the FPÖ.
- Urban white-collar protest: consisting of better-educated and younger voters, who give the LIF a plurality ahead of the FPÖ and the ÖVP.
- Populist protest against the system: a small segment with a clear FPÖ majority; it represents especially the older FPÖ voters who are disillusioned with the political system in general.
- Urban, bourgeois, female protest: by far the smallest cluster, but with some distinct characteristics, very mobile with an ÖVP plurality and the Greens as number two.

The first three clusters represent the traditional political system. The factors responsible for electoral preferences within these clusters can be explained by class or religion, that is by the two cleavages that dominated the history of Austrian politics in the past. Another characteristic the three have in common is that they are still clearly dominated by either the SPÖ or the ÖVP.

The other six clusters indicate the future of Austrian politics. No party has a significant lead over the others in any of the clusters except in the rather small "populist protest" group. That is the new openness: Each of the clusters consists of voters with social and ideological similarities. But despite these parallels, there is no evidence of significant party preferences.

New cleavages cut through the old. Generation, education, and gender are dividing the electorate not so much along the old lines of class and religion but into "winners" and "losers" of modernization. The losers tend to be more defensive and more inclined to exclude "others"; they therefore represent the new type of ethnic cleavage. This new cleavage defines "we" as "Austrians" and not as "Germans" as traditional pan-Germanism does. And "them" now includes "foreigners" as a socioeconomic category: as wage-dumping competition on the labor market and as rent-increasing competition in the housing market.

But there is also the regional cleavage. The traditional camps were able to guarantee maximum integration. Social Democrats from Vienna and Vorarlberg were united by their party loyalty, as were ÖVP activists from Tyrol and Styria. When anticentralist emotions began to effect politics, they were channeled through party lines. The initiative "pro Vorarlberg," for example, was organized in the westernmost state in 1979 and 1980 and directed against the federal government, against "Vienna," at that time associated with the SPÖ. Thus the ÖVP, which dominated Vorarlberg's political system, was able to use this anticentralist initiative for its own purposes (Barnay 1983).

But with the decline of party concentration, the party system's capacity to integrate regional divergencies also declined. Regional antagonism came into the open. One example of this new type of regional diversity that had nothing to do with the left-right dimension of political conflicts is the concept of the "Euro-Region Tyrol." In 1995, the Austrian state Tyrol and the two Italian provinces Bolzano and Trentino—the latter two both part of pre-1918 Austrian Tyrol—declared themselves a region under the terms of the EU's Maastricht Treaty and opened a joint office in Brussels to lobby for their common interests as a region autonomous from both Italy and Austria.

This "Euro-Region" has a delicate ethno-national aspect: the possible reconciliation of the German- and Italian-speaking parts of old Tyrol (Luverà 1996). But its attitude is also distinctly anti-Rome and anti-Vienna, although the latter has nothing to do with the old party loyalties. When, in 1994, Tyrolean Governor Wendelin Weingartner spoke of Tyrol as being equidistant from Rome and Vienna (Luverà 1996: 132), the leaders of his own party were in power in Vienna. An ÖVP representative, Alois Mock, was the foreign minister responsible for Austria's foreign policy. Austrians thus identified the ÖVP as strongly with "Vienna" as they did its coalition partner, the SPÖ. The foreign minister and other ÖVP cabinet members had to tolerate Weingartner's pan-Tyrolean "equidistant" approach, but they clearly did not promote it. It was also Weingartner's Tyrolean People's Party that avoided campaigning as "ÖVP" for the state diet elections in 1994, instead preferring the semi-official label "Wir Tiroler" ("We Tyroleans").

The Tyrolean governor, whose state had been ruled by Habsburg Austria for centuries, stirred up anti-Vienna sentiments by equating Italian rule over South Tyrol with Austrian rule over North Tyrol. As the German-speaking majority in the province of Bolzano has always considered Italian rule a direct infringement on their right to self-determination, Weingartner's message was clear: The relationship between Tyrol and Austria is also the dominance of a center over a resentful periphery.

This type of regional conflict cuts across the cleavage that separates the traditional camps. It indicates a new cleavage, Tyroleans against Austria, which can be also applied to Styrians, Carinthians, and others. As traditional loyalties break down, the absence of their integrating effects is being felt. The rise of regional controversies is one of the foreseeable results.

The old antagonism has been "decoded" (Loewenberg 1983: esp. 97–204). The basic conflict between the Christian-conservative and the Socialist camp is now "comprehensible" to Austrians. And with an understanding of the dynamism behind the conflict has come a realistic view of the facts, which has destroyed the myths (Loewenberg 1995). A naive belief in the legends of the past has been replaced by a sober and analytical understanding of historical reality. The irrationality of pseudo-religious creeds and loyalties has been consigned to the museum.

The greatest success of the Second Republic is that the old cleavages are dying out. But this success is releasing new energies and creating new cleavages. New types of antagonism now need to be "decoded." New types of interests are mobilizing certain segments of Austrian society. And even if the pseudo-religious character of the new forms of political mobilization is less visible, it still exists. It can be seen in the way the losers of modernization have rationalized their fears by placing the blame on "foreigners."

But it is a trend that is eradicating Austria's distinguishing characteristics. The existence of the gender conflict does not distinguish Austria from other developed European countries. Migration is also provoking new waves of xenophobia in other parts of Europe, where the underprivileged are afraid of the even more underprivileged. The process of emancipating regions from central governments is a much more common phenomenon in countries such as Italy or Belgium. The new energies that are pushing Austrian politics forward are more pan-European than specifically Austrian.

A Different Austria?

Austrians are rather proud to be Austrians. They profess a kind of national pride unlike that of most other nations. Austrians are prouder of their country's culture and landscape than of its political profile. The latter was an integral part of the Austrian self-esteem during the Kreisky era but has lost its relevance in the 1980s (Bruckmüller 1996: 70 f.). If politics is part of the Austrian image in the 1990s, it is politics not so much in the sense of government but in the sense of political culture. Social peace and political stability are still values Austrians associate positively with their country.

This is also reflected in Austria's image in the world. Austria is seen as being especially defined by its culture, first and foremost by its association with classical music. The most prominent Austrians are Wolfgang Amadeus Mozart and Johann Strauss. Second to culture are the tourist attractions for which Austria is famous (Schweiger 1992: esp. 294–300).

The past still casts its shadow over Austria. The Austria of the eighteenth and nineteenth centuries still defines the image of Austria at the end of the twentieth century, an image that is both geographically and politically out of date. The world bases its perception of Austria not on the small republic that exists today, but on an Austria that has long since ceased to exist.

But even the aspects of post-1945 Austria that are seen as "typical" for Austria in a positive sense are disappearing. The Kreisky era, which combined social stability with an unmistakable identity, is over. Austria's remaining positive qualities are not the result of the present generation's efforts but vestiges of the past.

The Second Republic has been both praised and criticized for its stability. Stability is the highest priority of consociational democracy, which integrates all major organized interests into government in order to maximize that stability. But like any political product, stability has its price. According to Gerhard Lehmbruch's analysis of the Swiss and Austrian systems, consociational democracies tend to inhibit innovation and participation (Lehmbruch 1967: 47–49). Both—innovation and participation—are secondary to stability. Stability, innovation, and participation form the magic triangle of functions every modern political system must fulfill.

With the decline of consociationalism and the increase in competitive elements, priority is no longer given to stability, but to a more balanced mix of stability, innovation, and participation. The increase in innovation is reflected in the Westernization and Europeanization of the Austrian political system, especially since the 1980s. More participation is expressed in the greater number of political activities outside traditional party organizations. The decline in stability is evident in the decline in political predictability: The mere existence of five parties instead of three in parliament multiplies the number of possible majority coalitions. And the complexity of new cleavages cutting through the old ones creates an electoral volatility never before known in the Second Republic.

Today democracy in Austria is less consociational and more competitive. That means it is democracy less according to Arend Lijphart and more according to Anthony Downs (Downs 1957). Austrian democracy is less "liberal" and more "populistic," according to William H. Riker (Riker 1982), less elite oriented and more mass oriented, less predictable and more open to various options and developments.

If Austrian democracy is indeed democracy à la Downs, it needs to heed Robert Dahl's warning against becoming too exclusive. Dahl accuses the democratic model as described by Joseph Schumpetrer and Anthony Downs of being insensitive to the basic rights of those who must abide by its rules but have no political entitlements (Dahl 1989: 119–131).

It is precisely this exclusion from citizenship that makes migration one of the major issues of democratic quality in Austria. About 10 percent of the adult population is excluded from political participation. This is a direct consequence of Austria's policy of not recognizing migration as immigration, and of accepting foreign labor but not granting the workers full citizenship as soon as possible.

The decline in predictable stability has one advantage: It makes the system more open to the participation of all those who are included. But there is also a disadvantage: The number of those excluded from participation is higher than at any time since 1949, when the former members of the NSDAP were reenfranchised. And these two situations are correlated in a causal relationship: The political elites, now more dependent than ever on the input of the electorate, do not dare to include those who are currently excluded because xenophobic sentiments are too strong. The elitist, cartel-like style of consociationalism was strong enough to make decisions that were too unpopular to win majority support on the political market. Now, however, the rules of the political market no longer allow for decisions that may be unacceptable to quantitatively decisive segments of the electorate. The quantitative, input-oriented character of the political market overshadows the qualitative, output-oriented character of the Second Republic's traditional elite cartel.

This is the second transformation the Republic of Austria has undergone. The first was an elite-governed transformation from centrifugal to consociational democracy, made possible by the experience of authoritarian and totalitarian rule between the First and the Second Republics. Austria's current transformation is to "autopoiesis," a system that is not ruled in the traditional sense by powerful groups or persons but that is part of a global system of self-regulating mechanisms (Beyme 1994: 33 f.). The Europeanization of politics and the globalization of the economy are merely the most visible aspects of this tendency, which is by no means uniquely Austrian.

Politics is becoming less important, at least politics in the sense of the overall regulation of society. The power of the powerful is less impressive if unemployment figures depend not on government decisions but on an economic logic nobody seems to be responsible for. But the electorate must feel betrayed. Its voting power, now freed from traditional paternalism, is weaker than ever. The political decisionmakers are more dependent than ever on electoral moods but no longer make so many important decisions. Austria's four farewells—to Catholicism, to socialism, to corporatism, to neutrality—at the end of the twentieth century are very important social trends that are not the result of political priorities set by powerful figures. The negative side effect of these developments, decreased security for an increasing number of Austrians, cannot be blamed on certain persons or political parties.

Austrian democracy has become more democratic and less important at the very same time. Its new openness and unpredictability have given the electorate more power over the elected. But political power as such seems to be vanishing, absorbed by anonymous "systems" and mechanisms beyond Austrian borders. The power of the oligarchies, both the socialist and the Christian-conservative, has been broken or at least significantly diminished. But who has stepped into the power vacuum left by the traditional oligarchies?

Austria is facing the end of an illusion, the idea that this small country still retains more of its former "greatness" than its size would indicate. The outcome of World War I put an end to an Austria that was truly "great" in many respects. The Nazi years put an end to the illusion of greatness based on being German. The post-1945 years were marked by efforts to preserve a borrowed greatness: Austria as a cultural power that enjoyed worldwide acceptance not as a rather small country but as the country in which the spirits of Mozart and Strauss were still alive.

This borrowed greatness was accompanied by the "blessed island" syndrome. Smallness was considered great as long as it set Austria apart from the others; from Communist dictatorships in the East and from intensive political conflicts and social unrest in the West. Corporatism and neutrality fit perfectly into the pattern of that syndrome. The Austria of the 1950s, 1960s, and 1970s appeared to have mastered the trick of being small and great at the same time.

The "blessed island" syndrome was the escape route for the dreams of greatness. After the imperial greatness of not-so-multinational Austria, after the greatness of the German Empire of which Austria was briefly a part, the "blessed island" syndrome provided post-1945 Austria with a way to reconcile its smallness with the idea of another kind of greatness: the greatness of being distinctive. Small only in size, Austria wanted to be considered great in the following ways:

- Culture. Austria managed to preserve the Austrian State Opera in Vienna, the Salzburg Festivals, and other traditions of highbrow culture, thus saving its image as a "cultural power" in the same league with France or Italy.
- Economy. Especially in the 1970s, Austria seemed to have found the magic formula of full employment, economic growth, and hard currency. The terms Austro-Keynesianism and Austro-corporatism are used to describe this period of economic success, which is attributed to specific Austrian policies (Bischof and Pelinka 1996).
- Society. Austria's ability to avoid dramatic conflicts along existing cleavages was attributed to a specific "Austrian mind," which distinguished the peace-loving Austrian from other national stereotypes (Bruckmüller 1996: 129–131).
- Politics. Others may have their disruptive power struggles. You, felix (happy) Austria, combine and reconcile and harmonize: SPÖ and ÖVP, labor and business, Vienna and the provinces, the young and the old, men and women. Harmony through power sharing became part of both the autostereotype and the heterostereotype of post-1945 Austria.

In the 1990s, there is still reason to insist that some of those perceptions are more than just illusions. But in general, the impact those Austrian qualities have had on making Austria distinct has been grossly overrated. The escape route from the smallness Austria has so long refused to accept is closed. Austria has lost most of the features that make it unique.

If present political culture is any indicator, Austria has started to accept its smallness. All the political trends are pointing in one direction: Austria is becoming less distinguishable; in that sense, it is becoming less Austrian. It has started to come to terms with the fact that it is playing in the European league with countries like Denmark and Belgium and Greece—the league of small and medium-sized countries. Austria is becoming more like Finland and should be compared with countries like the Netherlands and Portugal. It should not be seen as the country of the Habsburgs or compared primarily with the First Republic.

Austria's past greatness and remaining vestiges of it may be still effective in promoting the country's tourism industry, but they have nothing to do with the reality of present-day Austria and Austrians. It has become obvious that Austria is not different.

The acceptance of smallness put an end to the nostalgia of the imperial past and the pan-German imperial dreams. Now another dream is also ending: the dream that Austria, despite its small size, could still be a power: culturally, politically, socially, economically. The belief that Austria might be a kind of a model for anything has been proved naive. The "blessed island" syndrome has lost its usefulness.

The future has already begun. And this future is open—with regard to electoral results, to the party system, to parliament and government, to social conflicts and political attitudes. But there is a blueprint for the future: Whatever form the new Austria will take, it will be less Austrian and more European, less distinctive and more similar to other European countries.

References

Aarons, Mark, and Loftus, John. 1991. *Unholy Trinity. How the Vatican Nazi Networks Betrayed Western Intelligence to the Soviets.* New York.

Adamovich, Ludwig K., and Funk, Bernd-Christian. 1985. *Österreichisches Verfassungsrecht.* 3rd edition. Vienna.

Adamovich, Ludwig K., Funk, Bernd-Christian, and Holzinger, Gerhart. 1997. *Österreichisches Staatsrecht,* vol. 1: *Grundlagen.* Vienna.

Adorno, Theodor, et al. 1950. *The Authoritarian Personality.* New York.

Aiginger, Karl. 1996. "Wirtschaftsstandort Österreich." In: Trautl Brandstaller, ed., *Österreich 2 1/2. Anstöße zur Strukturreform,* 105–126. Vienna.

Albrich, Thomas. 1987. *Exodus durch Österreich. Die jüdischen Flüchtlinge, 1945–1948.* Innsbruck.

Angebert, Jean-Michel. 1974. *The Occult and the Third Reich. The Mystical Origins of Nazism and the Search for the Holy Grail.* New York.

Antisemitism World Report, 1995. The Institute of Jewish Affairs, London, and the American Jewish Committee, New York.

Appelt, Erna. 1993. *Sozialpartnerschaft und Fraueninteressen.* In: Tálos 1993, op. cit., 243–266.

Atzmüller, Karl F. 1985. *Die Kodifikation des kollektiven Arbeitsrechts.* Vienna.

Bader, William B. 1966. *Austria Between East and West, 1945–1955.* Stanford.

Bailer, Brigitte. 1993. *Wiedergutmachung kein Thema. Österreich und die Opfer des Nationalsozialismus.* Vienna.

Bailer, Brigitte. 1995. *Haider wörtlich. Führer in die Dritte Republik.* Vienna.

Bailer, Brigitte, and Neugebauer, Wolfgang. 1994. "Die FPÖ. Vom Liberalismus zum Rechtsextremismus." In: Dokumentationsarchiv 1994, op. cit., 357–494.

Barnay, Markus. 1983. *Pro Vorarlberg. Eine Regionalistische Initiative.* Bregenz.

Berchtold, Klaus, ed. 1967. *Österreichische Parteiprogramme, 1868–1966.* Vienna.

Berger, Karin. 1988. "'Hut ab vor Frau Sedlmayer!' Zur Militarisierung und Ausbeutung der Arbeit von Frauen im nationalsozialistischen Österreich." In: Tálos, Hanisch, and Neugebauer 1988, op. cit., 141–162.

Bergmann, Kurt, and Wögerbauer, Harald. n.d. "Julius Raab als Klubobmann, 1945–1953." In: Brusatti and Heindl n.d., op. cit., 128–142.

Beyme, Klaus von. 1994. *Systemwechsel in Osteuropa.* Frankfurt am Main.

Bielka, Erich, Jankowitsch, Peter, and Thalberg, Hans, eds. 1983. *Die Ära Kreisky. Schwerpunkte der österreichischen Außenpolitik.* Vienna.

Bischof, Günter. 1992. "The Anglo-American Powers and Austrian Neutrality, 1953–1955." In: *Mitteilungen des Österreichischen Staatsarchivs* 42: 368–393. Vienna.

Bischof, Günter, and Leidenfrost, Josef, eds. 1988. *Die bevormundete Nation. Österreich und die Alliierten, 1945–1949.* Innsbruck.

Bischof, Günter, and Pelinka, Anton, eds. 1993. *Austria in the New Europe. Contemporary Austrian Studies,* vol. 1. New Brunswick.

Bischof, Günter, and Pelinka, Anton, eds. 1994. *The Kreisky Era in Austria.* With Oliver Rathkolb as editorial consultant. *Contemporary Austrian Studies,* vol. 2. New Brunswick.

Bischof, Günter, and Pelinka, Anton, eds. 1996. *Austro-Corporatism: Past, Present, Future. Contemporary Austrian Studies,* vol. 4. New Brunswick.

Bischof, Günter, Pelinka, Anton, and Steininger, Rolf, eds. 1995. *Austria in the Nineteen Fifties. Contemporary Austrian Studies,* vol 3. New Brunswick.

Bluhm, William T. 1973. *Building an Austrian Nation: The Political Integration of a Western State.* New Haven.

Böhm, Johann. 1964. *Erinnerungen aus meinem Leben.* Vienna.

Born, Hanspeter. 1987. *Für die Richtigkeit Kurt Waldheim.* Munich.

Botz, Gerhard. 1978. *Wien vom "Anschluss" zum Krieg. Nationalsozialistische Machtübernahme und politisch-soziale Umgestaltung am Beispiel der Stadt Wien 1938–1939.* Vienna.

Boyer, John. 1981. *Political Radicalism in Later Imperial Vienna: Origins of the Christian Social Movement 1848–1897.* Chicago.

Boyer, John. 1995. *Culture and Political Crisis in Vienna: Christian Socialism in Power, 1897–1918.* Chicago.

Breuss, Susanne, Liebhart, Karin, and Pribersky, Andreas. 1995. *Inszenierungen. Stichwörter zu Österreich.* Vienna.

Bruckmüller, Ernst. 1994. *Österreichbewußtsein im Wandel. Identität und Selbstbewußtsein in den 90er Jahren.* Vienna.

Bruckmüller, Ernst. 1996. *Nation Österreich. Kulturelles Bewußtsein und gesellschaftlich-politische Prozesse.* Vienna.

Brusatti, Alois, and Heindl, Gottfried, eds. n.d. *Julius Raab. Eine Biographie in Einzeldarstellungen.* Linz.

Bunzl, John, and Marin, Bernd. 1982. *Antisemitismus in Österreich. Sozialhistorische und soziologische Studien.* Innsbruck.

Cap, Josef. 1989. *Sozialdemokratie im Wandel.* Vienna.

Cede, Franz, and Pahr, Willibald. 1996. "De-facto-Ende für Österreichs Neutralität." In: *Die Presse,* July 27, 4.

Childers, Thomas. 1983. *The Nazi Voter: The Social Foundations of Fascism in Germany, 1919–1933.* Chapel Hill.

Cohen, Bernard, and Rosenzweig, Luc. 1986. *Le mystère Waldheim.* Paris.

Cronin, Audrey Kurth. 1986. *Great Power Politics and the Stuggle over Austria, 1945–1955.* Ithaca.

Dachs, Herbert. 1988. "Schule und Jugenderziehung in der 'Ostmark.'" In: Tálos, Hanisch, and Neugebauer 1988, op. cit., 217–242.

Dachs, Herbert, et al., eds. 1997. *Handbuch des politischen System Österreichs.* 3rd edition. Vienna.

Dahl, Robert A. 1989. *Democracy and Its Critics.* New Haven.

Daim, Wilfried. 1958. *Der Mann, der Hitler die Ideen gab.* Munich.

Diamant, Alfred. 1960. *Austrian Catholics and the First Republic: Democracy, Capitalism, and the Social Order 1918–1934.* Princeton.

Dippelreiter, Michael. n.d. "Julius Raab und der Gewerbebund." In: Brusatti and Heindl n.d., op. cit., 97–105.

Dokumentationsarchiv des österreichischen Widerstandes, ed. 1988. *"Anschluss" 1938. Eine Dokumentation.* Vienna.

Dokumentationsarchiv des österreichischen Widerstandes, ed. 1994. *Rechtsextremismus in Österreich.* Revised edition. Vienna.

Downs, Anthony. 1957. *An Economic Theory of Democracy.* New York.

Edmondson, C. Earl. 1978. *The Heimwehr and Austrian Politics 1918–1936.* Athens, Georgia.

Embacher, Helga. 1995. *Neubeginn ohne Illusionen. Juden in Österreich nach 1945.* Vienna.

Esterbauer, Fried. 1995. *Das politische System Österreichs. Eine Einführung in die Rechtsgrundlagen und die politische Wirklichkeit.* Graz.

Etzersdorfer, Irene. 1995. *Arisiert. Eine Spurensicherung im gesellschaftlichen Untergrund der Republik.* Vienna.

Falter, Jürgen W. 1991. *Hitlers Wähler.* Munich.

Fassmann, Heinz. 1993. *Arbeitsmarktsegmentation und Berufslaufbahn. Ein Beitrag zur Arbeitsmarktgeographie Österreichs.* Vienna.

Fassmann, Heinz, and Münz, Rainer. 1995. *Einwanderungsland Österreich? Historische Migrationsmuster, aktuelle Trends und politische Maßnahmen.* Vienna.

Fessel+GFK Institut für Marktforschung. 1995. *Eurostyles-Politik. Research Report.* Vienna.

Fischer Almanach. 1995. *Der Fischer Weltalmanach 1996.* Frankfurt am Main.

Fischer, Ernst. 1973. *Das Ende einer Illusion. Erinnerungen 1945–1955.* Vienna.

Fischer, Heinz. 1993. *Die Kreisky-Jahre.* Vienna.

Fischer, Heinz. 1997. "Das Parlament." In: Dachs 1997, op. cit., 96–117.

Fischer, Heinz, ed. 1966. *Einer im Vordergrund: Taras Borodajkewycz. Eine Dokumentation.* Vienna.

Freund, Florian, and Perz, Bertrand. 1988. "Industrialisierung durch Zwangsarbeit." In: Tálos, Hanisch, and Neugebauer 1988, op. cit., 95–114.

Funder, Friedrich. 1952. *Vom Gestern ins Heute. Aus dem Kaiserreich in die Republik.* Vienna.

Gallhuber, Heinrich. 1994. "Rechtsextremismus und Strafrecht." In: Dokumentationsarchiv 1994, op. cit., 625–647.

Gärtner, Heinz. 1979. *Zwischen Moskau und Österreich. Analyse einer sowjetabhängigen KP.* Vienna.

Gärtner, Reinhold. 1996. *Die ordentlichen Rechten. Die "Aula," die Freiheitlichen und der Rechtsextremismus.* Vienna,

Gatterer, Claus. 1972. *Erbfeindschaft Italien-Österreich.* Vienna.

Gehler, Michael, and Sickinger, Hubert, eds. 1995. *Politische Affären und Skandale in Österreich. Von Mayerling bis Waldheim.* Thaur, Tyrol.

Gerlich, Peter. 1992. "A Farewell to Corporatism." In: Luther and Müller 1992, op. cit., 132–146.

Gerlich, Peter, and Ucakar, Karl. 1981. *Staatsbürger und Volksvertretung. Das Alltagsverständnis von Parlament und Demokratie in Österreich.* Salzburg.

Goldhagen, Daniel. 1996. *Hitler's Willing Executioners: Ordinary Germans and the Holocaust.* New York.

Goodrick-Clarke, Nicholas. 1985. *The Occult Roots of Nazism: The Ariosphists of Austria and Germany, 1890–1935.* Wellingborough.

Gottweis, Herbert. 1997. *Neue soziale Bewegungen in Österreich.* In: Dachs 1997, op. cit., 309–324.

Grausgruber, Alfred. 1995. *Wählertypen und Parteienwettbewerb nach der Nationalratswahl 1994.* In: Müller, Plasser, and Ulram 1995, op. cit., 407–434.

Gulick, Charles F. 1948. *Austria: From Habsburg to Hitler.* 2 vols. Berkeley.

Haider, Jörg. 1993. *Die Freiheit, die ich meine. Das Ende des Proprzstaates. Plädoyer für eine Dritte Republik.* Frankfurt am Main.

Hamann, Brigitte. 1996. *Hitlers Wien. Lehrjahre eines Diktators.* München.

Hanisch, Ernst. 1994. *Der lange Schatten des Staates. Österreichische Gesellschaftsgeschichte im 20.Jahrhundert.* Vienna.

Heer, Friedrich. 1968. *Der Glaube des Adolf Hitler. Anatomie einer politischen Religiosität.* Munich.

Heindl, Peter. 1994. "Positionen und Maßnahmen dere Sicherheitsbehörden im Kampf gegen den Neonazismus." In: Dokumentationsarchiv 1994, op. cit., 616–624.

Herzstein, Robert Edwin. 1988. *Waldheim: The Missing Years.* New York.

Hitler, Adolf. 1938. *Mein Kampf.* 352nd–354th edition. Munich.

Höbelt, Lother, Mölzer, Andreas, and Sob, Brigitte, eds. 1994. *Freiheit und Verantwortung. Jahrbuch für politische Erneuerung 1995.* Vienna.

Hofinger, Christoph, and Ogris, Günther. 1996. *Achtung, gender gap! Geschlecht und Wahlverhalten 1979–1995.* In: Plasser, Ulram, and Ogris 1996, op. cit., 211–232.

Höll, Othmar. 1994. "The Foreign Policy of the Kreisky Era." In: Bischof and Pelinka 1994, op. cit., 32–77.

Holzer, Gabriele. 1995. *Verfreundete Nachbarn. Österreich-Deutschland. Ein Verhältnis.* Vienna.

Howell, Susan, and Pelinka, Anton. 1994. "Duke and Haider: Right Wing Politics in Comparison." In: Bischof and Pelinka 1994, op. cit., 152–171.

Hudal, Alois C. 1936. *Die Grundlagen des Nationalsozialismus.* Vienna.

Hudal, Alois C. 1976. *Römische Tagebücher. Lebensbeichte eines alten Bischofs.* Graz.

Hummer, Waldemar, and Schweitzer, Michael. 1987. *Österreich und die EWG. Neutralitätsrechtliche Beurteilung der Möglichkeiten der Dynamisierung des Verhältnisses zur EWG.* Vienna.

Institute of Jewish Affairs and the American Jewish Committee. 1995. *Antisemitism World Report 1995.* London, New York.

Jahrbuch der Österreichischen Wirtschaft 1994. 1995. *Tätigkeitsbericht der Wirtschaftskammer Österreich.* Vienna.

Janik, Allan. 1987. "Viennese Culture and the Jewish Self-Hatred Hypothesis: A Critique." In: Oxaal, Pollak, and Botz 1987, op. cit., 89–110.

Johnston, William M. 1972. *The Austrian Mind: An Intellectual and Social History, 1848–1938.* Berkeley.

Jones, J. Sydney. 1980. *Hitlers Weg begann in Wien.* Wiesbaden.

Journal für Sozialforschung. 1991. *Journal für Sozialforschung* 4. Vienna.

Kann, Robert A. 1950. *The Multinational Empire: Nationalism and National Reform in the Habsburg Monarchy, 1848–1918.* 2 vols. New York.

Karazman-Morawetz, Inge, and Pleschiutschnig, Gerhard. 1997. "Wirtschaftsmacht und politischer Einfluß." In: Dachs 1997, op. cit., 418–431.

Karlhofer, Ferdinand. 1996. "The Present and Future State of Social Partnership." In: Bischof and Pelinka 1996, op. cit., 119–146.

Karlhofer, Ferdinand, and Tálos, Emmerich. 1996. *Sozialpartnerschaft und EU. Integrationsdynamik und Handlungsrahmen der österreichischen Sozialpartnerschaft.* Vienna.

Kasemir, Gerard. 1995. "Spätes Ende für 'wissenschaftlich' vorgetragenen Rassismus. Die Borodajkewycz-Affäre 1965." In: Gehler and Sickinger 1995, op. cit., 486–501.

Katzenstein, Peter J. 1984. *Corporatism and Change: Austria, Switzerland, and the Politics of Industry.* Ithaca.

Kennedy, Paul. 1976. *The Rise and Fall of British Naval Mastery.* London.

Kernbauer, Hans, and Weber, Fritz. 1988. "Österreichs Wirtschaft, 1938–1945." In: Tálos, Hanisch, and Neugebauer 1988, op. cit., 49–68.

Keyserlingk, Robert H. 1988. *Austria in World War II: An Anglo-American Dilemma.* Kingston and Montreal.

Khol, Andreas, Ofner, Günter, and Stirnemann, Alfred, eds. 1978–1997. *Österreichisches Jahrbuch für Politik.* 20 vols. Munich and Vienna.

Kindley, Randall W. 1996. "The Evolution of Austria's Neo-Corporatist Institutions." In: Bischof and Pelinka 1996, op. cit., 53–93.

Kirchschläger, Rudolf. 1983. "Integration und Neutralität." In: Bielka, Jankowitsch, and Thalberg 1983, op. cit., 61–96.

Kissinger, Henry A. 1957. *A World Restored: Metternich, Castlereagh, and the Problems of Peace, 1812–1822.* Boston.

Klaus, Josef. 1971. *Macht und Ohnmacht in Österreich. Konfrontationen und Versuche.* Vienna.

Klemperer, Klemens von. 1972. *Ignaz Seipel: Christian Statesman in a Time of Crisis.* Princeton.

Klose, Alfred. 1970. *Ein Weg zur Sozialpartnerschaft. Das österreichische Modell.* Vienna.

Klose, Alfred. n.d. "Julius Raab und die Sozialpartnerschaft." In: Brusatti and Heindl n.d., op. cit., 167–179.

Knight, Robert, ed. 1988. *"Ich bin dafür, die Sache in die Länge zu ziehen." Die Wortprotokolle der österreichischen Bundesregierung über die Entschädigung der Juden.* Vienna.

Konrad, Helmut, and Lechner, Manfred. 1992. *"Millionenverwechslung." Franz Olah. Die Kronenzeitung. Geheimdienste.* Vienna.

Kreisky, Bruno. 1981. *Reden.* 2 vols. Vienna.

Kreisky, Bruno. 1986. *Zwischen den Zeiten. Erinnerungen aus fünf Jahrzehnten.* Berlin.

Kreisky, Bruno. 1988. Im Strom der Politik. Der Memoiren zweiter Teil. Berlin.

Kreisky, Eva. 1981. "Thesen zur politischen und sozialen Funktion des Föderalismus in Österreich." In: *Österreichische Zeitschrift für Politikwissenschaft* 10: 261–277.

Kreissler, Felix. 1984. *Der Österreicher und seine Nation. Ein Lernprozeß mit Hindernissen.* Vienna.

La Palombara, Joseph. 1987. *Democracy, Italian Style.* New Haven.

Lauber, Volkmar. 1992. "Changing Priorities in Austrian Economic Policy." In: Luther and Müller 1992, op. cit., 147–172.

Lazarsfeld, Paul F., Berelson, Bernard, and Gaudet, Hazel. 1944. *The People's Choice: How the Voter Makes Up His Mind in a Presidential Campaign.* New York.

Lehmbruch, Gerhard. 1967. *Proporzdemokratie. Politisches System und Politische Kultur in der Schweiz und in Österreich.* Tübingen.

Lehmbruch, Gerhard, and Schmitter, Philippe C., eds. 1982. *Patterns of Corporatist Policy-Making.* London, Beverly Hills.

Lendvai, Paul. 1983. "Der 'Kreisky-Effekt' und die internationalen Medien." In: Bielka, Jankowitsch, and Thalberg 1983, op. cit., 323–346.

Leser, Norbert. 1968. *Zwischen Reformismus und Bolscshewismus. Der Austromarxismus als Theorie und Praxis.* Vienna.

Lichtenberger-Fenz, Brigitte. 1988. "Österreichs Hochschulen und Universitäten und das NS-Regime." In: Talos, Hanisch, and Neugebauer 1988, op. cit., 269–282.

Lijphart, Arend. 1977. *Democracy in Plural Societies: A Comparative Exploration.* New Haven.

Lijphart, Arend. 1994. *Electoral Systems and Party Systems: A Study of Twenty-Seven Democracies, 1945–1990.* Oxford.

Linder, Wolf. 1994. *Swiss Democracy: Possible Solutions to Conflict in Multicultural Societies.* New York.

Lipset, Seymour Martin. 1960. *Political Man: The Social Bases of Politics.* New York.

Loewenberg, Peter. 1983. *Decoding the Past: The Psychohistorical Approach.* New York.

Loewenberg, Peter. 1995. *Fantasy and Reality in History.* New York.

Loewenstein, Karl. 1965. *Political Power and the Governmental Process.* Chicago.

Ludwig, Michael, Mulley, Klaus Dieter, and Streibel, Robert, eds. 1991. *Der Oktoberstreik 1950. Ein Wendepunkt der Zweiten Republik.* Vienna.

Luif, Paul. 1995. *On the Road to Brussels: The Political Dimension of Austria's, Finland's, and Sweden's Accession to the European Union.* Vienna.

Luther, Kurt Richard. 1997. "Bund-Länder Beziehungen. Formal- und Realverfassung." In: Dachs 1997, op. cit., 816–826.

Luther, Kurt Richard, and Müller, Wolfgang C., eds. 1992. *Politics in Austria: Still a Case of Consociationalism?* London.

Luverà, Bruno. 1996. *Oltre il confine. Euregio e conflitto etnico: Tra regionalismo europeo a nuovi nazionalismi in Trentino-Alto Adige.* Bologna.

Luza, Radomir. 1975. *Austro-German Relations in the Anschluss Era.* Princeton.

Luza, Radomir. 1984. *The Resistance in Austria, 1938–1945.* Minneapolis.

Mantl, Wolfgang, ed. 1992. *Politik in Österreich.* Vienna.

Marin, Bernd. 1982. *Die Paritätische Kommission. Aufgeklärter Technokorporatismus in Österreich.* Vienna.

Marko, Josef, and Poier, Klaus. 1997. "Die Verfassungssysteme der Bundesländer: Institutionen und Verfahren repräsentativer und direkter Demokratie." In: Dachs 1997, op. cit., 817–832.

Markovits, Andrei S. 1996. "Austrian Corporatism in Comparative Perspective." In: Bischof and Pelinka 1996, op. cit., 5–20.

Mastny, Vojtech. 1986. *Helsinki, Human Rights, and European Security: Analysis and Documentation.* Durham, N.C.

Mathis, Franz. 1995. "Between Regulation and Laissez Faire: Austrian State Industries After World War II." In: Bischof, Pelinka, and Steininger 1995, op. cit., 79–90.

Matzner, Egon. 1996. "Österreich in Europa—Kooperation oder Desintegration? Eine spieltheoretische Betrachtung der EU." In: Trautl Brandstaller, ed., *Österreich 2 1/2. Anstöße zur Strukturreform,* 311–330. Vienna.

May, Arthur J. 1966. *The Passing of the Hapsburg Monarchy, 1914–1918.* 2 vols. Philadelphia.

Meissl, Sebastian, et al., eds. 1986. *Verdrängte Schuld–verfehlte Sühne. Entnazifizierung in Österreich 1945–1955.* Vienna.

Mitten, Richard. 1992. *The Politics of Anti-Semitic Prejudice.* Boulder.

Mommsen, Hans. 1963. *Die Sozialdemokratie und die Nationalitätenfrage im habsburgischen Vielvölkerstaat.* Vienna.

Mommsen-Reindl, Margarete. 1976. *Die österreichische Proporzdemokratie und der Fall Habsburg.* Vienna.

Mooslechner, Michael, and Stadler, Robert. 1988. "Landwirtschaft und Agrarpolitik." In: Tálos, Hanisch, and Neugebauer 1988, op. cit., 69–94.

Müller, Wolfgang C. 1996. "Wahlsysteme und Parteiensysteme in Österreich, 1945–1995." In: Plasser, Ulram, and Ogris 1996, op. cit., 233–272.

Müller, Wolfgang C. 1997. "Regierung und Kabinettsystem." In: Dachs et al. 1997, op. cit., 122–137.

Müller, Wolfgang C., Plasser, Fritz, and Ulram, Peter A., eds. 1995. *Wählerverhalten und Parteienwettbewerb. Analysen zur Nationalratswahl 1994.* Vienna.

Mulley, Klaus-Dieter. 1988. "Modernität oder Traditionalität? Überlegungen zum sozialstrukturellen Wandel in Österreich 1938 bis 1945." In: Tálos, Hanisch, and Neugebauer 1988, op. cit., 25–48.

Natter, Bernhard. 1987. "Die 'Bürger' versus die 'Mächtigen.' Populistischer Protest an den Beispielen Zwentendorf und Hainburg." In: Pelinka, Anton, ed., *Populismus in Österreich.* Vienna.

Neuhofer, Hans. 1997. "Gemeinden." In: Dachs 1991, op. cit., 774–784.

Neuhold, Hanspeter. 1995. "Austria Still Between East and West?" Austrian Institute for International Affairs. AP 10/July 1995. Laxenburg.

Neuhold, Hanspeter, and Luif, Paul, eds. 1992. *Das außenpolitische Bewußtsein der Österreicher. Aktuelle internationale Probleme im Spiegel der Meinungsforschung.* Vienna.

Nick, Rainer. 1995. "Die Wahl vor der Wahl. Kandidatennominierung und Vorwahlen." In: Müller, Plasser, and Ulram 1995, op. cit., 67–118.

Nick, Rainer, and Pelinka, Anton. 1996. *Österreichs politische Landschaft.* 2nd edition. Innsbruck.

Olah, Franz. 1995. *Die Erinnerungen.* Vienna.

Oxaal, Ivar, Pollak, Michael, and Botz, Gerhard, eds. 1987. *Jews, Anti-Semitism, and Culture in Vienna.* London.

Palumbo, Michael. 1988. *The Waldheim Files: Myth and Reality.* London.

Parkinson, F., ed. 1989. *Conquering the Past: Austrian Nazism Yesterday and Today.* Detroit.

Pauley, Bruce F. 1972. *Hahnenschwanz und Hakenkreuz. Steirischer Heimatschutz und österreichischer Nationalsozialismus 1918–1934.* Vienna.

Pauley, Bruce F. 1981. *Hitler and the Forgotten Nazis: A History of Austrian National Socialism.* Chapel Hill.

Pauley, Bruce F. 1992. *From Prejudice to Persecution: A History of Austrian Anti-Semitism.* Chapel Hill.

Pelinka, Anton. 1981. *Modellfall Österreich? Möglichkeiten und Grenzen der Sozialpartnerschaft.* Vienna.

Pelinka, Anton. 1983. *Social Democratic Parties in Europe.* New York.

Pelinka, Anton. 1989. *Karl Renner zur Einführung.* Hamburg.

Pelinka, Anton. 1990. *Zur österreichischen Identität. Zwischen deutscher Vereinigung und Mitteleuropa.* Vienna.

Pelinka, Anton. 1993. *Die Kleine Koalition. SPÖ-FPÖ, 1983–1986.* Vienna.

Pelinka, Anton, ed. 1994. *EU-Referendum. Zur Praxis direkter Demokratie in Österreich.* Vienna.

Pelinka, Anton, and Plasser, Fritz, eds. 1989. *The Austrian Party System.* Boulder.

Pelinka, Anton, Schaller, Christian, and Luif, Paul. 1994. *Ausweg EG? Innenpolitische Motive einer außenpolitischen Umorientierung.* Vienna.

Pelinka, Anton, and Smekal, Christian, eds. 1996. *Kammern auf dem Prüfstand. Vergleichende Analysen institutioneller Funktionsbedingungen.* Vienna.

Pelinka, Peter, and Steger, Gerhard, eds. 1988. *Auf dem Weg zur Staatspartei. Zu Geschichte und Politik der SPÖ seit 1945.* Vienna.

Perner, Markus, and Zellhofer, Klaus. 1994. "Österreichische Burschenschaften als akademische Vorfeldorganisationen des Rechtsextremismus." In: Dokumentationsarchiv 1994, op. cit., 270–277.

Pfabigan, Alfred. 1976. *Karl Kraus und der Sozialismus. Eine politische Biographie.* Vienna.

Pflichterfüllung. 1986. *Ein Bericht über Kurt Waldheim.* Edited by Neues Österreich. Vienna.

Pilz, Peter. 1982. *Die Panzermacher. Die österreichische Rüstungsindustrie und ihre Exporte.* Vienna.

Plasser, Fritz. 1987. *Parteien unter Streß. Zur Dynamik der Parteiensysteme in Österreich, der Bundesrepublik Deutschland und den Vereinigten Staaten.* Vienna.

Plasser, Fritz. 1997. "Massenmedien." In: Dachs et al. 1997, op. cit., 463–482.

Plasser, Fritz, and Ulram, Peter A. 1994. "Meinungstrends, Mobilisierung und Motivlagen bei der Volksabstimmung über den EU-Beitritt." In: Pelinka 1994, op. cit., 87–120.

Plasser, Fritz, and Ulram, Peter A. 1995. "Wandel der politischen Konfliktdynamik. Radikaler Rechtspopulismus in Österreich." In: Müller, Plasser, and Ulram 1995, op. cit., 471–504.

Plasser, Fritz, and Ulram, Peter A. 1996. "Wandel der politischen Konfliktdynamik: Radikaler Rechtspopulismus in Österreich." In: Müller, Plasser, and Ulram 1995, op. cit., 471–504.

Plasser, Fritz, Ulram, Peter A., and Ogris, Günther, eds. 1996. *Wahlkampf und Wählerentscheidung. Analysen zur Nationalratswahl 1995.* Vienna.

Plasser, Fritz, Ulram, Peter A., and Seeber, Gilg. 1996. "(Dis-)Kontinuitäten und neue Spannungslinien im Wählerverhalten: Trendanalysen, 1986–1995." In: Plasser, Ulram, and Ogris 1996, op. cit., 155–209.

Powell, G. Bingham, Jr. 1970. *Social Fragmentation and Political Hostility: An Austrian Case Study.* Stanford.

Powell, G. Bingham, Jr. 1980. "Voting Turnout in Thirty Democracies: Partisan, Legal, and Socio-Economic Influences." In: Richard Rose, ed., *Electoral Participation: A Comparative Analysis,* 5–34. Beverly Hills, London.

Prisching, Manfred. 1996. *Die Sozialpartnerschaft. Modell der Vergangenheit oder Modell für Europa? Eine kritische Analyse mit Vorschlägen für zukunftsgerechte Reformen.* Vienna.

Pulzer, Peter. 1988. *The Rise of Political Anti-Semitism in Germany and Austria.* Revised edition. London.

Purtscheller, Wolfgang. 1993. *Aufbruch der Völkischen. Das braune Netzwerk.* Vienna.

Rabinbach, Anson. 1983. *The Crisis of Austrian Socialism: From Red Vienna to Civil War.* Chicago.

Rathkolb, Oliver. 1994. "Bruno Kreisky: Perspective of Top Level U.S. Foreign Policy Decision Makers, 1959–1983." In: Bischof and Pelinka 1994, op. cit., 130–151.

Rauchensteiner, Manfried. 1979. *Der Sonderfall. Die Besatzungszeit in Österreich 1945 bis 1955.* Graz.

Reiterer, Albert F. 1988. *Die unvermeidbare Nation. Ethnizität, Nation und nachnationale Gesellschaft.* Frankfurt am Main.

Reiterer, Albert F. 1995. *Gesellschaft in Österreich. Sozialstruktur und sozialer Wandel.* Vienna.

Riedlsperger, Max E. 1978. *The Lingering Shadow of Nazism: The Austrian Independent Party Movement Since 1945.* New York.

Riedlsperger, Max E. 1996. "The FPÖ and the Right." In: Bischof and Pelinka 1996, op. cit., 351–386.

Riekhoff, Harald von, and Neuhold, Hanspeter, eds. 1993. *Unequal Partners: A Comparative Analysis of Relations Between Austria and the Federal Republic of Germany and Between Canada and the United States.* Boulder.

Riker, William. 1982. *Liberalism Against Populism: A Confrontation Between the Theory of Democracy and the Theory of Social Choice.* Prospect Heights, Ill.

Rosenberger, Sieglinde. 1992. *Frauenpolitik in Rot-Schwarz-Rot.* Vienna.

Rosenberger, Sieglinde. 1997. "Frauen- und Gleichstellungspolitik." In: Dachs 1997, op. cit., 690–699.

Rot-Weiss-Rot-Buch. 1946. *Gerechtigkeit für Österreich! Darstellungen, Dokumente und Nachweise zur Vorgeschichte und Geschichte der Okkupation Österreichs. Erster Teil (nach amtlichen Quellen).* Vienna.

Sandgruber, Roman. 1995. *Ökonomie und Politik. Österreichische Wirtschaftsgeschichte vom Mittelalter bis zur Gegenwart.* Vienna.

Schaller, Christian. 1994. "Die innenpolitische EG-Diskussion seit den 80er Jahren." In: Pelinka, Schaller, and Luif 1994, op. cit., 27–270.

Scharsach, Hans-Henning. 1992. *Haiders Kampf.* Vienna.

Scharsach, Hans-Henning. 1995. *Haiders Clan. Wie Gewalt entsteht.* Vienna.

Schermann-Richter, Ulrike. 1996. "Frauen im Bundesdienst oder Der gläserne Plafond." Research Report. Vienna.

Schlesinger, Thomas O. 1972. *Austrian Neutrality in Postwar Europe: The Domestic Roots of a Foreign Policy.* Vienna.

Schmitter, Philippe C., and Lehmbruch, Gerhard, eds. 1979. *Trends Toward Corporatist Intermediation.* London, Beverly Hills.

Schneider, Heinrich. 1990. *Alleingang nach Brüssel. Österreichs EG-Politik.* Bonn.

Schorske, Carl E. 1980. *Fin-de-Siècle Vienna: Politics and Culture.* New York.

Schweiger, Günter. 1992. *Österreichs Image in der Welt. Ein weltweiter Vergleich mit Deutschland und der Schweiz.* Vienna.

Schwimmer, Walter. 1993. "Das neue Parlamentsmitarbeitergesetz. Aufwertung des Parlamentarismus?" In: Khol, Ofner, and Stirnemann 1993, op. cit., 387–414.

Secher, Pierre H. 1993. *Bruno Kreisky: Chancellor of Austria.* Pittsburgh.

Seidel, Hans. 1996. "Social Partnership and Austro-Keynesianism." In: Bischof and Pelinka 1996, op. cit., 94–118.

Shell, Kurt L. 1969. *Jenseits der Klassen? Österreichs Sozialdemokratie seit 1934.* Vienna.

Sickinger, Hubert. 1995. "Partei- und Wahlkampffinanzierung in Österreich. Ein Überblick." In: Müller, Plasser, and Ulram 1995, op. cit., 265–294.

Sickinger, Hubert. 1996. "Der Nationalrat auf dem Weg zum Arbeitsparlament." Research Report. Institute for Conflict Research, Vienna.

Sickinger, Hubert. 1997. *Politikfinanzierung in Österreich. Ein Handbuch.* Thaur.

Sieder, Reinhard, Steinert, Heinz, and Tálos, Emmerich, eds. 1995. *Österreich 1945–1995. Gesellschaft. Politik, Kultur.* Vienna.

Siegfried, Klaus-Jörg. 1974. *Universalismus und Faschismus. Das Gesellschaftsbild Othmar Spanns.* Vienna.

Sottopietra, Doris. 1997. *Variationen eines Vorurteils. Eine Entwicklungsgeschichte des Antisemitismus in Österreich.* Vienna.

Spannocchi, Emil. 1976. *Verteidigung ohne Selbstzerstörung.* Munich.

Speer, Albert. 1969. *Erinnerungen.* Berlin.

Stauber, Leland G. 1987. *A New Program for Democratic Socialism: Lessons from the Market-Planning Experience in Austria.* Carbondale, Ill.

Steger, Gerhard. 1982. *Der Brückenschlag. Katholische Kirche und Sozialdemokratie in Österreich.* Vienna.

Steiner, Kurt. 1972. *Politics in Austria.* Boston.

Sternfeld, Albert. 1990. *Betrifft: Österreich. Von Österreich betroffen.* Vienna.

Stiefel, Dieter. 1981. *Entnazifizierung in Österreich.* Vienna.

Stourzh, Gerald. 1975. *Kleine Geschichte des österreichischen Staatsvertrages.* Graz.

Stourzh, Gerald. 1988. "The Origins of Austrian Neutrality." In: Alan T. Leonhard, ed., *Neutrality: Changing Concepts and Practices,* 35–58. Lanham, Md.

Sully, Melanie A. 1982. *Continuity and Change in Austrian Socialism: The Eternal Quest for the Third Way.* New York.

Sully, Melanie A. 1990. *A Contemporary History of Austria.* London.

Svoboda, Wilhelm. 1990. *Franz Olah. Eine Spurensicherung.* Vienna.

Svoboda, Wilhelm. 1993. *Die Partei, die Republik und der Mann mit den vielen Gesichtern.* Wien.

Tálos, Emmerich. 1995. "Der Sozialstaat. Vom "goldenen Zeitalter" zur Krise." In: Sieder, Steinert, and Tálos 1995, op. cit., 537–551.

Tálos, Emmerich, ed. 1993. *Sozialpartnerschaft. Kontinuität und Wandel eines Modells.* Vienna.

Tálos, Emmerich, and Kittel, Bernhard. 1996. "Roots of Austro-Corporatism: Institutional Preconditions and Cooperation Before and After 1945." In: Bischof and Pelinka 1996, op. cit., 21–52.

Tálos, Emmerich, Hanisch, Ernst, and Neugebauer, Wolfgang, eds. 1988. *NS-Herrschaft in Österreich, 1938–1945.* Vienna.

Tálos, Emmerich, and Neugebauer, Wolfgang, eds. 1988. *"Austrofaschismus." Beiträge über Politik, Ökonomie und Kultur, 1934–1938.* 4th edition. Vienna.

Taschenbuch. 1997. *Wirtschafts- und Sozialstatistisches Taschenbuch 1997.* Bundeskammer für Arbeiter und Angestellte. Vienna.

Thalberg, Hans. 1983. "Die Nahostpolitik." In: Bielka, Jankowitsch, and Thalberg 1983, op. cit., 293–322.

Tributsch, Gudmund, ed. 1994. *Schlagwort Haider. Ein politisches Lexikon seiner Aussprüche von 1986 bis heute.* Vienna.

Tweraser, Kurt K. 1995. "The Politics of Productivity and Corporatism: The Late Marshall Plan in Austria, 1950–1954." In: Bischof, Pelinka, and Steininger 1995, op. cit., 91–115.

Uhl, Heidemarie. 1992. *Zwischen Versöhnung und Verstörung. Eine Kontroverse um Österreichs historische Identität fünfzig Jahre nach dem "Anschluss."* Vienna.

Ulram, Peter A. 1990. *Hegemonie und Erosion. Politische Kultur und politischer Wandel in Österreich.* Vienna.

Vranitzky, Franz. 1992. *Franz Vranitzky im Gespräch mit Armin Thurnher.* Frankfurt am Main.

Waldheim, Kurt. 1996. *Die Antwort.* Vienna.

Warren, Donald I. 1996. "The Institutionalization of Protest Politics: The Case of Austria's Freedom Party 1986–1995." Working Paper, Initial Draft, May 1996. Oakland University.

Weininger, Otto. 1916. *Geschlecht und Charakter.* 15th edition. Vienna.

Weinzierl, Erika. 1969. *Zu wenig Gerechte. Österreicher und Judernverfolgung 1938–1945.* Graz.

Weiss, Hildegard. 1984. *Antisemitische Vorurteile in Österreich. Theoretische und empirische Analysen.* Vienna.

Welan, Manfried. 1992. *Der Bundespräsident. Kein Kaiser in der Republik.* Vienna.

Welzig, Elisabeth. 1985. *Die 68er. Karrieren einer rebellischen Generation.* Vienna.

Whiteside, Andrew G. 1975. *The Socialism of Fools: Georg Ritter von Schönerer and Austrian Pan-Germanism.* Berkeley.

Widder, Helmut. 1997. "Rechnungshof und Volksanwaltschaft." In: Dachs 1997, op. cit., 164–174.

WIFO (Österreichisches Institut for Wirtschaftsforschung), ed. 1995. *Umverteilung durch öffentliche Haushalte in Österreich.* Coordinated by Alois Guger. Vienna.

Wiltschegg, Walter. n.d. "Julius Raab und die Heimwehr." In: Brusatti and Heindl n.d., op. cit., 76–86.

Wistrich, Robert S. 1989. *The Jews of Vienna in the Age of Franz Joseph.* Oxford.

Wodak, Ruth, et al. 1990. *"Wir sind alle unschuldige Täter!" Diskurshistorische Studien zum Nachkriegsantisemitismus.* Frankfurt am Main.

Zohn, Harry. 1971. *Karl Kraus.* New York.

Zulehner, Paul F. 1995a. "Die Kirchen und die Politik." In: Sieder, Steinert, and Tálos 1995, op. cit., 525–536.

Zulehner, Paul F., ed. 1995b. *Kirchenvolks-Begehren und Weizere Pfingstvision. Kirche auf Reformkurs.* Düsseldorf.

Zulehner, Paul F., et al. 1996. *Solidarität. Option für Modernisierungsverlierer.* Innsbruck.

Zulehner, Paul, and Denz, Hermann. 1993. *Wie Europa lebt und glaubt. Europäische Wertstudie.* Düsseldorf.

Index